Steen Ledet Christiansen is Associate Professor of English at Aalborg University, Denmark. His research focuses on popular visual culture, particularly film and the burgeoning field of post-cinema, on which he has written numerous articles and book chapters. Additionally, he is co-editor of a number of anthologies including *Monstrologi: Frygtens manifestationer* (2012) and *Spøgelser: Genfærdet som kulturel og æstetisk figur* (2012).

.

"This extraordinary book combines lucid philosophical insight with careful analysis of film technique. Steen Christiansen shows us how recent action films actually work; and he speculates on why we are drawn to such films, and what this tells us about the state of digital culture."

– Steven Shaviro, Wayne State University, USA;
author of *Post Cinematic Affect*

"*Drone Age Cinema* compellingly argues – through detailed analyses of blockbusters like *Sucker Punch* and the Dark Knight trilogy– that the contemporary action genre projects its power through an assault on the senses, situated within a cultural context of fear. A 'must read' for anyone interested in action cinema, visual effects, spectatorship, and technologies and global power."

– Angela Ndalianis, University of Melbourne

STEEN LEDET CHRISTIANSEN

DRONE AGE CINEMA

ACTION FILM AND SENSORY ASSAULT

I.B. TAURIS

LONDON · NEW YORK

Published in 2017 by
I.B.Tauris & Co. Ltd
London • New York
www.ibtauris.com

Copyright © 2017 Steen Ledet Christiansen

The right of Steen Ledet Christiansen to be identified as the author of this work
has been asserted by the author in accordance with the Copyright, Designs and
Patents Act 1988.

All rights reserved. Except for brief quotations in a review, this book, or any
part thereof, may not be reproduced, stored in or introduced into a retrieval
system, or transmitted, in any form or by any means, electronic, mechanical,
photocopying, recording or otherwise, without the prior written permission
of the publisher.

Every attempt has been made to gain permission for the use of the images in
this book. Any omissions will be rectified in future editions.

References to websites were correct at the time of writing.

International Library of the Moving Image 38

ISBN: 978 1 78453 640 4
eISBN: 978 1 78672 076 4
ePDF: 978 1 78673 076 3

A full CIP record for this book is available from the British Library
A full CIP record is available from the Library of Congress

Library of Congress Catalog Card Number: available

Printed and bound by CPI Group (UK) Ltd, Croydon, CR0 4YY

MIX
Paper from
responsible sources
FSC® C013604

Contents

List of Plates

Acknowledgements

Although my keyboards did all the writing, many others had an influence on this book. Sarah Juliet Lauro and Meredith McCarroll, who accepted the paper from which everything grew. Gray Kochhar-Lindgren for early support and optimism when this book was only a paper. Anna Coatman for urging me to send in a proposal and guiding the book in its infant stages. Steven Shaviro for enthusiasm and drone music videos – I'll use them in my next book. Madeleine Hamey-Thomas for her commitment to this project. Patrick Casey for improving my writing.

And LeAnne, of course, who believed in this book even when I did not.

An earlier, quite different, version of parts of chapter three was published in *Akademisk kvarter* 7 as "Hyper Attention Blockbusters."

1

War of the Senses

Contemporary cinema is entering the drone age. There are two entry points. The first is the inevitable integration of drones into film production.[1] The second entry point, and the more important one, is cinema's response and adaptation to a new cultural and technological environment. What will cinema be in the drone age? And more urgently, what will cinema be able to do our senses? As Rey Chow has pointed out, our world has "been transformed into – is essentially conceived and grasped as – a target. To conceive of the world as a target is to conceive of it as an object to be destroyed."[2] Chow argues that we have transitioned into a mindset where war is not *a* solution, it is *the* solution, evident in phrases such as war on poverty, war on terror and so forth. Another way of phrasing the "world as target" is that perception has increasingly become power, because perceiving facilitates destruction. Cinema remains one of our dominant technologies of perception and so expresses how we conceive of the world as a target, and how perception and power fold together.

Nowhere is perception and power as intensely entangled as in contemporary action cinema. Action cinema works through bodily forces that stun our senses, and for more than a decade the genre's audiovisual barrage has taken on an unprecedented intensity and speed, adapting to shifting cultural and technological environments. Contemporary action cinema's power is thus of utmost importance: its impact on our senses, its affective entrainment of our bodies and its ramifications for our preconscious sensibilities. Contemporary action cinema's affordances, potentialities and relations as it responds and adapts to cultural transitions is my primary interest here. The only way to understand these films' cultural force is to first understand their aesthetic force. In fact, their aesthetic force *is* their cultural force; the way action films make us feel determines how they impact us. Cinema has weaponized our senses so that all we see are targets.

Often an overlooked genre, the past decade especially has brought much needed scholarly attention to action films as a serious mode of cinematic expression, although earlier forays do exist. Most of this work, both earlier forays and the past decade, has focused on representational issues, such as gender norms, the idealization of bodies and sexualities, the whitewashing of ethnicities or the delegation of minorities to marginal positions of either support or threat. Action films have been seen as structures of containment or repression, usually reinforcing dominant ideologies and expressing cultural symptoms and malaises. I commend this work and find it useful and important. This book, however, is not that.

Instead, I am interested in how action cinema in the twenty-first century responds to what I will call the culture of fear. In what ways does contemporary action cinema function as an affective reprieve in a culture suffused with fear, in a constant state of terror? Furthermore, how can contemporary action cinema be viewed as affective entrainment for living through, for enduring, this culture of fear? My argument hinges on the crucial contradiction of fear's redistribution of power through affective projections of power. That is to say, action films work by instilling sensations of power and agency in us as a form of recompense for the atmosphere of fear that permeates our everyday lives. Action films, I argue, are about power and agency, and so in what follows I am interested in what action films *do* (how they affect our sensory experience and bodily engagement) rather than what they represent (in terms of gender, sexuality and race politics). Only by investigating the redistribution of power and agency that action films enact can we begin to understand action cinema's position in contemporary culture.

The book proceeds in six movements, each chapter following the same rhythm: opening with a central concept, two or three close readings of films follow, concluding with how these films entrain us. Each conclusion works across the chapters to form a discussion of how our sensory experience is reconfigured and retrained by contemporary action films. Imminently, I will turn to how sensory assault functions as bodily innervation in a culture of fear. The pre-eminent expression of this cultural climate is the action film, and I will briefly outline how action films have been studied academically and how this genre has transformed in recent years, before correlating this transformation with the emergence of the culture of fear.

After this introductory chapter, I broach the crucial subject of *vectors*, how feeling is transported from there to here. I argue that computer-generated imagery, and particularly computer-generated animation, plays a central role in the way digital images connect to a broader field of energies for us, what I term *machinic sensations*. I follow up on the conception of transfer of energy in the next chapter on *kinetics*, where I discuss the production of audiovisual energy through camerawork, object movement and stereoscopic effects. This acceleration of action cinema's audiovisuals results in *hyper-perception*, a pluralized and distributed form of perception to keep up with such acceleration. *Volatility* is the fourth chapter, and discusses the bodily mastery achieved through a post-cinematic body of hypermediacy. As I show, the end results are *body assemblages*, where human and nonhuman capacities entwine and vibrate together. In chapter five, I discuss *corporeal projections*, films were the human body is replaced with a drone body in order to adapt to a dangerous environment. What emerges from such a body relation is *telesomatics*, a paradoxically intimate distance to our environment, in which we cede power and agency in favor of innervation. Finally, I discuss *droning* as an audiovisual process that overwhelms and dominates our sensory experience. As a compensatory process, droning facilities *anaisthesis*, a form of non-perception that renders us inert. I conclude the book with a reflection on how action films enhance power and agency, while simultaneously siphoning power and agency from us, in favor of technological projections of power and agency. In this way, I argue, action films help us adapt to a culture of fear.

My theoretical framework is film-philosophy, a diverse set of approaches. As the hyphen indicates, we are not dealing simply with the study of film, nor with philosophy, nor even with the philosophy of film, but rather a specific philosophical argument: that films do things. What films do becomes the whole question, which does not make it a simple question. Film-philosopher Daniel Frampton argues that the purpose of film-philosophy (what he terms filmosophy) is to "organicise the relationship of form and meaning."[3] Frampton's argument centers on the fact that feeling and thought are not separate or distinct but rather articulated together: "Meaning becomes immediate and immanent to the rhythm and motion and mood of the film's thoughtful forms."[4] Frampton rejects the separation of feeling and meaning as meaningful, which is why I correlated aesthetic force with cultural force above.

If, as Robert Sinnerbrink maintains, most work on film can be divided into either *culturalist-historicist* or *cognitivist-naturalist* approaches, I follow instead the third approach that he identifies as the film-philosophical, which "undoes the hierarchical orders of representation structuring more traditional regimes, opens up experience to a plurality of forms of presentation, and thus anticipates the possibility of an aesthetic critique of modern culture" that highlights "the significance of affect, pleasure and thought in our experience of film," providing new ways to "reflect upon, interpret, or extend the kind of aesthetic experience that film evokes. They seek not only to explain and comprehend but to question and understand the significance of film experience; they search for apt ways of expressing this aesthetic experience."[5] A vocabulary focusing on energies, flows and intensities is better able to express our experience, because it is through energies and intensities that our experience is formed.

Experience is a complicated term, since it is evident from Sinnerbrink's argument that experience is not solely cultural, historical, cognitive or naturalistic. Instead, although Sinnerbrink never comes out and says as much, experience is first and foremost aesthetic. Cautiously, Sinnerbrink always qualifies experience as aesthetic in his book, yet there is no need for this, since experience is always already aesthetic. As Steven Shaviro has argued, following process philosopher Alfred North Whitehead, "the primordial form of all experience, and thereby of all action and relation, is an aesthetic one."[6] Our experience of film is first and foremost rooted in feeling; all cultural and cognitivist superstructures remain just that: filterings and interpretations of immediate experience in order to translate experience into stable emotions and perceptions. Furthermore, any change in the cinematic sound-image produces equal change in our experience, which is also the reason why film experience is material. Film works as the expression of experience, always embodied in what Vivian Sobchack calls the film's body, which "functions to visibly *animate* perception and expression in existence. Thus, its primary function always already entails *movement*."[7] John Mullarkey agrees when he asserts that "movies have an *élan* rather than an essence – a divergent form of movement that participates in (rather than 'captures') processual reality in myriad ways; indeed, it can only so participate when it is myriad."[8] Films participate in the ways that our bodies move and the ways that we are moved, which is what constitutes the film experience. When experience is movement, energies, flows and intensities are better suited to grasp that movement than representational terms.

As we can see, experience is crucial as a bridge between a film and our reception of it. Experience is always emotional, or more accurately, experience "is the rise of an affective tone originating from things".[9] Watching a film generates affective tones in us, and the processual nature of experience indicates that there is more than one component involved in experience, which is why Whitehead argues that process is the becoming of experience.[10] The basic unit of experience for Whitehead is intensity, the way our bodies integrate relations.[11] The more relations we integrate, the more intense our experience. For this reason, intensity will be a highly significant concept throughout the book. Speed and acceleration, two important aspects of action cinema, are ways of changing relations, and so the acceleration of action cinema's audiovisuals intensify our experience.

Significantly, although Whitehead often speaks of individual responses ("subjective forms"), we can also think of experience in a more collective manner. Early film theory, as Miriam Bratu Hansen points out, also focused on what cinema does, i.e. "the kind of sensory-perceptual, mimetic experience it enabled."[12] Importantly, this experience is not individual but collective "sensorily, bodily transmitted rhythms".[13] What I am getting at here is that contemporary action cinema generates collective, bodily transmitted rhythms that reconfigure experience. Yet this experience is to be understood as a pre-individual, collective experience that we are all part of, yet do not all share. As I discuss later, we may feel apart from collective experience.

Here we can see how film-philosophy is different from classical versions of film theory. Film theory has traditionally been interested in issues of reproduction and the ontology of the cinematic image. Certainly André Bazin paved the way for this long debate in his articles "The Ontology of the Photographic Image" and "The Myth of Total Cinema". Far from wanting to add to this debate, especially since Bazin has often been mis-read to bolster positions he never meant to take, I simply remark that film-philosophy cares less about what cinema *is* than what cinema *does*. This position also sidesteps issues of any difference between analog and digital sound-images. Digital cinema is equally as real as photographic cin-ema, since the reality of images is located in their actions rather than any connection to an anterior reality.

In an age of digital overload, we can no longer take seriously the charge that the digital is somehow "virtual", or less real than earlier, analog media. For this reason, I find the notion of reproduction to be of less interest than that of *rendering*. Michel Chion, the French audiovisual theorist, makes a distinction between the real and the rendered in several of his books, arguing that we recognize "sounds to be truthful, effective, and fitting not so much if they reproduce what would be heard in the same situation in reality, but if they render (convey, express) the feelings associated with the situation."[14] In a later work, Chion insists that rendering is not limited to the auditory but that the rendered is "a product of the film's auditory and visual texture and articulation."[15] The fact that rendering also indicates the process of generating an image from a 2D or 3D model simply makes the argument for a shift of focus from reproduction to rendering even more forceful. For digital sound-images, there is no relevant distinction between reproduction or rendering; it is the same process.

Furthermore, what is rendered is a "clump of sensations" that "'attracts' affects for which they are not especially responsible."[16] This poses the ques-tion of *affect* and *sensation*, two significant concepts for the present project. While affect has a long and complicated pedigree, including several differ-ent and contradictory meanings, I follow Brian Massumi in understand-ing affect as presubjective intensity that traverses our bodies.[17] Affect is the inescapable ground from which we emerge as subjects with emotions and is "something that comes before the subject has arrived, or that sub-sists after the subject has departed, or that happens alongside the subject, affecting it but not being integrated within it."[18] We should keep in mind that affect is not a matter of personal opinion, taste, or preference. Affect traverses everyone "independently of their individuation and the forms of their personality."[19] Affect is also what connects us to the collective field of forces and energies that we call culture.

Likewise, sensation is essential to our experience but broader than and prior to perception. Significantly, sensation does not belong to a specific sensory channel. As Chion puts it, "most of our sensory experiences consists of these clumps of sensations."[20] In other words, sensation is how we feel specific events, which is always a mix of sensory input: tactile, auditory, visual and so forth. In fact, we should understand sensation as an environmental process that does not distinguish between individual senses and the surrounding environment. Sensation is a state of mixing, not only of action, perception and thought, as Massumi argues, but also of objects in the world.[21] We cannot meaningfully separate our sensations from the cinematic rendering of these sensations, which is why we should think of sensations as pulses between entities. Sensation, therefore, is not defined as a subjective experience but as a process of what Whitehead calls prehension in a boundless ecology of pulses that animate sensory responses and render bodies.

Affect and sensation converge in what Mark B.N. Hansen has termed "feed-forward," an operation that makes experience present to consciousness.[22] As Steve Goodman has condensed it, "affect becomes emotion as sensation becomes perception," after which we emerge as subjects who are these emotions and perceptions.[23] Before there is an "I perceive," there are pulses of feeling and throbs of passion that determine *how* we perceive. These pulses and throbs determine the environment in and through which our experience unfolds, what Hansen refers to as worldly sensibility.[24] Such a perspective is imperative because films modulate this worldly sensibility. In this sense, films are not simply discrete texts or works, but instead participate in the production of "structures of feeling," which Raymond Williams famously defined as the "characteristic elements of impulse, restrain, and tone" and "their connections in a generation, or period" and how "meanings and values as they are lived and felt" can be negotiated and articulated.[25] Cinema thus participates in and expresses structures of feeling through the cinematic rendering of sensations.

Through this process of participation and expression, cinema also pertains to war and the world becoming a target. As Paul Virilio has provocatively declared, "cinema is war pursued by other means."[26] While this may sound like an astounding oversimplification of an indefensible thesis, Virilio is certainly not the only one to make such an argument. Friedrich Kittler: "The entertainment industry is, in any conceivable sense of the word, an abuse of army equipment."[27] Yet what does it mean that the entertainment industry abuses army equipment and that cinema is war pursued by other means? There are several ways of answering this.

First off, there is the historical fact that the movie camera is based on Étienne-Jules Marey's chronophotographic gun, which was shaped like a rifle and is the reason why the basic unit of film is called a shot, as well as why the film industry still speaks of "shooting a film". From this historical anecdote follows a host of cross-pollinations between military research and film research. Virilio outlines some of these in *War and Cinema*, such as the use of the camera's peep-hole as an indirect sighting device for bomber planes, or the use of cameras to surveil enemy territory. Kittler points out that Marey's invention was based on an earlier device: the multi-chambered Colt revolver.[28] The revolving mechanism of the bullet chamber and the photographic chamber started as the same. More significant, however, is the idea of mechanized death of nonhumans. Automated weapons were designed to destroy indigenous peoples who were not considered humans, while Marey's chronophotographic gun shot birds in fight.[29] All we see are nonhuman targets. Furthermore, both weapons and film became components in a much larger mass industry that emphasizes seriality and serial production at a pace that operated "even below the smallest difference that would still be physiologically perceptible."[30] Serial production overtakes human perception.

Secondly, cinema has often functioned as disseminator of propaganda, whether in direct, non-fictional form of newsreels and documentaries, or in the more or less subtle forms of war films to support the war effort – whether we think of films such as *God Is My Co-Pilot* (Robert Florey 1945) and "Der Fuehrer's Face" (Jack Kinney 1942) that are meant to bolster morale in a time of war; films meant to rinse off the national shame of war, like *We Were Soldiers* (Randall Wallace 2002); or war fantasies such as *Rambo: First Blood Part II* (George P. Cosmatos 1985), or many other films that portray war as a necessary or just cause. In a similar vein, the US military often works with film producers and film directors to lend an air of authenticity as well as crucial material support (helicopters, tanks, troops, etc.), as long as the military is allowed to approve the script.[31]

Thirdly, and most significantly for me, war and cinema share an interest in the production of audiovisual spectacle and the distortion of perception that goes along with this spectacle. For Virilio, both cinema and war deal with "radically changing fields of perception".[32] In this way, cinema is *like* war because they both take the same object: human perception. This is not to say that war and cinema are the same but that they work according to similar logics: to captivate the audience (cinema) or enemy (war).[33] Cinema and war must both be regarded as integrated into the process of producing new forms of machinic perception, a perception suffused with media technologies. Media technologies become integral to human perception, to the extent that we can no longer meaningfully distinguish between technological or non-technological perception. As Jonathan Crary argues, "vision and its effects are always inseparable from the possibilities of an observing subject who is both the historical product *and* the site of certain practices, techniques, institutions, and procedures of subjectification."[34] I would extend Crary's argument to encompass not just vision but the whole range of human perception and sensation. We emerge as perceiving, sensing subjects through a historical process of cultural, institutional and technological processions.

That is also Kittler's point, when he argues that the entertainment industry is abuse of army equipment: the entertainment industry produces combat as inner experience.[35] Cinema thereby becomes one of the contemporary technologies of the body, in Kittler's phrase, where films render new sensations and prime our sensorium for new experiences.[36] But in this way, the world is also rendered as a target, a confluence of perception and power. The impact this junction of cinema and war has on our worldly sensibility is what is really at stake, the way cinema makes us see and hear the world. What happens when we are captivated by the cinematic spectacle, and what structures of feeling are produced by the confluence of cinema and war? Steve Goodman, writing primarily about sound, but still applicable more broadly, expresses exactly what is at stake:

> If war saturates modern societies right down to the microphys-
> ical fabric, then it does so using an array of distributed processes

of control, automation, and a both neurophysical and affective mobilization: the military-entertainment complex as a boot camp therefore, optimizing human reaction speeds, fabricating new reflexes for a postcybernetic condition. Media technologies discipline, mutate, and preempt the affective sensorium. Entertainment itself becomes part of the training.[37]

Cinema trains us for war. Our bodily sensations are modulated to perceive the world in a particular way, thus shaping our experience. As one component in a larger process, cinema participates in the production of a culture of fear, a culture that captivates us through audiovisual spectacle. Nowhere is this culture expressed more clearly than in contemporary action films, a cinema that excels in astounding audiovisual spectacles. The function of these spectacles is less to inure us to images of war, death and destruction than to habituate us to the fold of perception and power. If we collectively come to accept the fact that perception is power, then the projection of power through technologies of perception becomes the logical progression. Through action cinema's affective entrainment, that is exactly what we all come to need.

Action Films

Action films are compactions of energies. Action films move us physically, electrify us, grip us and pull us along with their frenetic drives. This sensation of energy is achieved by all manners of cinematic devices, whether through rapid editing, swirling camera movements, death-defying stunts, or elaborate digital animations. A body leaps across the reflecting glass of the Burj Khalifa hundreds of feet above the ground with nothing anchoring it; giant robots spin before us in a fluid movement with no sense of gravity; a sonic blast reverberates with a force that physically unsettles us. Such scenes, and a host like them, all hinge on bodily sensations of energy and speed achieved through the deployment of new cinematic technologies. These new technologies that hook into our sensory experience are at the center of this book.

Action films have both a long and a short film history. While spectacular sequences have been part of action cinema since its inception, when that inception occurred is contested. The short history of action cinema emphasizes the intensity and predominance of spectacular sequences emerging in the 1970s, solidifying in the 1980s, and achieving prominence at the box office through the 1990s onwards. Spectacles and elaborate set pieces are the primary motivation for making and watching action films. This fact also stresses the increasing deployment of visual effects. By contrast, the long history of action cinema points to the constant presence of spectacle in cinema, from its early beginnings on. Yvonne Tasker makes this argument in her concise *The Hollywood Action and Adventure Film*, where she also points to the fact that any case for either the long or short history of action cinema runs the risk of obscuring salient points: action has always been part of narrative cinema, but has also taken on particular prominence and coherence since the 1970s.[38]

Rather than develop another cultural history of action cinema's emergence that identifies continuities and variations across different films, I argue that action cinema is a cinema of speed, force and energy. In arguing for action films as the production of energy, I also argue that action films *do* things. One might simply say that action cinema is a cinema of actions, that these films perform actions on us, that our experience of watching these films change us in some way, however minimally. My argument is that *action films themselves have power and agency*. Action films have the ability to affect us and make us feel. The cinematic intensities of action films make them intimately involved with our bodies, and these intensities are their very definition. Action films' bodies and our bodies co-mingle in what Vivian Sobchack has called the film experience.[39] This argument falls along the lines of Linda Williams' argument in her groundbreaking article "Film Bodies: Gender, Genre, and Excess," where she posits a corporeal relation between viewer and film in three 'body genres' – horror, melodrama and pornography – a relation defined by "a body caught in intense sensation".[40] Williams emphasizes the contiguity of the actor's body on screen and our body, whereas Sobchack and others instead speak of the film body or cinematic body's contiguity with our body.[41] There exists, either way, a generative relation between bodies, human and cinematic, that produces intensities, sensations and moods that constitute our film experience.

Action films clearly belong to this category of body genres, although Williams never discusses action films. Whether this is because action films had not yet reached the level of intensity they did later, especially considering that Williams primarily discusses classical Hollywood, or if it is for some other reason, is trivial. Being caught up in intense sensation certainly describes action films well. We find in Williams' expression of a body caught in intense sensation also an interesting wavering between agency and power. Clearly, as I stated, I see action films having power and agency over us. Not complete and utter control, but the films have a force that exceeds our subjective control. Much of action cinema's impact comes through its intensive force, a force that registers affectively and bodily rather than cognitively.

Power, agency, and mastery are all key terms for action films. Yvonne Tasker's central concerns in *Spectacular Bodies*, her first book on action films, are "issues of cultural power that are at stake in thinking about the status and the operations of action cinema."[42] Similarly, Harvey O'Brien suggests in his *Action Movies* that agency is central to action cinema, agency understood as action in action, the capacity to exert transformation.[43] Lisa Purse asserts in *Contemporary Action Cinema* that "action films trade in spectacles of physical mastery, in fantasies of empowerment."[44] Such an emphasis on these three interrelated concepts is easy to understand, considering their self-evidence in both the spectacular sequences of action films' focus on able-bodied heroes, and in how central the white, male, muscular body is for action cinema as a cultural expression of power.

Yet at the same time, there is a distinct wavering between action cinema as extending our power and agency and us being subjected to the film's power and agency. The relation between film and viewer is more complicated than the straightforward model of the screen body as prosthetic extension for the viewer's body. I wish to suggest *aisthesis* as the primary model for our relation to film, rather than prosthetic extension. *Aisthesis* means sense perception or "the perception of the external world by the senses."[45] Significantly, *aisthesis* suggests a bodily engagement with the world, that we apprehend the world. In *The Tactile Eye*, Jennifer M. Barker suggests apprehension as a good model for how action film interacts with our bodies. Apprehension means "fear of what may happen," "the action of seizing upon," and "the action of laying hold of with the senses."[46] *Aisthesis* and apprehension express a confluence of how we sense the world, how we grasp the world, and how fear reverberates through those two conjoined actions: a model that is eminently suitable for action films. For Barker, the central concern is how "film inspires our desire to grasp even as it instills and exacerbates our fear of losing our grasp."[47] So action films are not simply about the expression and exertion of power, they are also about being subjected to power, although in an exhilarating form, which begins to explain why so many critics compare action films to rollercoaster rides: we are not in control of a rollercoaster but we are also not out of control. Similarly, action films depend on trepidatious apprehension, the liminal sense of teetering on the edge of catastrophe.

Action cinema's sense of empowerment, however, is increasingly shifting to a different sensation, one that has less to do with empowerment and more to do with overpowering tractability. Since action films are louder than hell, going along for the ride can be an innervating experience, as well as an enervating one. Tasker points to action cinema's central trait being "the movement of the body through space; the body is central to action whether it is superhuman or simply enhanced."[48] Tasker emphasizes the screen body too much and also unnecessarily limits the movement aspect too much. Existing on a continuum, enhanced bodily movement would be Ethan Hawke (Tom Cruise) crawling and leaping around the Burj Khalifa enhanced with (digitally removed) wires. Superhuman would be Neo (Keanu Reeves) slowing down time in a twirl as he dodges bullets. Yet what are we to do with the tracking shot in *Sucker Punch* (Zack Snyder 2011) that circles around the women in the burlesque club, only to continue the circling movement *into* mirror space, where we literally move through the looking-glass, as it were. Such a movement is neither enhanced nor superhuman (since not even Superman could manage this tracking shot).

Contemporary action cinema increasingly relies on camera positions, movements and other devices that are literally impossible for a camera to make. Only the advent of digital image technologies can accomplish such shots. William Brown has dubbed this new digital cinema *supercinema* in his book of the same name. A new iteration of cinema, supercinema only pretends to have limitations similar to analog cinema, but it can do things that were previously impossible.[49] In the same vein, Barker points to the fact that "Steadicam cinematography and computer-generated or -enhanced camera movements (or illusions of camera movements, in some cases) take us beyond our own abilities, moving in ways and to places that no human could reasonably expect to go."[50] Cinema is increasingly abandoning any kind of human model of perception in the images it produces, and the contemporary action film blazes the trail away from this stability into a faster-paced sensory assault produced by introducing new – especially digital – technologies into their filmmaking. Instead of a human or superhuman body, we increasingly find a nonhuman body capable of moving through solid space, speeding across time in a continuous shot or gazing into other spectra of light. As Angela Ndalianis argues, "the motion of the body, in fact, has shifted to the stylistic tools of the cinematic body, as sound, editing and cinematography combine with the muscular, hyper physiques in breathless displays of hyperkinetic motion."[51]

The increasingly non-anthropocentric nature of cinematic images is what is at stake here. As Edward Branigan has pointed out, anthropomorphism as analytic category is a matter of how much a camera or shot simulates a feature of human embodiment.[52] Vivian Sobchack, similarly, points to the structural homology between camera movement and the human body in her early film phenomenology: an embodied relation between spectator-projector and camera-world, a relation where the machine is also incorporated into our human embodiment of sensing the world.[53] Increasingly, films employ non-anthropocentric embodiments and movements in order to produce what Shane Denson has termed "discorrelated images."[54] We find instead a nonhuman cinema that privileges shots that not only puts us in positions that no human can be in, but even more radically in positions that no thing can be in. Sobchack's structural homology between human body and film body breaks down. Our embodiment is reduced or enhanced depending on the sound-images we encounter. Action films emphasize physical empowerment and bodily mastery and so conventionally enhance our embodiment. But what happens when there is no longer a camera involved in the process? Increasingly, contemporary cinema, and contemporary action cinema in particular, does not depend solely on a camera in order to produce images. That is, images that do not correlate to human embodiment but instead take up nonhuman positions, such as on the front of cars, the corners of rooms, floating above a city looking straight down, and similar shots. Contemporary action cinema is a thoroughly nonhuman cinema that willfully abandons its basis in human bodily perception and instead boldly goes where no human has gone before. Yet this is exactly the exhilarating apprehension we get from watching such films: we get to partake in something other than ourselves, even if only for a few hours (and usually only a few minutes out of those few hours). In the original sense of the word, contemporary action cinema is awesome, which is to say, filled with a sensation of dread mingled with veneration.

New image technologies have expanded cinema in terms of what cinema can do. Even the briefest list of these new image technologies suggests the change cinema is currently undergoing: motion capture technologies, computer-generated animation, digital image compositing using so-called synth cameras or virtual cameras, LIDAR (Light Detection and Ranging) technologies, Kinect motion sensing input devices (originally designed for the Xbox game console), and many other devices. The cameras used for filmmaking have also changed, ranging from digital video cameras including commercial DSLR cameras not designed for filmmaking, night vision cameras, infrared cameras, surveillance cameras, and more. Not only can these cameras record images from positions that humans cannot occupy, but they can also perceive things that we cannot perceive, as in the case of night vision cameras. More importantly, however, some of these new image technologies do not even perceive images but rather motion (as in the case of Kinect devices) or distance and light (as in the case of LIDAR devices). These recordings then have to be rendered visually as images in order for humans to perceive them. Similarly, computer-generated images do not require a camera, even if animators often use the term in order to specify things such as point of view. Compositing images increases the potential for cameras to move in ways that humans could never do.[55]

Our embodiment is stretched, amplified and distorted in the process; impossible spaces unfold and our perception becomes increasingly plastic as a result. Our embodiment with new image technologies is a historical one, and the shock perceptions elicited when cinema was young has long since been naturalized into perception, eliciting recognition rather than shock. However, the perceptual technologies listed above have not yet been assimilated into our embodiment. Therefore, they register a different kind of image regime than the cinematic one. Hence, post-cinema. As Shaviro notes in *Post-Cinematic Affect*, not only has digital network media displaced cinema as the cultural dominant, but new articulations of lived experience have also emerged as a result.[56] Instead of registering as shocks, post-cinema registers as intensity effects that "help and train us to endure – and perhaps also to negotiate" our contemporary culture.[57] These intensities occur as what Deleuze has termed micro-perceptions, "little folds that unravel in every direction, folds in folds, over folds, following folds".[58] What is folded? All the new imaging technologies that produce post-cinematic sound-images are folded into our bodies below conscious perception.

The conventional cinematic embodied relation of spectator-projector plus camera-world produced a transformational moment from photography to cinema as the lived momentum of a fleshing out of the image.[59] Similarly, as the camera-world relation shifts to CGI-(world) and spectator-projector relation shifts to spectator-screen, so too does the ensuing embodiment. Let me unpack this a little. We no longer necessarily have a camera-world relation but a relation where images are *generated* (rather than recorded and subsequently rendered). Even when images are shot with a conventional camera, post-production holds the potential to radically transform the recorded images. Similarly, we can no longer distinguish between recorded or computer-generated images, meaning that there is no camera. The same thing goes for *world*. When images are not necessarily recorded any more, are no longer indexical images but may well be entirely simulated, world becomes bracketed: it is no longer the recording of an anterior reality but the production of a new reality.

We find in this technological revolution of new media technologies also a perceptual revolution, Sobchack argues.[60] But since these post-cinematic images do not correlate with human embodiment, in that they do not have a structural homology with our bodies, this perceptual revolution should be understood as a *micro-perceptual revolution*. The integration, extension and stretching of our bodily experiences that these new media technologies exacts informs us differently. Micro-perceptions register bodily but not consciously and in this way color our macro-perceptions, "our conscious, clear and distinct apperceptions."[61] One way in which we can register a shift in perception is the concept of drone vision. As Anna Munster points out regarding drone vision, such vision "is not first person point of view or narrative action but instead a sense of being in the midst of transmission, buoyed by a network of multiple signal flows, subject to fluctuations, transitions, instabilities."[62] In other words, drone vision is eco-logical rather than perspectival, which expresses very well the reconfigura-tion of post-cinematic images that often do not employ perspectival shots but rather dynamic environments produced by digital media: the camera has splintered into multiple processes, rather than a single apparatus. New media technologies generate new forms of affects in us and through this process effectuate changes in our larger, conscious perceptions. It is impor-tant to keep in mind that digital images no longer suggest an anterior real-ity but instead participate in producing realities; these images are realities because they still have an effect on the viewer that is just as real as photo-graphic images: they have power and agency.

Post-cinema has the ability to project power, what we may also call power-to. Post-cinema functions under a different logic than cinema: we may call this logic operational rather than a logic of reproduction. Post-cinema does not reproduce an anterior reality but produces new reali-ties through its intensity effects. Such projection of power as intensities of new realities converges exactly in the crux of a drone culture. The drone stands as the central object of power today, a conjunction between human and nonhuman agencies, which binds images, intensities, flows and cul-ture together. Contemporary cinema's emphasis on nonhuman embodi-ment, the production of images rather than the reproduction of reality, automated processes, the decoupling of bodily perception and cinema's imbrication in operational images and machinic vision instantiate a new mode of cinema, one that I will term drone age cinema. Drone age cinema expresses the convergence between these varied forces.

Drone Age Cinema

As Adam Rothstein argues, the drone is a "cultural node – a collection of thoughts, feelings, isolated facts, and nebulous paranoias related to a future-weird environment."[63] In this way, Rothstein goes on, it is best to view drones as existential forces, forces that shape us and the environment we live in. The word drone carries several meanings and does not only indicate a piece of technology. Significantly, the word "drone" functions both as a noun and a verb, a fact that allows us to cross a divide between being and action. Drone as a concept thus points to the fact that being and

17

action are never distinct, but that we are what we do; we are being-action. In other words, drone stands as an assemblage of perception and action – perceiving as a form of doing, or as Massumi argues, "perceptions are possible actions."[64] While there is a distinction between perception and action, rather than being different in kind, they are different in degree, lying on a continuum. Harun Farocki has termed this confluence "operative images."[65] For Farocki, operative images' purpose is not to inform or entertain (though they may do either) but to perform an operation, i.e. to do something. The drone relation thus entangles power, agency and dominance with fear, trauma and terror.

Nasser Hussain has pointed to a central contradiction of the drone age: drones are both nodes of dominance and power as well as fear and trauma. For drone operators, drones are agents of power: what we see we can kill. For those who live in a drone environment, the relation is reversed: if we can be seen, we can be killed.[66] Hussain underlines the diffuse sense of dread that people living in a drone environment feel, while those who operate drones feel completely safe. Gregory Chamayou, one of the most prominent drone theorists, has argued that the drone's advantage is that it allows one to project power without projecting vulnerability.[67] The reverse, then, is also true: drones make us vulnerable without having had any power to project. Or as Warren Ellis argues, "drones are extensions of human agency."[68] But by the same logic, drones are also contractions of human agency; those who live in a drone environment "all attest to widespread occurrence of PTSD and anticipatory anxiety."[69] Drone, as both power and fear, being and action, functions as metaphor for our relation to the environment and how we sense that environment. For Hussain, the central issue for drones is the distribution of the senses: do we experience sensations of power or sensations of fear? A different way of phrasing that would be to say that the drone functions as a node expressing a modulation of body as well as new bodily dispositions.

Drone becomes an orientation within a larger environment, a way of understanding how power is articulated. Shaviro regards post-cinema as deeply embedded in neoliberal flows.[70] I would argue that contemporary action cinema is deeply imbricated in what Virilio has termed the environment of fear.[71] Environment here is a crucial concept because it connects to Michel Foucault's late argument that power has become environmental, a "governmentality which will act on the environment and systematically modify its variables."[72] Modifying variables is essentially what Deleuze picks up on in his "Postscript to Control Societies", where he argues that "controls are a *modulation*, like a self-transmuting molding continually charging from one moment to the next."[73] Modulation, then, is how pressures are exerted on us as a collective as well as individuals. Much as drone vision is ecological because of its fluctuations, transitions and instabilities, so is our current drone era a flux of forces and energies that move transversally across different fields. Such a view allows me to tie together films and embodiment and cultural forces in a complex torsion.

Fear and the culture of fear has become a central concern in our post-9/11 age. Virilio argues that fear has become universal, that it permeates our space-time and as a result permeates our bodies.[74] More than any other feeling, fear has dominated contemporary assessments of our era. Virilio talks about an administration of fear, which for him means that "fear is now an environment, a surrounding, a world. It occupies and preoccupies us. Fear was once a phenomenon related to localized, identifiable events that were limited to a certain timeframe: wars, famines, epidemics. Today, the world itself is limited, saturated, reduced, restricting us to stressful claustrophobia."[75] Fear has become a structure of feeling and a collective affective quality. Similarly, Anderson outlines many different critics' and theorists' arguments that we are living in a culture of fear.[76] Massumi, likewise, points to fear and threat as two intertwined affects that impact entire populations through affective modulation.[77] Fear, for Massumi, is a future event that requires an action in the present, even though the event has not yet happened. The shadows of futurity, of potential disasters, darken the brightness of the present day. Yet for this very reason, fear cannot be rational, cognitive or knowable, since if we knew what would happen, we would no longer need to be afraid but could simply act. Instead, fear is a burden, something that reduces movement and induces paralysis, an inability to act based on what might happen. As Massumi states, "fear can now operate as the nonphenomenal background of existence, or outside in-which of experience, in its role as the affective tone or generic context for a way of life."[78] Fear, in other words, has power-to. Fear has the power to change our ecological relation and perception, to redistribute our senses and attune them differently.

19

Just like the drone is a technological response to a culture of fear, trying to keep the operator safe while projecting power and force, so too is contemporary action cinema an aesthetic response to the culture of fear. Contemporary action cinema participates in fear's affective modulation, but it does so primarily through recompense and shielding. We are protected from affects of fear and the ensuing sensations of reduced movement and paralysis through the intensity of movement, speed and force induced by action films. Their sensory assault instills motion in our bodies, and so we get a reprieve from fear through the intense experience of action films. As Joanna Bourke has shown in her *Fear: A Cultural History*, fear works to disturb the nervous system, and for this reason, bodily movement has always been the way that fear has been overcome. Where speed, acceleration and power reside, fear cannot exist. In that process, intensity substitutes fear with a sense of power. The vicarious movements of action films dispel the inertia of fear.

A central argument for Bourke is that fear is not simply an emotion (or what I would call an affect, since fear is never cognitive or rational but always something that impinges on our cognitive behavior). Instead, fear is a redistribution of power. Fear correlates to suffering in the sense that we too often visit our fear on others as their suffering.[79] Furthermore, fear is not simply an individual state of being, but rather mediates between the individual and the social, body space and social space.[80] As a redistribution of power, fear must be expressed in a variety of ways and forms. If bodily movement is the only way that fear can be modulated, then it follows that bodily movement must be elicited. In other words, action films project power into us. For this reason, contemporary action films are not about drones specifically, nor about the culture of fear that we live through or how fear is administered. Action films are about doing away with fear. As muscular actions provide relief from fear, so too do sensations of motility, even though this motility is experienced intensively rather than extensively. Fear is still administered via affective modulation, but we are presented with an antidote, or *pharmakon*, in the form of action films. As we know, *pharmakon* is both poison and antidote and so works in a dual torsion between giving and taking. Bourke points to the same paradox at work for fear: "the pain at the heart of fear could simultaneously constitute part of the pleasure".[81]

Action films, then, give us a reprieve from fear, but only by taking away our agency and modulating our bodies. That modulation is what turns the pain of fear into the pleasure of power and agency, even as that power and agency only manifest vicariously.

We should not, of course, make the leap from affective modulation to the idea that everyone will respond in the same way. Attunement renders structures of feeling, not individual responses. As Massumi points out, "jacked into the same modulation of feeling, bodies reacted in unison without necessarily acting alike. Their responses could, and did, take many forms. What they shared was the central nervousness. How it translated somatically varied body by body."[82] Instead, as Ben Anderson has shown, the "idea that discreet periods of time can be characterised in terms of a single, identifiable, nameable emotion leads to some important starting points for an account of affective conditions. It acts as a counterpoint to any tendency to see a body's 'force of existing' as an exclusively individual phenomenon."[83] For Anderson, we must pay attention to structures of feeling and/as affective atmospheres, because such a view of affect also allows us to understand that some people may be "out of sync" with a dominant structure of feeling.[84]

For this reason, it is useful to consider that action films participate in the production of structures of feeling, because that means that the affects and sensations expressed and rendered by the films need not manifest in every single viewer. Structures of feeling thus help us understand how films can participate in what Williams argues are "palpable pressures" that set "effective limits on experience and action."[85] First of all, not only do structures of feeling set limits and exert pressures, they also expand options and induce vigor. As such, structures of feeling are not only oppressive but may just as easily be confident: the force of movement says nothing about where the movement will go. What matters is that structures of feeling are collective, shared across members of a culture. Affects connect us to the cultural environment, "where sensations and sensory organs, bodies and desires, social groups and mediating formations become connected in specific ways."[86] Action films thus engage us at a pre-individual level, which designates "the limit between the individual and collective".[87] What we must pay attention to, then, are the effects of action films, their affective engagement and sensory articulation.

Sensory Assault

Contemporary action cinema is resplendent with sequences that overload our senses. In doing so, their sound-images exert power and agency over us by injecting us into a flow of energy too fast-paced for us to keep up. Tim Blackmore terms this visual velocity the "speed death of the eye," suggesting that this situation is a kind of entropic state where information breaks down.[88] Yet it seems to me that the situation is not exactly one of death, since that suggests complete collapse, but rather a different kind of visual regime defined by an immediacy of perception where "our eyes become indistinguishable from the camera's optics, and critical consciousness, along with the body, goes missing."[89] Speed overtakes our senses, presenting images and sounds at such velocities that our conscious perception can no longer keep pace.

Critical consciousness recedes as there is no longer time for reflection, and our bodies go missing not because they vanish, but because we lose control of them: the speed of action cinema's audiovisuals makes everything an affective blur, or what Paul Virilio terms emoting-power: the impact of speed on the senses.[90] The end result for Virilio is a situation of automated perception; we are so overwhelmed by the speed of images, that we no longer have time, space, or capacity for reflection. Consciousness goes missing in the immediacy of images, and crucially these images have lost all reference to anterior reality for Virilio. Again, we are faced with a changed relation to digital video and computer-generated images, or what Virilio dubs synthetic images. The logical progression is that "after *synthetic images*, products of info-graphic software, after the digital image processing of computer-aided design, we are on the verge of *synthetic vision*, the automation of perception."[91]

Contemporary action cinema becomes one iteration of Virilio's vision machine, where stable, embodied human perception is deterritorialized by the accelerating, proliferating and nonhuman capacities of the sound-images that can go above and beyond human perception and human embodiment. For Virilio, "information comes to the fore as an entirely separate form of energy: *sound and image* energy, the energy of long-distance touch and contact."[92] If we unpack this notion of audiovisual energy, it is worth noting that Virilio regards any machine as a producer of speed, which is also a motor of attack.[93] Any machine, then, challenges the ground of the human body and suggests that we may become unmoored by machines. That cinema produces a particular kind of energy is really only a specification of Virilio's earlier thesis. As Virilio goes on in *Pure War*, "the prostheses of automotive audio-visual movement create a subliminal comfort. Subliminal, meaning beyond consciousness. They allow a kind of visual – thus physical – hallucination which tends to strip us of our consciousness. Like the 'I run for you' of automobile technology, an 'I *see* for you' is created."[94] The emphasis here is on the physical nature of kinematic energy; this is an energy that crosses from the purely visual into a tactile sensation. Virilio proposes kinematic energy as a third energy next to potential and kinetic energies. The significance here is that Virilio draws on physics to express what cinema does. In this way, Virilio, although never expressing it in so many words, crosses from a purely informational view of cinema to a view based on the flow of energies. For this reason, we never actually lose our body with the acceleration of images, only that we lose conscious control of our body, which for Virilio's nostalgic phenomenology is a distinctive loss. As he laments in *The Aesthetics of Disappearance*, "turned causal by its excessive speed, the sensation overtakes the logical order."[95] We find ourselves in a frenzy of the sensible.

One part of sensory assault, then, is precisely the way that cinema's acceleration of images escapes any critical response to them: we are caught up in a bodily immediacy that precludes reflection. Our senses are overtaken by technology and perception becomes automated. Yet as John Johnston has show in his article "Machinic Vision," human vision has never been distinguishable from technological mediation as a strict binary opposition.[96] Instead, vision is conceived of as a machinic process that does not separate the human from the technical. Machinic vision "presupposes not only an environment of interacting machines and human-machine systems but a field of decoded perceptions that, whether or not produced by or issuing from these machines, assume their full intelligibility only in relation to them."[97] Sensory assault is identifiable by the intrusion of new technologies on our sensorium, but it is an intrusion that transforms and renders anew our sensorium.

23

Any kind of new technological affordance that can make a film more intense, more immediate, filled with more sensations is vital to the production of contemporary action cinema, where the emphasis has shifted so exclusively to the nonhuman capacities of the sound-images. Capacities that are designed to distort our pre-existing sensorium, making them a matter of *aisthesis* not prosthesis. Our sense perceptions are not simply extended or added to but reconfigured by the affordances of new image technologies. This aesthetic reconfiguration becomes the basis for our embodied perception, but it is a perception that is no longer unified or based only on the human body. Rather, it is a distributed perception, "because what is perceived is not located at any single place and moment in time, and the act by which this perception occurs is not the result of a single or isolated agency but of several working in concert or parallel."[98] We must also understand *aisthesis* as being inherently a different regime of perception, a regime that Shaviro terms affective or presubjective.[99] This affective argument stands in sharp contrast to Virilio's insistence on conscious perception as the very basis for our human condition, as anything that is preconscious is anathema to him.

Miriam Bratu Hansen employs the concept of mimetic innervation in her book *Cinema and Experience* in order to explicate the conversion or transmission of psychic excitation to somatic stimulation.[100] Taking the concept from Walter Benjamin, Hansen emphasizes that mimetic innervation is a two-way process, "not only a conversion of mental, affective energy into somatic, motoric form but also the possibility of reconverting, and recovering, split-off psychic energy through motoric stimulation."[101] If Virilio can only see the human subject drain away as kinematic energy impacts the body, Hansen, channeling Benjamin, argues that this bodily stimulation may awake new sensations and energies in the subject through the process of mimetic innervation.

Central to this process stands movement. Hansen argues that there are three primary movements that produce innervation: the movement of actors and objects, camera movement, and editing rhythm.[102] The exclusion of sound is immediately obvious, which in itself can produce innervation. Not only can sonic effects such as contrast or counterpoint color our impression of the image, but sonic qualities such as tone, density, and amplitude can also produce innervation through sonic vibrations. Much

24

contemporary action cinema today employs sound at extreme degrees of amplitude, using pure volume to intensify its images. Through these movements, the nonhuman capacities of sound-images can incorporate into our human capacities at the level of sensation. Cinema opens up to a broader realm of the senses through movement, a nonhuman world of perception which is as exciting and invigorating as it can be intimidating and menacing.

That action films accelerate us is an argument connected to the conjoining of affect and sensation: we feel ourselves sped up by the sensory assault of contemporary action cinema. However, it is also important to recognize that the sheer speed of these sound-images mean that our experience of them is not fully within perceptual consciousness: the vital trait of contemporary action cinema is that its speed is such that it bores below our perceptual threshold and so alters our perception. The key question here is not only whether or not perception is transformed while watching the film, but also to what extent this perceptual transformation telescopes out and impacts our general perception of the world. Virilio terms this impact "subliminal comfort" since it can be a pleasant "relative acceleration, that is, within the boundaries of my consciousness; but these boundaries are very narrow, and if, as in certain cases of 'invasion of privacy,' someone should use speed to go beyond this, I am conditioned."[103] Now, Virilio employs the peculiar phrase 'invasion of privacy' from a very strict phenomenological understanding of the subject. For Virilio, we are subjects that intend and perceive phenomena, such as films. If these films move too fast, they condition us as subjects *before* we become subjects, which is why it is an invasion of privacy: the most sacred, inner core of who I am is invaded by the speed of images.

The processual nature of our experiential becoming is what matters here. Pulses and throbs of sensation produce drops of experience that feed-forward to what our consciousness becomes. At extreme velocities, films transmit "affective energies to us, some of which pass below intellectual attention while still influencing emotions, judgments, and actions."[104] These affective energies can best be understood as the process of *priming*. Priming is a way of understanding how affects and sensations have an impact on our conscious experience. Dirk Eitzen argues that "priming is easily understood in the light of the basic function of the nervous system, which is to guide the body's interactions with the environment."[105] We are prepared for action via priming, although as Eitzen goes on to show, just because one might be primed for certain actions and behaviors, that in no way indicates that one will act or behave in that way. As Massumi phrases it, "priming *conditions* emergent awareness (creatively modulates its formation) rather than *causing* a response."[106] There is no way in which priming affects everyone equally, nor can priming overturn deliberate conscious choice.

What priming does, however, is to induce, incite and orient.[107] We could also term priming a lure for feeling, the urge we feel to step into and articulate certain sensations and experiences. There is no disciplinary power at work here, only a vague whispering that things feel better over here: a modulation. Sensory assault, then, is priming because the forces and energies thrust at us hold an allure in themselves; their intensities are fascinating and hold a promise of sensations of bodily mastery, power and agency. As modulation and entrainment, action cinema readies us for action: not direct action for our own bodies, but rather through projections of power. Essentially, our modulation starts off with vectoral forces that begin to direct the kinetics of our bodies, becoming entrainment through volatility, which in turn opens up new modes of action at a distance, all of which converge in a recognition of drone power, the reprieve we get from the culture of fear. What I turn to now, then, is the beginning of this process – the vectoral power of action films' audiovisual energies and how vectors function as transfers of affect. This approach lays the groundwork for how films work when considered as compactions of energies and forces rather than informational and representational structures.

2

Vectors and the Transfer of Affect

When action films are considered as priming our bodies' energies, transfer becomes central to our understanding of how these films work. I wish to discuss this particularly in relation to the new digital imagery employed so often in contemporary action films that rely heavily on spectacular effects. The films have incorporated new image technologies in order to intensify their action sequences. How audiovisual energy is transferred is central for how films work on and prime our bodies. While motion has always been central to cinema, the simulated and virtual movement created by digital animation and vector graphics produce a completely different form of autonomous movement. Furthermore, digital cinema technologies are not about the traditional reproduction of images but about the intensification of images, often achieved through animation. Motion capture and digital animation are among the foremost of these technologies and through a study of the Iron Man films (Jon Favreau 2008 and 2010, Shane Black 2013) and *Sucker Punch* (Zack Snyder 2011), I wish to emphasize how computer-generated imagery generates nonhuman energies.

I will employ the term *vector* to specify how intensity moves from screen to us. As a term, vector has a variegated history. Employed in mathematics to indicate any quantity having direction as well as magnitude, representable by drawing a line from one point to another, vector can also work as a verb for directing an aircraft (or another vehicle, such as missile or drone) towards its destination or target. Quite conceivably for this reason, Paul Virilio employs vector to describe the velocity of vehicles, bodies and images, drawing his definition from Albert Einstein: "Force and the change of speed are vectors that have the same direction."[1] Vectors are defined by change in quantity, magnitude and position and so help us better articulate the direction of acceleration.

When considering film, we can use the logic of the vector as change to explain how intensity is generated as a formal process. Deleuze does so in *Cinema 1*, where he defines vector as an instance of the action-image, the "broken line which brings together singular points or remarkable moments at the peak of their intensity."[2] Any change between screen elements (sound, color, lighting, composition and so forth) produces a change in intensity and so a change in sensation in the viewer. Rather than consider formal properties in isolation, we must understand them in relation to each other and through the change they effect. This is what Sean Cubitt means when he argues in his extensive history of cinema, *The Cinema Effect*, that the vector "does not represent, it communicates."[3] What matters for Cubitt is the transformation that the vector traces.

We should not regard the vector as simply the "in-between" of two fixed points but instead regard it as a process of becoming.[4] The vector is not a simple line but rather an unfolding of variation. Such unfolding cannot be contained within the sound-image but becomes an oscillation between film and viewer, the constant adjustment and adaptation to each other. For this same reason, Cubitt suggests that we are not dealing with one transmission so much as a weave of transmissions. We, as viewers, are part of this weave, not as end points but "as media: as people who make sense, but only as nodes in interweaving trajectories of signification."[5] The vector shifts emphasis away from a simple communication model of sender – channel – receiver to a field of metamorphosis. Such a field is traversed by energies in all directions. In this way, the aesthetic and the social interweave as different forces. Although Cubitt does argue that the vector communicates rather than represents, I do not agree that a vector communicates in the sense of an exchange of information. Rather, I regard the vector as the transfer of energy, irrespective of content.

McKenzie Wark discusses the vector as a power relation that regulates *how* energies are transferred. For Wark, what matters is the material form relations take; thus relation has certain definable qualities without having a fixed position.[6] Vectors are lines of force that limit or guide where meaning can go, how fast or how wide. The vector field translates and transforms energies and forces along certain lines, and in doing so exerts control over the flow of energies, although not their intensity. Redirection becomes a powerful tool and an important issue for the aesthetic production of forces, since social and cultural conditions may divert disruptive forces to harmless ends. Control the vector and you control the outcome, no matter the intensities the sound-image may produce.

What the vector clarifies is how every change in the sound-image registers a change in our sensate experience of this sound-image, but also how we are tied into a larger social milieu through the trajectories and lines of force that every film is composed of. We are riveted to material, cultural conditions, as Wark suggests. While we cannot directly equate new image technologies with the forms of sensations that they produce, we can argue that new image technologies afford new nonhuman sensations, i.e. sensate experiences that we could not otherwise have. All sensation starts out as nonhuman and only becomes human as it is folded into the process of experience that becomes us. As the screen and our bodies fold together along the vector, our range of sensate experience is broadened, converting the nonhuman into new human forms. That is the job of the vector, to transform nonhuman experience into human experience, but in that same process what constitutes human experience is also transformed.

Object Desire: *Iron Man*

Today's digital animation, also called computer-generated animation or CGA, has become the preferred method for animating spectacular sequences due to the way it reproduces a plunge into space that is concomitant with regular camera perspective. In other words, CGA makes us feel as if we are in the middle of the environment, while still allowing for movement that would otherwise be impossible. Such intensive movements are part of producing new cinematic sensations that go beyond traditional negative parallax movement (the movement of objects towards the camera). Through vectorized animated images, things take on life, which fills us with a sense of wonder at the images in themselves. This cinematic sense of wonder opens up a desire for the nonhuman as a form of cinematic transgression.

In the Iron Man films, Tony Stark (Robert Downey Jr.) pilots different versions of a military combat suit, necessitating digital animation to produce the superhuman feats that Iron Man regularly performs. Due to Downey's breezy, charming performance, we are strongly aligned with the Iron Man character, but also with the suit, since so much of Downey's performance is a matter of bringing life to the suit, both in animated sequences as well as in close-ups where he controls the suit. There is a tight enmeshing of man and machine which suggests that the binary opposition makes little sense in these films.

The most fascinating aspect of the films are the suit sequences whose wondrous liveliness fascinate us. This animate-ness of the battle suits suggests a wonder and desire for being more-than-human, moving beyond human bodily capacity. This nonhuman capacity is achieved through several computer-generated animation sequences and composited sequences that blend computer-generated animation and traditional footage. Briefly, computer-generated animation works by creating characters or objects with three-dimensional values across the X, Y and Z axes. Using a technique termed vector graphics, these objects and characters are turned into 3D wire models that are then finally rendered into 2D final versions that become the cinematic image. The advantage of vector graphics is that scale is irrelevant, as opposed to earlier methods employing raster graphics, making it easier to integrate animations into cinematic space.

Computer-generated animation works as a way to produce different forms of cinematic space, especially a more fluid rendition of three-dimensional space and movement through it. However, animating the Iron Man battle suit is another imperative function for the films, enabling an unusual form of alignment or identification. At its most basic, as Beth Coleman points out, "animation adds life to objects, albeit a synthetic life."[7] This synthetic life works in all the Iron Man films to infuse us with the clear sense that the suit has a life of its own, a fact that becomes clearer through the sequels as the different suits begin to move on their own, either remote-controlled (in the second film) or operating of their own accord (in the third film). This automation culminates in the third film with the suits coming to Stark's rescue. Reversed are the usual notions of man controlling machines, or even of machines controlling man, into an experience of machines living their own lives, divested from ours. That becomes a deeply wondrous sensation.

Our first introduction to the Iron Man suit comes in the first film, after Tony Stark has been captured by the Ten Rings terrorists in Afghanistan. After his friend Yinsen (Shaun Toub) has sacrificed his life for Stark, Stark employs his new crudely built Iron Man suit, called Mark I, and walks out of the cave to face the terrorists. As their bullets bounce off the suit's steel plates, Iron Man stands still, waiting. In a close-up, we hear Stark's voice echo "My turn", after which he proceeds to sear the terrorists with his built-in flame throwers. We shift to a wide shot of more terrorists running towards Iron Man, firing on him in medium shot reverse shots of the terrorists, medium-wide shots of Iron Man, after which Iron Man falls to his knees in a medium close-up, emphasizing the steel plating and bulky joins of the suit. Heroically, Iron Man sits up, bursting the terrorists with his flame throwers and stands up with a mighty heave, only to be engulfed in flames as explosives go off. We shift again to an extreme wide shot of the fireball explosion, relieved to see Iron Man fly out of the explosion, safe.

A scene full of digital effects, not least the Iron Man suit's computer-generated animation, this first scene of the Iron Man suit is revealing on several counts. The majesty of technology is paraded in sharp contrast to the terrorists, both in terms of the suit's weaponry and also the damage the suit can take without Stark being injured. Technology here becomes a force in its own right, but this is especially so considering the computer-generated animation. Originally shot as a mix between a still photo of the Mark I suit and motion-capture images, the suit's powerful stance is a product of animation. Animation provides synthetic life to the still image but significantly takes over when the motion-capture footage is not enough.

As Mihaela Mihailova has summarized, animation in general and digital animation in particular is strongly linked to notions of mastery and control, fulfilling the omnipotent dream of a "cinema fully and exclusively subservient to human imagination."[8] It's no surprise, then, that superhero films are filled with computer-generated animation, since CGA allows bodily movements that are impossible. The tension between bodily movement and static postures of mastery are central for action movies, as Lisa Purse has pointed out.[9] But when Iron Man in the above scene stands up in a posture of mastery, bullets spraying off the armor, his flame throwers belching fire and smoke, the human body cannot keep pace. The motion capture actor was unable to stand up in a way that suggested enough physical force, simply because human knees cannot bend that way. Computer-generated animation had to be used to produce the proper, forceful posture. In other words, the human body is overtaken by a nonhuman body of digital animation to suggest power beyond what we can do. And to be clear, the adjustment is not directly noticeable, and most will not see the augmentation, yet I believe it is felt as a vector that renders a larger potentiality for our embodiment, a sense of power and mastery indicated in the overlapping processes of digital bodies, cinematic bodies and our bodies.

Such scenes, and there are many of these nonhuman sequences in all the Iron Man films, pose a challenge to the way that we understand cinematic identification. Traditionally understood to connect to a specific character through the pleasure of looking, Barbara Creed points out in an early piece on "synthespians" that such identification becomes untenable: "Asked to identify with a cyberstar, the spectator would be haunted by a sense of uncanny: the image on the screen appears human, and yet is not human. The glamorous other is a phantom, an image without a referent in the real, an exotic chimera, familiar yet strange."[10] However, I do not agree with Creed's notion that our identification is located in the pleasure of looking, although I do agree that cinematic identification alters in the case of digital animated characters.

My conception of identification is one of embodiment, residing more in the force of movement, the sensations of moving along with the actor's body and the film's body. Yet even with embodied identification, digitally animated characters indicate a shift, although I believe a pleasurable shift rather than a specifically uncanny one. When a digitally animated character moves in ways that not only go beyond what we can do, but go beyond what any human body can ever do, such as the digitally animated body movements of the Iron Man suit, we encounter a nonhuman embodiment. So, in order to maintain our alignment with Iron Man, we must detach from our embodied logic and extend into what Ian Bogost has termed alien phenomenology: to be subsumed entirely in the uniqueness of the cinematic object's native logic of motion capture and animation effects that allow for nonhuman movements.[11] Our embodied desire for the nonhuman movements of the Iron Man suit is one of vector transformation: we are made to desire these movements, despite the fact that they are beyond our human embodiment.

Bogost proposes wonder as the term for how objects orient; that is to say, how things fascinate us in and of themselves. I believe this is precisely what the Iron Man suit does – it offers a cinematic object worthy of interest on its own accord, not necessarily subsumed to narrative logic, emotional character investment or any other human concern. This is not to suggest that narrative pleasures are not part of our interest in the Iron Man suit, but rather to say that the Iron Man suit is in itself interesting.[12] The film-makers realized that such identification is problematic in the long run and so opted for intermittent close-ups of Stark's face to humanize the film and make a more conventional identification available. Yet I will maintain that this simply opens up a kind of dual identification located in either Stark or the suit. We find here a plural form of identification, no longer unitary, and one that does not necessarily privilege the male, human character but opens up for a thoroughly nonhuman form of identification. Whether or not such an identification should be termed exactly "identification" is a different question.

Cinematic objects are wonders in their own right. The desire to watch the latest and greatest audiovisual special effects that cinema has to offer is one expression of this sense of wonder. Too often such spectacles are denigrated as mindless, useless trivialities, or the presence of narrative in action films is emphasized, as if to ensure that people still prefer nar-rative films. Scott Bukatman, in his piece "Spectacle, Attractions and Visual Pleasure," strikes a happy medium, arguing that while narrative endings may indeed contain spectacle, overly favoring narrative pleas-ures negates the inherent pleasure of disruption.[13] Much as traditional identification is disrupted with the introduction of the Iron Man suit's spectacular, nonhuman embodiments, narrative can be disrupted by spectacle, and an attachment to the fascinating objects within the film develops.

Objects matter in film, and not just symbolically. In her *Savage Theory*, Rachel O. Moore points out that cinematic objects may be "different from those daily-life objects from whence they came, but that nonetheless these objects are no less but rather even more alive than those objects. Objects burn bright as constellations of meaning and crackle with tactile effects; things take on life."[14] Moore's argument is in part that an affective form of life imbues these cinematic objects, a source that is a double of our own. This formulation is entirely congruent with Bogost's argument that things have agency in themselves. The crackle of tactile effects is the way an object acts on us beyond our knowledge or understanding. There is a production of desire for the Iron Man suit through the vector transfer of sensation. This production of desire comes in part also from the autonomous nature of the Iron Man suit. Not only is the suit a nonhuman agent in terms of providing plural embodiments and identifications, we also experience the suit as a living object on several occasions. Such a living object infuses us with a sense of wonder, and it is the vector that directs this trajectory of wonder towards the suit rather than Tony Stark (or Robert Downing, Jr).

Most intensely, such autonomous agency occurs at the end of *Iron Man 3*, when a host of Iron Man suits of different capabilities show up to help Stark and James Rhodes (Don Cheadle) fight the Extremis virus-infected minions of Aldrich Killian (Guy Pearce). Clearly summoned by Stark and operated by J.A.R.V.I.S. (Stark's Paul Bettany-voiced AI butler), these drone suits, however, also move and act of their own accord. The suits show up at a crucial moment in the narrative, just in time to save Stark, Rhodes and Pepper Potts (Gwyneth Paltrow), indicating that these objects clearly do have narrative functions. However, the suits' actions also indicate a sense of wonder for their actions. Not only do the suits fly and fight as well as Stark in a suit, they also perform actions that no human can do, yet feel wondrous to participate in. One suit disassembles itself to take out minions, only to reassemble itself after. *(See Figure 2.1 in the insert.)*

All these movements suggest an earlier era of animation where objects come alive, something that Vivian Sobchack calls the incredible lightness of being, drawing on Eisenstein's notion of the plasmatic nature of animation.[15] Similarly, Bukatman argues that animation opens up new sensations and experiences through a "renewal of perception through an act of estrangement" and a "conscious decision to 'play along' with a world that operates differently."[16] Wonder is an acceptance of a world that works differently, that allows objects to crackle with tactile energies, where we try on what it is like to be a thing, even just for a little while. This cinematic room for play opens up a much larger world of sensation that is in no way grounded in human bodily experience but stretches wide across a range of plural, distributed embodiments. As Beth Coleman insists, "in the face of an autonomous animation of things, instead of what has been theorized as a seemingly unstoppable progression toward an inertia of the human subject, one may also engage other modalities of agency."[17] If things are alive, we can try what it is like to live as such a thing, what it feels like to be Iron Man's suit. Far from being somehow a misanthropic denigration of a human subject, it allows the recognition that the world of sensation is wider and deeper than human sensation.

As the world of sensation opens up for us, surely this new realm of the nonhuman is something we desire. Yet such desire is not traditional sexual desire but instead an eradication of human desire in favor of nonhuman desire, a desire to merge with a larger machinic process. The vector field modulates our experience and our desire towards the fluid bodies of the Iron Man suits. The way the suits merge and fold over human bodies or perform actions of their own suggests an attraction to such nonhuman metamorphoses. In *Iron Man 3*, Stark loses interest in Pepper Potts in favor of the suits, a desire for transformation and change that goes beyond a desire of the human. Irrespective of the fact that Stark renounces the suits at the end of the film, recognizing that he must accept who he is and choose the woman he loves, our desire in the film is at least as tied to the suit embodiment as any fixed sexual desire.

We find thus a strong reverberation between human desire and the nonhuman suit. The desire, what I would essentially term the affect, we feel in the case of the Iron Man films cannot be contained within a sense of human affect. Rather, what these films show is that affect is not limited to us as humans, but that affect necessarily traverses between humans, nonhumans and machines. This nonhuman affective reverberation is what Patricia MacCormack terms cinesexuality, the ambiguous state of desire in cinema, in which we cannot say no to the affect of cinematic images, a desire that "involves human participations with inhuman entities – animals, machines, anything that does not reflect or affirm the dominance of the human."[18] The nonhuman nature of the Iron Man suits is what attracts us to them, the fact that they have a different life from our own, their sleek and sexy bodies, able to do things we can only desire.

We should keep in mind that the nonhuman desire for the Iron Man suits is closely intertwined with destruction, which seduces us into a state of wonder at the destructive capacities of the suits. I see these films as drawing on what Sarah Wanenchak refers to as drone sexuality: "a sexualized drone is transgressive, and that transgressiveness is erotic. A drone is not literally an enmeshing of organic and mechanical in the way that a cyborg is, but in terms of power, that's exactly what it is."[19] I would make explicit that Wanenchak's argument includes desire alongside power, which I believe she implicitly argues. Iron Man is a drone from this perspective, as an enmeshing of organic and mechanical, just as the cinematic image of the Iron Man films is an enmeshing of digital and physical bodies. It is this enmeshed object that we cannot help but desire in its transgressiveness and its crackle of tactile effects. We are insatiably drawn to the nonhuman enfleshment of the animated object of the Iron Man suit. The Iron Man films thus celebrate the sexy destructive capacities of war machines, turning violent spectacle into seductive dance. Certainly the films insist on the sexiness of the Iron Man suit and play up the enmeshing of sexualized bodies, the suit and its destructive capacities. Desire, nonhuman bodies and power mesh together as a powerful force that is vectorized to culminate in our experience. We are brought into the same seductive dance of the Iron Man suit, sexy, destructive capacities and violent spectacle.

Consider the first appearance of Iron Man in *Iron Man 2*. After a suitably ominous scene with Mickey Rourke as Ivan Vanko, we get the title image and then a black screen with distant booms and a staticky radio voice giving the all-clear for a plane, suggesting a war zone. A guitar riff sets in – for most people, instantly recognizable as AC/DC – which slightly shifts our impression of the shot into probably being about Iron Man rather than a military aircraft. Considering this is the second film, the audience has been trained to expect AC/DC and similar hard rock guitar riffs to signify Iron Man. And sure enough, in beat with the music, we cut to Iron Man standing inside an air carrier, ready to jump. Outside the plane, we see an explosion, although the music remains in the foreground of the soundtrack. More explosions go off as Iron Man courageously runs out of the aircraft and leaps through the air down towards a large metropolis at night; we see the street lights illuminate our horizon as the camera follows Iron Man down. Then suddenly we recognize that the explosions are fireworks, not actual explosions. In a long continuous take, the camera swirls and swerves around Iron Man as he descends towards the ground. While there are no cuts, there are several swoosh pans that work in a similar way, particularly when Iron Man is struck by a firework, making us hesitate for a moment: are the fireworks flak or fireworks? Boosting his rockets, Iron Man shoots down towards the ground and lands on a stage with several scantily clad female dancers behind him. We are at the Stark Expo, not in a war zone.

The scene continues in a far lighter mood, with close-ups of Iron Man and Stark, cross-cutting to the dancing women, with the cheers of the crowd in the background. Along with the sexual innuendos of AC/DC's cock rock and the wriggling dancers, this is clearly a sexually charged scene. What is interesting, however, is that there are relatively few shots of Stark's face. Instead, the camera seeks out the suit, giving us close-ups of boots, joins, and chest plate, all happening while mechanical tentacles slip the suit off Stark. The Iron Man suit functions as an intensive figure of overflowing sexuality that conflates and shifts desire between Stark, the dancers and the machines. The transgression between technological body and human body is what gives the scene its erotic charge, but rather than privileging the male or female body, the technological body is what is shown off here. As Wanenchak points out, such desire for the non-human is both frightening and arousing. In fact, it is arousing *because* it is frightening. This is a deeply queer scene that reveals the intensity of affect as traversing all domains, conflating them experientially through the force of the vector.

An intense blurring of dominance and submission is at work in the scene. The Iron Man suit is exceedingly dominant, forceful in its hard, metallic body that both protects and controls Stark's body. While in principle Stark is in control as he hurtles through the air towards the expo center, we get none of the typical close-ups of Stark's face, thus making the descent a purely digitally animated scene. Here, we are aligned with the technological body and its nonhuman capacities through a long take that can only occur through computer-generated animation. Once Iron Man lands, the dancers behind him provide the clearest example of human bodies in action, and the dancers' bodies' gyrating is certainly a spectacular display of physical prowess, even as it is also sexualized. At the same time, the dancers' synchronized moves also suggest a kind of machinic, relational body beyond the merely human. At one and the same time, there are the individual dancers and the dancers as synchronized whole: there are bodies and one body moving at the same time.

As Iron Man rotates on a platform, the floor folds away and the mechanical arms extend to peel off the suit. The face plate comes off first, revealing that there is a human underneath. Yet even after this is revealed, that only makes Stark even more at the mercy of the mechanical arms, since he cannot move or do anything but let them remove the suit. The more the machines work, the more of Stark's soft, vulnerable body is exposed. As we can see, there is an overwhelming display of boundaries and their transgression. While much of this display is self-evidently gendered, significantly the Iron Man suit transgresses any easy gendering. Obviously, as an object of violence, hard and impenetrable, we would code the suit as masculine. Yet at the same time, the suit envelops and protects Stark, almost akin to a womb. And certainly J.A.R.V.I.S.'s voice (although not present in this scene) is more airy and effeminate than Stark's melodic baritone, opening up for a further queering of the suit (since the suit is associated with J.A.R.V.I.S. more than anyone else).

The pulses of nonhuman desires emanating from the screen and sound system become vectors of power that fold into our bodies, generating resonances in us. The sound-images consist of what we can call, following Goodman, audiovisual affectiles.[20] For Goodman, affectiles are conflations of affect and projectiles and are primarily associated with sound vibrations. Sound, especially music, is significant in the scene – AC/CD's riffs provide the rhythmic pounding that makes everything else vibrate – yet the computer-generated animations are as much a part of the affective tone of the scene, as are the movements of human bodies. Audiovisual affectiles become the convergence point of all these affects, hurled at us at high velocities. Affectiles are thus condensed energies that make our bodies vibrate.

This scene activates overlapping zones: the machinic and nonorganic desire of the suit, but also the overlapping of this desire with that of war as spectacle. The fluid sensation we experience in the opening of the scene, where we transition from the assumption of being in a war zone to that of being in a celebration at an expo, conflates the two into a clear sensation of semblance. The way we are first accelerated into thinking of the scene as a combat scene primes us for a radically different affect than the one we get from the celebration. Yet considering the intensity of the fireworks, the machinic desire for the Iron Man suit and male sexualized desire embodied by the dancers, we find a fully charged experience that activates all these modes into an affective worlding of the nonhuman sexual desire for war. Rather than presenting war as a terrifying situation, we are shifted into a titillating ensemble of war as desirous spectacle. Such is the force of the vector. (*See Figure 2.2 in the insert.*)

Such priming early in the film sets us up for experiencing later scenes in the same titillated state of affect. Our desire for the Iron Man suit, and the nonhuman capacities the suit facilitates, rivets us to the screen. The final, climactic battle squares off Iron Man, now employing the Mark VI version, and Rhodes in the confiscated Mark II suit against Vanko in an altered Mark II suit and Vanko's automated drones. This scene becomes the pinnacle of our desire for the computer-generated animated body, considering that it is essentially a five minute animated sequence interspersed with close-ups of Stark and Rhodes' faces, while, significantly, Vanko never gets a close-up but instead fights with his helmet off to increase recognition. The camera loops and zooms at breakneck paces to infuse the animated bodies with even more movement, increasing the embodied identification we feel. Tense and harried, the scene accelerates us into a tight loop between these animated bodies and our own sensations, producing a distinct machinic assemblage of experience that is entirely congruent with the drone sexuality expressed by Wanenchak.

We are riveted to the Iron Man suit and its constant metamorphoses show that drone sexuality is ideologically reproductive. Conflating the desire for the nonhuman suit's excessive capacities with war-as-sexualized-spectacle produces an affective atmosphere which is attenuated by Downey's charming performance. War is spectacle-spectacle is sexy-sexy is fun becomes the vector of force that the suit renders clear for us. But there is certainly also a freedom in the way that a larger sensory world has been opened up for us, a freedom that can assert itself resistantly by focusing on the new sensations afforded by the nonhuman desire of drone sexuality. As I have already argued, priming never determines outcomes, priming only ever elicits. And the Iron Man films are full of elicitations of sex, war, potency and spectacle.

What seems to me undeniable are the ways that computer-generated animation produces not only human sensations but also a larger scope of nonhuman sensations, and that our enjoyment of these films are entirely contingent on these nonhuman sensations. Clearly there is a tension between these sensations and the directions in which they pull us. We do, however, emerge with a broader understanding of how embodied identification works in these films. We can no longer argue that identification is unitary or depends only on the subsumption of spectacular irruptions in narrative closures. Nor can we argue that embodiment is singular or predominantly human. At the very least, the embodiment that we find in these films is plural, dispersed across human bodies but also digitally animated bodies. And these digitally animated bodies may not have real-world referents but they do produce movement and sensation in us, making their presence equally as real as any other body. This is the first step in arguing that contemporary action cinema functions as an assemblage of human and nonhuman sensations.

Vectorized Space: *Sucker Punch*

While computer-generated animation is usually thought of in terms of characters or objects, another significant aspect of digital visual effects is the environment through which characters move. Usually relegated to digital matte paintings, compositing or similar background details in films such as *The Lord of the Rings* (Peter Jackson 2001, 2002, 2003), computer-generated imagery can take on even more of the mise-en-scène. In films such as *Sin City* (Frank Miller and Robert Rodriguez 2005) or *Sky Captain and the World of Tomorrow* (Kerry Conran 2004), the entire film has been shot on green screens and the environment is entirely digitally generated. However, even in such unusual cases, the environment remains static, a backdrop for character actions to unfold. Rare are the films where the environment becomes an active participant in the narration of the story and takes on degrees of agency. *Sucker Punch* is one of these, producing a digitally animate space that shifts and transforms in response to the narrative action. As such, the film's space emerges as a dynamic vector space that alters relations within it.

Traditionally, space changes only in a sequential manner. The continuity system exchanges one space for another based on logical progression, one place after another joined through editing. We move between radically different locales only through parallel editing, where two distinct storylines unfold. We can move from placid Hobbiton to ominous Mount Doom in *The Fellowship of the Ring* in only one cut, yet we recognize that these are two different places. This is the basis of the narrative exchange of space, where, as Aylish Wood points out, "space only gains meaning from the actions of the characters within it, and so is seamlessly embedded within a narrative organization."[21] Other traditions of montage may conjoin separate places through metaphoric or other symbolic meanings, such as the ambiguous places in Lars von Trier's *Element of Crime* (1984) that register an uncanny tone for the entire film. Such non-sequitur exchanges of space often function as similes, producing symbolic resonances between spaces.

Literal, physical transformation of space is highly unusual. We can think of examples such as *Inception* (Christopher Nolan 2010), where most of the film (and possibly all of the film) takes place within dreams, thus permitting space to dissolve into a dream logic, where the environment itself takes on threatening qualities. What is challenged in *Inception* is primarily Cartesian space, and instead the dream powers of the characters produce Escher-like spaces that fold in on themselves. Yet even this shifting space is under the control of characters, and so works as an extension of the narrative conflict. By contrast, *Sucker Punch* reneges on the idea that space is anything other than another resource to be exploited, producing a dynamic space that shifts almost at whim. Rather than following a dream logic, *Sucker Punch* follows a game logic, in which space, as well as time, becomes mutable and produces vectors that change and overturn relations just as suddenly as these same vectors are instated. Game logic allows for this transformation of space and time into things that do not follow the causal logic of physics but instead become what Alexander Galloway has termed an "actionable space".[22] Space is not defined by its dimensions but by the actions that are possible within it. Unlike the Iron Man films, *Sucker Punch* vectorizes space as a challenge to overcome in itself. Space becomes dynamic or performative in an irruption of what we can term agential space.

41

Sucker Punch is, by all accounts, a pubescent dream turned into multi-million dollar blockbuster vehicle. The story itself is as minimal as it is predictable and generic. Babydoll (Emily Browning, we never learn the character's actual name) is unfairly institutionalized for accidentally having caused her sister's death. In the asylum, Babydoll faces lobotomy and slips into a fantasy world, in which she works in a burlesque club alongside other women – Amber (Jamie Chung), Blondie (Vanessa Hudgens), Rocket (Jena Malone) and Rocket's sister, Sweet Pea (Abbie Cornish). In this fantasy world, Babydoll orchestrates an escape from the burlesque club, an escape set up as the quest for five items. The items are achieved through three major set pieces: an attack on a World War I bunker, an assault on an Orc castle and fighting robots on a speeding train. These three set pieces are stand-ins for Babydoll's impressive burlesque dancing (which we never see), and also represent the other women finding the quest items. The fourth item, a key, is found in the burlesque club, while the last item is Babydoll sacrificing herself for her friends, which parallels Babydoll being lobotomized. Back in the asylum, the doctor in charge realizes that Babydoll was only lobotomized because his signature was forged. The plot is unveiled, and although Babydoll is now lobotomized, it is strongly indicated that she has produced another fantasy world, where she will live in happiness.

As is evident from the above, narrative and realistic portrayal of place and characters matter less to the film than spectacular permutations of space and the intensities of experience that follow. The variegated nested worlds function as ways of producing new spectacular displays. For this reason, we should distinguish between the story world (where Babydoll is in a psychiatric hospital), her fantasy world (where she is in the burlesque club) and the game-worlds (different levels where Babydoll and her friends must vanquish foes to find the quest item they are looking for). The narrative follows a clear quest structure that also borrows heavily from computer games and the idea of levels or stages through which the player must move, defeating hordes of mooks before taking on the final boss. The quest structure and the game logic of progression are tightly entwined and help articulate each other. Game logic interjects in the way that there is little correlation between one stage and the next, drawing on a rich tradition of fantastic worlds that have little to no interest in reproducing a preexisting reality. While most people will recognize the narrative structure and its clear-cut goals, fewer might be willing to accept the unmotivated shifts in narrative reality that keep occurring. Yet these shifting worlds, with their own internal logic and new challenges, also present the way that *Sucker Punch* innovates the production of cinematic space by making it dynamic. With this in mind, I will examine three examples of how space becomes agential: first, the burlesque club in an otherwise dialog-driven scene; second, the assault of the Orc castle and the slaying of the dragon; and third, the attack on the train – especially the first sequence, where the women gain access to the train.

The first example of agential space is a relatively calm scene, considering the hectic pace of *Sucker Punch's* narrative and sound-image organization: Babydoll has just insisted that they must all escape the clutches of Blue Jones and the burlesque club. After Babydoll has left, the others debate Babydoll's plan. Primarily a dialog-driven scene, it works well to show how space can participate actively in how we experience a film, what Wood refers to as spaces with incipient agency.[23] Space begins to exhibit agency when it exceeds limits conventionally placed on it by narrative organization, i.e. when space becomes excessive. Spatial excess typically manifests in terms of an intensity of space rather than the conventional extensive expression of space.

In the burlesque club, the madam has just said that the women must get ready for rehearsal in fifteen minutes. Sweet Pea and Rocket sit in front of their make-up mirrors with the camera placidly tracking around them. They discuss whether or not Babydoll's plan of escape is good; Sweet Pea is adamantly against it. As the camera tracks around them, we can see the other women in the mirrors, following the conversation. Both women sit with their backs to us, but because of the mirror, we can also see their faces in a medium wide shot. The camera keeps tracking past them, and then past Blondie, as Sweet Pea asserts that they are on their own and they will not agree to Babydoll's plan. The tracking shot brings Blondie into frame and we can see Rocket in Blondie's mirror, looking down despondently. And then the camera tracks into the mirror, still in the same shot, and we slowly move into the reverse space, or more accurately, the mirror space on the *other side* of the mirror. The camera continues around Blondie and tracks behind Rocket. We now see what used to be the real world as the mirror image, and what was the mirror image is now three-dimensional space. Rocket explains how Babydoll saved her, and just then, Babydoll steps into the mirror image, stops and looks at Sweet Pea. Cut. *(See Figures 2.3 and 2.4 in the insert.)*

The tracking shot is one long, continuous take, and the spatial illogics it produces are highly complex. We have to accept that this is not a regular, three-dimensional space but is rather a product of compositing together at least two shots in order to produce the mirror space. Furthermore, once we cut and Babydoll explains what items they need for their escape, Sweet Pea is now to the left of Rocket, so they have switched positions. While this change in position might be regarded as a minor continuity error, it is just as conceivable that we are now in yet another nested world, considering all the nested worlds that the narrative employs. We find here an example of what Brown has dubbed "digital cinema's conquest of space": we experience paradoxical, impossible movement through space facilitated only by the nonhuman capacities of computer-generated animation.[24]

I argue for computer-generated animation over imagery because this is an instance of movement rather than static images. More than simply a space that characters move through, this is a matter of space as movement, a fluid continuity that can only be achieved by the conjoining of moving images, not a layering of movement across static images. From the stand-point of narration, this spatial plunge is a matter of making a static, expository scene engaging, where movement overtakes the purely narrative information dispersed in the scene. As fascinating as this tracking shot is, a similar shot would be hard to pull off during a scene that contained several movement trajectories. Since all the actors' bodies sit still, space can be allowed to churn without spatial relations completely collapsing.

We traverse a space that cannot exist anywhere outside of cinema. The sensation of traversal through impossible space is at first unsettling, quite literally, since we lose our embodied location within the tracking shot. Secondly, once we reorient, there is a sense of deep fascination and curiosity about spatial relations and the shifting position between actors. This is the vectorization of space: relations become charged with energy and crackle as they shift in front of us. We can agree with Wood's argument, in which this scene would be an example of how "technologies are framing space, participating in organizing what we see and how it is seen."[25] A shot like this could never be made without computer-generated animation and digital compositing. Although in fact shot entirely on celluloid, *Sucker Punch* went through a digital intermediary process in order to join the shots together into one seamless whole.

What we find, then, in the tracking shot that goes behind the looking-glass, is transforming space, what we can also call, more accurately, a spatial morph. Traditionally, morphs are thought of in terms of characters who morph into a different character, such as *An American Werewolf in London* or *Dr. Jekyll and Mr. Hyde* or a host of other films.[26] When we talk of a spatial morph, however, immediately agency and action shift onto space rather than character. When space changes, especially if it changes unexpectedly within the shot, our perception shifts from its usual focus on the characters and their actions to that of space and its actions. Of course, there exists a rich tradition of spatial morphs: animation. But the classical animation shorts have always enjoyed a completely different relation to the production of reality, much less space. However, even for animation, literally changing embodied perspective on the viewer has been negligible. And as Wood argues, "as has been true of animation since its beginnings, digital technologies can now be used within live-action cinema to create transforming space."[27] And yet she still does not go far enough. Space can even be inverted, as in this scene, where space and perspective are shifted and turned on their sides, if not on their heads. I suggest the term *burlesque space* here, because this spatial morph is an exaggerated imitation of three-dimensional space, as well as being comedic in the sense that the morph here gleefully rejoices in the disruption of boring old space, reveling in the complete and intoxicating freedom of a space with no boundaries. One can almost sense the perverse pleasure taken in parodying stable conceptions of space and the continuity system idea that space must remain coherent for the viewer. Space does not need to remain coherent as long as it produces intensities, vectors that change our relation to the screen and the cinematic space produced by the screen.

Mastery of movement is key for burlesque space; to the extent that we are always aligned with the camera, here we are allowed to go where literally no one can ever go. On a thematic level, such a mastery of movement exists in stark contrast to the spatial confinement that all the women live under.

We never see the outside of the burlesque club, and in fact most of the action takes place in the dressing room, the kitchen or the hallways, making for a relatively claustrophobic environment. The women are not free to leave, and all their dreams manifest as dreams of the outside: expanses of wilderness and vast, open skies are the images that serve to represent their desires to be free. In the same way, every single set-piece game-world that they must conquer in order to recover another quest item is precisely displaced onto massive spaces that stretch far into the horizon. Similarly, only through mastery of these spaces and spatial movements within them do the women win. Conquering space is the central metaphor for freedom for this film, and the mirror scene's brief excursion into burlesque space has merely begun to open the wider issues of space expressed throughout the film. The two next scenes I discuss surpass each other in spatial morphing and mastery of movement.

A good example of extreme spatial mastery comes in the second game-world, where the women must now locate fire. While in the burlesque club fire is represented by something as mundane as a lighter, within the game-world fire comes in the far more evocative shape of two stones located in a baby dragon's throat, which, when struck together, produce the most wonderful fire anyone has ever seen. But the baby dragon resides in an Orc fortress with its mother, and the Orcs are waging a bloody battle against a human army. The only way to get to the baby dragon is to fly a bomber over the fortress, so the women can jump inside the castle. The scene kicks into gear when the bomber plane swoops in over the fortress in a wide following shot that cuts to a close-up of a red blinking light, then to a medium shot of the women jumping out of the plane. The camera tracks out of the door, zooms down with Rocket, cuts to an upward medium shot of the women falling, tilting down as they hit the ground in a kneeling pose, the ground cracking and splitting beneath them, debris spraying around them as the camera zooms in on Babydoll, who looks up. Cut to a reverse shot of surprised Orcs and the fight is on. As the women twist and tumble around the fortress courtyard, the camera often moves in a counter-trajectory against the direction of the women's movement, providing even more energy of movement. The women here are shown to be in control of space, able to move in any way that they want. But the same can be said of the camera's movements, which so often articulate space counter to the women's movements. This unmotivated camera movement helps produce what Wood refers to as dynamic space, a space that has its own form of agency, because we are forced to align movement across two axes at the same time: the women's limber acrobatics and the camera's ditto.[28] Unlike conventional spatial choreography, the camera does not help provide a stable space through which we can follow the characters' actions unfolding. Instead, the camera produces its own spaces, spaces that "have meaning beyond that given to them by character actions."[29] The articulation of space becomes its own unique sensation, one that is not limited to simply following character movements and actions.

Such dynamic space thus works to expand and augment the already spectacular bodily displays of the women. When Babydoll, Rocket and Sweet Pea find the baby dragon, they inadvertently wake the mother. Filled with righteous fury, the mother gives chase but is cut off by the bomber plane piloted by Amber (Jamie Chung). A brief, break-neck chase sequence follows, where the dragon hurtles after the plane, billowing fire. Only masterful flying allows Amber to evade the dragon fire, fearlessly navigating past bridges and other objects in her path. Once again, space becomes a threat to be vanquished, just like the Orcs and the dragon. Furthermore, the angered dragon and the bomber chase set up the clearest example of spatial mastery and the production of space as nonhuman capacity in the scene: when Babydoll slays the dragon.

Amber flies the bomber plane over the courtyard where Babydoll is still fighting. The dragon belly flops at high speed into the courtyard, sliding towards Babydoll with stones and tiles flying all around. Babydoll runs in a slow-motion medium shot from above behind towards the fortress gate, intercut with a medium close-up from below in front, showing the dragon sliding towards her. As she clears the gate, the dragon's head towering over her, she turns around and leaps upward. In a wide shot, we see a burst of flame scorch the ground as Babydoll clears the it, her sword at the ready. A close-up of her high-heeled foot shows how close the flames are to her. Then we cut to an extreme close-up of Babydoll's sword as a tracking shot that moves down the blade, close enough to see the elaborate engravings of dragons. As we reach the cross-guard, the camera swerves so we can see Babydoll below and the flames below her. The shot rotates along its own axis while Babydoll grips the sword with two hands and the dragon's head comes into focus below. Cut to a medium shot level on with Babydoll holding the sword with two hands in front of a fireball, gracefully twirling in slow-motion. A reverse angle close-up of Babydoll's face from below shows us her readiness and steely resolve, eyes looking off-screen at the dragon. Two quick medium shots of Babydoll falling down, hands moving down in a chopping motion towards the dragon with the fire on the left screen side opposite Babydoll. Close-up of Babydoll's grimly determined face as she chops down, and a medium shot of Babydoll stabbing the sword through the dragon's forehead with flames billowing all over. The camera tracks back as the flames die out, the dragon's head lolls and Babydoll relaxes. The dragon is slain.

As it takes longer to read this description than watch the scene, it may take away some of the imposing use of space in the scene. The combination of slow-motion and the impossible tracking zoom across Babydoll's sword opens up a majestic sense of spatial mastery, and again it is a sense of spatial mastery that augments Babydoll's impressive movement. Space itself becomes a vector that pulls us along, primarily by placing us in places that no one could ever be in. In opposition to what has so often been discussed as a kind of muscular cinema, no human body could ever move in this way. Instead, what we find in the dynamic space of the Orc fortress scene is a thoroughly nonhuman space, and subsequently, a nonhuman embodiment that nonetheless instills a powerful sensation of mastery in us. This mastery is parallel to the affectiles generated in *Iron Man*, though here in the form of intense spatial movements – especially the movement of the camera and the way that animation of space overtakes regular camera shots. Most of the shots are produced through techniques conjoining the conventional shots with computer-generated animations. The use of these computer-generated animations is what allows for the sense of spatial mastery rendered in this scene.

Space is vectorized, becoming a movement of its own kind that reaches beyond character movement and beyond even the magnificent movement of Steadicam rigs or similar superhuman movement. The vectors of the synthetic camera need not obey any kind of Newtonian physics, since there is no gravity in the spacetimes of computers. Correlating to the use of vectors in the Iron Man films, we find a similar sense of bodily innervation from *Sucker Punch's* affectiles, only more radically so, in that the tactile sensations of leaping and falling are no longer tied to a human body or an animated object but instead to the free-ranging movement of the synthetic camera. This is an actionable space, defined by the movements it produces and the effects these movements have on us.

The most excessive and impressive deployment of space in *Sucker Punch* comes, I believe, in the final game-world, where the women board a train to disarm a bomb, which correlates to stealing a knife from the Cook (Malcolm Scott). This game-world functions as the most extensive display of spectacle in the film, despite the quest item only being the third of four. However, as the final of the game-world set pieces, the film pulls out all the stops to produce a magnificent and overwhelming vectorized space. After the helicopter has flown over the train in a suitably vertiginous trajectory also followed by the camera, the women once again jump down in slow-motion, displaying an early command of space. Landing on the back of the train, they get ready to move into the train car that holds the bomb they must disarm.

One of the most impressive fight sequences in cinema ensues as they open the door and face the robots inside the train car. Too long to summarize here, the most important aspect of the sequence is the opening two and a half minutes which is done as one long continuous take of the women barreling through the train car, disposing of robots along the way. Of course, there is no way that the spatial manipulations could be done in one take. Instead the sequence is stitched together from numerous shorter shots alongside swoosh pans to ease the compositing, while also injecting several computer-generated animations to keep the momentum going. While a technical deconstruction of which shots are real and which are composites would be interesting as a kind of cinematic detective work, what matters is that the sequence is experienced as a seamless whole.

Not only do the women tumble around the way they did in the Orc fortress scene, the shot constantly ramps between regular speed and super-slow motion. Simultaneously whirling around its own axis, the camera also tracks back and forth inside the train car, as well as leaping up and down to follow the actors. Similarly, speed ramps down to allow us to experience movements more fully, seemingly also to allow the women more time to react, such as the moment when Rocket leaps up, freezes in mid-air to shoot three robots, after which she gracefully glides to the ground. Both space and time morph according to a sensorial logic rather than a narrative logic. While there is a clear overarching narrative goal – disarm the bomb – reaching this goal is made more tense through the sensorial logic of spacetime manipulation. (*See Figure 2.5 in the insert.*)

However, unlike the classic example of super-slow in *The Matrix's* bullet-time, where slowing down speed is an act of the characters, especially Neo as he learns to master the code of the matrix, the super-slow in *Sucker Punch* follows a different logic. Clearly meant to expand our sensorial experience of the sequence, we find that the image ramps down speed to increase tension. One example is when Rocket is punched in the face by a robot; we see the segment in super-slow, slow enough to see her face distort and even how the impact of the punch makes her cheek and nose ripple. While adding narrative tension, such super-slow moments also produce peaks of sheer intensity and fascination that go beyond narrative concerns. While the two aspects – visual fascination and narrative tension – do go together, there is a sense in which the sequence can be enjoyed without any interest in larger narrative issues. We find similar deployments of space in several action films, most recently *Hitman: Agent 47* (Aleksander Bach 2015), where space similarly warps to suggest the superhuman abilities of Agent 47 (Rupert Friend) and Katia (Hannah Ware).

With the way movement expressed through the camera functions as a seamless whole in this sequence, we must recognize that space becomes performative: it matters what space does in this sequence, not how it is constructed. Similarly, we do not so much care about clear, spatial choreography, as we do about the immediate sensory impact of movement through space. The performative aspect of space is thus a matter of how power and control are articulated, as Wood points out.[30] All the women are spatial masters, far more so than the robots, who all appear slow and lumbering in contrast. But in the way the movement constantly shifts between the women and the robots, spatial elements take on a more active role within the narrative. We can only understand the tension of the narrative with recourse to the spacetimes performed by the camera's movement and trajectory. This seamless whole becomes a *vector space* that rotates and revolves while maintaining a fluid motion. Space also expands its agency and capacity to act on us, as Wood argues, "creating a double point of attention, expanding dimensions of the narrative."[31] No longer limited to a static representation of space, movement vanquishes space and time to stretch our perception across multiple vectors: actors' bodies, slow-moving shell casings, twisting camera movements and more. Although still a rare sight, we find similar instances of vectorized space in a film like *Limitless* (Neil Burger 2011), which opens with a vertiginous fractal zoom through cars and along the streets of New York.

That the train's space has been entirely vectorized is made evident in the striking moment when Sweet Pea kicks a robot through the train car's wall, and the camera swerves out of the car as well in a languid super-slow. The speed ramps up, faster than regular speed, as the camera flicks around the robot and around the pole that the robot crashes into. The camera loops back into the train car, where Sweet Pea and Rocket are busy blasting more robots. Such an extreme swerve that is still kept as part of the continuous shot emphasizes not only the nonhuman capacity of this segment, but also the extent to which spacetime becomes an experience in itself, no longer tied to that of character movement or action. We are confronted with the intense vectorization of space as an actor in itself. The intensity of our experience comes from the traversal of spacetime and is not tied to any character but rather to the totality of the film's spatial articulation. Vector space pulses sensations at us: the immense, smooth articulation of space as movement rather than space as container. This vector is another audiovisual affectile that renders us through action. Space performs actions on us, primes us for seeing space as action, something we can impact, alter and transform. Space becomes a resource for sensation, something to be exploited as and through actions.

Machinic Sensations

Special effects of all kinds have always fascinated us and opened up new realms of experience. In that way, computer-generated imagery and animation are nothing new in their basic elicitation of wonder. What should be evident by now is the novelty of what digital images can do. That is to say, the vectors produced by digital means afford new sensations to flow from screen to viewer. Action cinema's potentialities have broadened considerably and it behooves us to understand what that means. While most commentaries on the state of contemporary action films acknowledge the predominance of spectacle and the dependence on digital effects, little attention has been paid to what these effects actually do on a larger scale. Sometimes lamented, sometimes celebrated, digital effects do in fact change our experience of films, because they allow us to see and hear things that we could not before.

For this reason, the concept of vector works well to understand how these new audiovisual experiences are transferred to us in the form of a changed relation. Whitehead employs the concept of vector in connection with the transmission of feeling. For Whitehead, "the experience of M is to be conceived as a quantitative emotion arising from the contribution of sensa from A, B, C and proportionally conformed to by M."[32] In other words, for process philosophy, M – the sensation experienced – arises proportionally from earlier changes elsewhere, so that small changes will result in low-intensity sensations, whereas larger changes will necessarily be quantitatively more effective (though not necessarily qualitatively). Whitehead also insists that this is a fully material process, in which feeling can simply be regarded as energy and otherwise conforms to the principles of physics. As he points out, "the direct perception whereby the datum in the immediate subject is inherited from the past can thus, under an abstraction, be conceived as the transference of throbs of emotional energy, clothed in the specific forms provided by sensa."[33] This rather dense passage simply argues that our sensations (direct perceptions before consciousness arises) arise from the transfer of emotional energies (affects), which take specific shape depending on the form of the sound-images. Computer-generated animations and vector spaces yield changes in my body relative to their impact. How I am made to feel these frenetic booms is a matter of the vectoral impact of the sound-images.

This is why, for Virilio, "the technology of vectors thus comes to replace the tactics of bodies," since the intensity of our feelings (and therefore bodies) is in part determined by vectors.[34] Virilio argues that films are *speed machines*: "they both give rise to mediation through the production of speed, both are as one since the functions of the eye and the weapon have come to be confused, linked up".[35] With regards to speed, Virilio later argues that the communication of dimension (i.e. space) is simultaneously the extermination of dimensions.[36] Space becomes trivial; what matters is the intensity of the moment. A vector is therefore, as both Whitehead and Virilio insist, the transfer of energy from there to here, a matter of intensity of feeling. This intensity of feeling that the vector transmits carries new potentialities in digital cinema, as opposed to analog, simply because digital cinema carries other affordances, new modes of producing sound-images.

When we consider computer-generated imagery and animation from the perspective of what they do, rather than how they are done or what they are, the significance shifts from a technical consideration to one of sensation and the importance of affective energies. In order to understand what these affective energies do, Erin Manning coins the term "preacceleration" as the virtual force of movement.[37] How we engage these energies is what interests Manning, the way our experience "becomes machinic in the sense that it is no longer a stable given in the process of exploring movement, but itself becomes a milieu through which experimentation takes place."[38] We inhabit films and experiment with different sensations as we flow through the sound-images, and the vectors of the films preaccelerate us. That is to say, action films preaccelerate us and prime us for certain actions and perceptions. Once again, keep in mind that affect straddles any distinction between perception and action, and so when we watch action films, our bodies are articulated in ways that elicit specific actions and perceptions. To reiterate, this is not to suggest that you react the way I do to a specific film, but that action films render cultural forces sensible. They explore structures of feeling, in this case an openness to nonhuman capacities through the force of vectors.

When our sensations become machinic, new nonhuman capacities unfold. We experience what it is like to move alongside the blade of a sword in super-slow; our desires are excited by dancing battle suits. Affective energies flow to us along vectoral paths to elicit these new, exciting sensations that no human could ever otherwise experience. These sensations do become human in the process of becoming ours, but in the same process our experience is also broadened and takes on new forms. These moments are what Whitehead dubs, "actual occasions," and describe the simultaneous constitution of a subjective interiority that reaches out to take hold of, or apprehend, these vectoral feelings and the objective construction of an exteriority that is apprehended.[39] In this view, the experience of a film participates in the constitution of the subject, and this is in part determined by the technological affordances of the medium itself. What is otherwise obscured when considering the ontology of special effects is that these effects are also bodily effects in us, which are not always accessible to consciousness. That is the final conclusion of preacceleration: energies and forces move us, and we are not fully in control of where that movement takes us, because those energies and forces are not accessible to consciousness.

The films I discuss, and others like them, achieve this through a digital augmentation of the cinematic body. As the cinematic body becomes an assemblage of multiple imaging technologies, it is no longer unitary but forms itself from a heterogeneity of presentational modes, becoming a post-cinematic body. The sensations that emerge and take shape from such a plural, dispersed process are likewise non-unitary: an assemblage of human and nonhuman sensations. The vectoral power of these films is such that we are rendered differently, opened to a machinic sensation that extends beyond earlier cinematic forms. Vectors, then, indicate movement and transformation; a vector is a line of force determining forms and their trajectories. What follows the vector is the direction of movement that the vector describes. The vectoral power of contemporary action cinema is such that it turns the entire cinematic field into a vibrant ecology rife with crackling, tactile sensations that all promise exhilarating experiences to expand our sensory realm. While this is undoubtedly an attractive proposition, what might be less attractive are the lines of force that we must inevitably follow if we step unfettered into this expanded sensory realm. Cinema's vectoral power elicits strong connections to collective reaction and ties us in to larger cultural shifts.

If Whitehead is content to let feelings be vectors that translate energy and intensity from one position to another, what matters for Wark is the way the vector redistributes power differently, elucidating what he terms the military-entertainment complex's offering of an elsewhere.[40] We can see this elsewhere emerging on a formal level in the ways that space becomes vectorized and our embodiment is stretched beyond normal capacity. The affectiles utilized by contemporary action cinema's vectoral power create a space that offers novel sensations and experiences. To enter into that space is to engage something entirely new and exciting, as long as one can keep pace with the cinematic vectors. When space becomes a resource, it has already been conquered, and the primacy of sensation becomes the way we are given free reign over space. As space becomes movement, it becomes an abstraction. Vectorized space is a changed relation that can irrupt anywhere. No longer anchored to a location, space is now an action, an expression of power.

The vectoral power of space as an action correlates with the continuity of space. As I have shown, space is regularly expressed as continuous to intensify sensations. Vectorized space is space given agency through computer-generated animation which in turn produces vectors of affect. For a drone, as Chamayou has pointed out, space is also continuous: "the drone counters the terrestrial forms of territorial sovereignty, founded upon the enclosure of land, with the continuity of air above it."[41] That is to say, drones and action films share the same conception of space as continuous and deterritorialized. Precisely this deterritorialization of space manifests in action cinema's modulation of our bodies, specifically in the way that the line between our bodies and the post-cinematic body is dissolved. In fact, the same sense of power, agency and mastery follows from both action cinema and drones. Our bodies are deterritorialized through intense spectacles, just as sovereign territories are deterritorialized by the drone's aerial force. The drone's transgression of borders through a continuity of space is what keeps us safe, because this transgression allows it to hunt terrorists anywhere. In the same way, we are entrained to allow action films to transgress our bodies through vectors, audiovisual affectiles.

I have already suggested how these films feed off a tension between sensory overload and bodily innervation. How that tension is expressed by setting new demands for our perception of films is integral to understanding the way these films integrate us into the culture of fear. In the cases I've used here, both films articulate fear for us only to later exceed or overcome that fear. As such, these films attempt to vectorize our fear into later sensations of power and mastery. But another way of thinking about the vectoral effects that produce sensations of power and mastery is to consider how energy is produced through camera movements. How do moments of power and mastery occur, and how does perception respond to the vectoral changes? Not all films employ computer-generated images or animations, yet they still succeed in inducing potency in the viewer. Camera movement, object movement and body movement are all methods to suggest energy, speed and force in ways that are manifestly different from CGI and CGA. I therefore wish to turn to a consideration of other ways of transferring affect from screen to viewer by examining formal properties like camerawork and editing. This will establish a broader foundation for movement and the production of energy.

3

Kinetics and the Force of Movement

Arguably, the greatest transformation in contemporary action cinema is its kinetics. By this I mean the sheer amount of movement and speed released through the screen, whether we are talking about object movement within the frame, camera movement or editing pace. Chase sequences exploit this sense of movement, in which it becomes difficult to separate cinematic movement and viewer motility. Grandiose spectacles propel movement in all directions, intent on evoking astonishing sensations in the viewer and providing a sense of being in the middle of the action and performing these astounding movements. A muscular evocation, our muscles twitch in response to audiovisual movement. Following on the concept of the vector, kinetics is more about the production of energy and less about transformation. While the vector produces change and transformation, kinetics produces movement and sensation. Rather than ask how far movement reaches, kinetics asks how intense it feels.

As speed machines, action films' preoccupation is to generate audiovisual energy, the energy that makes our bodies vibrate. Movement and speed are two different things, however. Movement is extension – a matter of how far we travel. Speed, on the other hand, is intensive – a matter of how movement feels. Whereas movement designates position, speed articulates a relation to other elements. A film can thus accelerate its

57

sensation of speed by altering the velocity of elements within its frame. The more elements that move, the higher the production of audiovisual energy, and thus the corresponding sensation of speed. Push this logic far enough, and things move too fast; all I can see is speed. As Enda Duffy has shown in *The Speed Handbook*, speed is modernity's new pleasure.[1] New technologies and new forms grew up around the desire for speed, speed and more speed. Everything from the roller coaster, cinematic journeys through mountains and the car chase are forms of speed. Duffy goes on to say that "to think of speed as a pleasure is to think of it strategically. It forces us to think of speed sensationally, that is, how it feeds our sensations, our senses, working on our bodies to produce physical as well as psychological effects."[2]

Duffy insists, alongside a host of other theorists, that our perception changes with new aesthetic forms and technologies.[3] Our sensory experience transforms through speed, so that our entire perception, conscious and non-conscious, is impacted by the velocity of sound-images. Virilio discusses cinema as a machine of attack, because it is also a producer of speed.[4] Cinema functions by giving our senses a particular direction or line of articulation, thus receiving sound-images in particular ways that are pre-given. This produces a tension in how we understand and perceive films in that the cinematic production of spacetime may influence how we perceive the world, once we emerge from the film experience.

Being pulled along by the film is what I will term *kinetics* rather than kinesis. "Kinesis" is Greek for motion, while "kinetics" is the study of relations between the motions of bodies and the forces acting on them.[5] We are worked on by the motion and force of the movie, which is what produces sensations in us. As Barker points out, "the film is to our bodies like car is to the driver: we live through it vicariously, allowing it to shape our own bodily image."[6] In the vocabulary of film phenomenology, body image designates our sensation of our body and not its visual appearance. Instead, a film actually takes us for a ride, which connects quite distinctly with Tom Gunning's aesthetics of astonishment and its presentational mode, with direct spectatorial address as sensual and psychological impact.[7] Kinetics aligns us with the movement of the film's body, creating the spectacle of movement, which throws us into the midst of things. These effects work as a form of direct address, engaging us bodily in the intensities of affect.

Kinetics, then, follows the line of the vector but adds bodily alignment in the space of movement.

Opposed to narrative cinema which privileges a rational (and often disembodied) viewer capable of recognizing cues and synthesizing actions into storylines, the moments of kinetics are moments "where the viewer is not recentred but is continually open and opened by movements (sensations) that pass through him/her and on which s/he is unable to attain the perspective of a disembodied consciousness capable of rational synthesis."[8] These moments of pure irrational bodily movement cannot be what makes up most of the film, nor can they exist without narrative scaffolding, but they can be why we seek out these films. An overemphasis on the cognitive pleasure of synthesizing cues into a narrative structure overlooks the generic nature of action films. Instead, we must recognize that a great part of our enjoyment of films, especially action films, comes from the impression of physical empowerment we get from spectacular sequences. If the vector is control and modulation, kinetics is innervation and unfolding, a frothing of the sensory bath of the film.

This is particularly important for contemporary action films because they pose a challenge to the classical model of how we perceive films. Many new action films depend on multi-angle camera setups that do not focus movement in one coherent direction, but instead produce a sense of dispersed fragmentation: movement in all directions at once. Such spectacular displays overwhelm our sense of direction, forcing us to immerse into the flow of the sound-images and follow them, rather than remain a detached viewer. As Scott Bukatman argues, "spectacular displays depended on a new mode of spectatorial address – essentially, you are there (even though you are not) – linked to new technologies of visual representation."[9] He goes on to argue that this spectatorial address depends on kaleidoscopic perception "comprised of equal parts delirium, kinesis, and immersion", which allows for a particular kind of "perceptual activity, kinesthetic sensation, haptic engagement, and an emphatic sense of wonder."[10] Bukatman also argues that there is a shift in perception that moves away from the purely visual and towards a haptic, bodily engagement with sound-images.

Action films are the locus of this transformation, where a form of this kaleidoscopic perception takes us away from the merely human and into the nonhuman. I am arguing that these new ways of perceiving are part of a larger shift in perception, a shift which N. Katherine Hayles calls hyper-attention, pointing to the co-evolution of the brain's synaptic connections and media-rich environments.[11] Increasing the velocity of sound-images becomes cinema's way of engaging this new form of hyper-perception, in which movement across several trajectories becomes paramount. The clearest example of this kinetic use of cinematic movement comes in the form of superhero films, where opportunities abound to present post-cinematic movement.

The most obvious way to move beyond the human body comes in the form of vehicular movement, where the vehicles can substitute our human bodies and perform nonhuman movements. This is evident in Christopher Nolan's Batman trilogy, where there is a steady supply of vehicular chase scenes. However, we also find that the use of camerawork and editing can induce a sense of multiple trajectories at work at the same time. A similar technique is notoriously employed in the Bourne series, which follow Jason Bourne's travails against a covert intelligence agency. Finally, our perceptual machinery is pushed to its limits in the kinetic masterpiece *Mad Max: Fury Road* (George Miller 2015). Here, we find the 3D stereoscopic effect pushed into abstract overdrive to provide trajectories that go beyond any kind of feasible movement. All these films feed off a tension between human, superhuman and nonhuman movements: sometimes we are provided stable movement, other times movements that are recognizably human but go beyond our capacities, and sometimes we are accelerated into completely nonhuman spatial positions. Taken together, these films provide a variety of kinetics that all converge on catapulting the human body into the cinematic frame.

Superhuman Force: The Batman Trilogy

Christopher Nolan's critically-acclaimed and popular Batman trilogy consists of *Batman Begins* (2005), *The Dark Knight* (2008) and *The Dark Knight Rises* (2012). Rather than the interest in temporal permutations that Nolan exhibits in his non-franchise films, the Batman trilogy instead focuses on the personal journey of Bruce Wayne (Christian Bale), the limits of morality and the constant mirroring of Batman in his antagonists: Ra's Al Ghul (Liam Neeson), The Joker (Heath Ledger) and Bane (Tom Hardy). Nolan appears fascinated by the resemblance between Batman and the villains he fights, also a constant undercurrent in many Batman comics. However, Nolan did much to pull Batman out of the campy and silly aesthetics established in the 1966 *Batman: The Movie* (Leslie H. Martinson) and mastered by Tim Burton in his two Batman films in 1989 and 1992, but fumbled by Joel Schumacher's *Batman Forever* (1995) and *Batman & Robin* (1997).

Nolan was thus responsible for rebooting the franchise in such a way that it provided DC Entertainment with a return to the box office and enabled more DC franchises to be put into production. This was especially so after the lackluster *Superman Returns* (Bryan Singer 2006), which saw DC's major franchise character shelved until 2013, when Nolan helped co-produce a reboot. What Nolan needed to balance the Batman franchise was an engaging story that did not experiment with narration the way his earlier films had done, primarily *Memento* (2000), but also later films such as *Inception* (2010) and *Interstellar* (2014). Yet the franchise still had to provide enough spectacular attractions and astounding effects to draw huge crowds. The Batman trilogy thus stands as emblematic of the challenges facing not only blockbusters but contemporary cinema in general: to strike the correct balance between narrative and spectacle to engage the audience.

Movement has always been significant for films, not only because movement distinguishes films from photography but also because movement allows for spectacle. As Richard Maltby points out, "American fiction movies have stressed movement from the outset, with early chase films providing the first synthesis of narrative and the attractions of spectacular movement."[12] Tom Gunning also locates spectacle in the chase film as part of a dialectics of spectacle and narrative: "The chase film shows how towards the end of this period (basically from 1903–1906) a synthesis of attractions and narrative was already underway. The chase had been the original truly narrative genre of the cinema, providing a model for causality and linearity as well as a basic editing continuity."[13] So, while a chase sequence provides a sense of astonishment and wonder due to hectic movement, it is also a mini-narrative of cause and effect and continuity. The viewer must understand where the vehicles are in relation to each other, the direction vehicles are moving in and so forth. Movement becomes paramount to solicit our attention.

Cinematic movement has always been tricky to define, since there are so many ways of achieving it. The movement of objects within the frame is the one which comes most readily to mind, but this refers to objective movement and keeps the viewer in her seat. Engaging the viewer bodily is more easily achieved via camera movement, because that production of kinematic energy is more easily converted to the sensation of bodily movement. David Bordwell, in an older article, discusses the use of camera movement, pointing out that

> the ability of subjective movement to endow static arrays with depth is usually called the 'kinetic depth effect.' As camera movement, the kinetic depth effect operates to some degree in panning, tilting, and all other rotational movements around the axis of the camera itself. But the kinetic depth effect achieves its greatest power to define space through the traveling shot.[14]

The camera's plunge into space allows for the greatest sensation of movement; and while Bordwell does not discuss the cinema of attractions (preferring to stay within narrative cinema), the sensation of movement through kinetic depth effects belongs properly to the aesthetics of astonishment as outlined by Gunning, which he describes as an experience of assault.[15] Because the camera's plunge through space feels as if we were plunging through space, this type of camerawork can also become precarious if we are not properly situationally oriented. In that case, we feel that we plunge into unknown space. Karen Pearlman refers to the rhythm of speed as "trajectory phrasing" – a matter not simply of how fast-paced the editing is, but rather the manipulation of energy in the narrative rhythm.[16] While pacing is often taken to mean the editing speed, Perlman points out that camera movement is also significant in terms of how fast narration feels. Pearlman's approach is innovative because it reveals how narrative sequences may be infused with a sense of movement by employing a traveling shot or similar camerawork.

Consider, about an hour into *Batman Begins*, the vertiginous visual assault when Flass (Mark Boone Junior) is grabbed by Batman and pulled up to the rooftop. The camera spins and lifts up, giving the impression of a subjective point-of-view from Flass while also completely disorienting us. Since the camera movement is not a plunge forward but a plunge backward, we have no information about what we might crash into, making for a gut-wrenching shot. Bordwell perceptively notes that "we can hardly resist reading the camera-movement effect as a persuasive surrogate for our subjective movement through an objective world."[17] While this is overwhelmingly true, it also marks the limit of Bordwell's theoretical horizon, because he refuses to discuss experience, discussing instead only the formal properties of positive or negative parallax (movement towards or past the camera) and thus deprives us of a significant element of understanding these films.

The force of this experience of camera movement is that we are moved into the zone between our own gaze and the camera's gaze, as Bordwell rightly points out, but he fails to recognize that this is a zone of immersion, in which we do not simplistically identify with one character but identify with the force of movement. The zone which blurs camera and viewer is precisely what Jennifer M. Barker identifies as apprehension, where "this constant feeling of being pulled and yet pushed leads us to the unique way we experience chase and suspense films, which is with a great sense of *apprehension*, in many senses of the word."[18] All cinematic experience shares in this sense of mingling our body with the cinematic body, of existing in the zone between camera and subject, which is also referred to as spectacle. We are, in other words, pulled along by the movie if not exactly into the movie. The upwards and backwards pull into the unknown is a precarious position to be in and disorients us. For this reason, we need an establishing shot after which orients us situationally.

The vertical axis of cinematic movement has itself been intensified in contemporary blockbusters, in part because vertical movement suggests power and control, but also because it suggests movements we human beings cannot perform. This becomes a form of disorientation, as is evident in the case of Flass and many of the movements Batman performs. As Sara Ross points out, "soaring through space (...) has historically been associated with progress and mastery, both literally and metaphorically, and thus can be used to structure the overall journey of a heroic protagonist."[19] This runs parallel to arguments put forth earlier by Kristen Whissel, who states that verticality is a technique for visualizing power.[20] That Batman can pull Flass up vertically visualizes Batman's superiority, and when Batman can also survive spiraling jumps to the ground, we recognize that he is beyond our capacities.

These moments are spectacles which cannot be reduced to narrative structure without missing the point: audiences long for the masterful disorientations that these superheroes perform. Although these spectacles fit within a larger narrative structure, our experience of the movement cannot be ignored in favor of narrative. The bodily sense of kinetics is imperative for these films, for without it they would not feel superheroic. While we know enough about blockbuster films to anticipate the general trajectory of the story, what makes each superhero film special is how it allows for the superhuman constructions of spacetime articulation. What makes superhero films engrossing is that we are allowed to feel superhuman for a brief moment of time, but the intensity of that moment is high, precisely because it is an unusual sensation, and one that goes beyond our everyday sensual register. This argument alone makes it evident why Singer's *Superman Returns* fared worse than Zack Snyder's *Man of Steel*. In Singer's version, Superman (Brandon Routh) uses his supervision to sit in a car and stalk Lois Lane (Kate Bosworth). In Snyder's version, Superman (Henry Cavill) battles tanks and aircrafts in all manner of epic shots. Which version *feels* more superhuman is self-evident.

When, in *Batman Begins*, James Gordon (Gary Oldman) gets into the Bat-Tumbler to control it, the Tumbler mostly takes control of him. The seat shifts and pulls him into the very belly of the vehicle while Gordon yells out in worry. That is the perfect metaphor for many of the action blockbusters in recent years, in which the movies take over and pull us along for the ride. Furthermore, there is pleasure in the submission to these sequences. I agree with Barker that there is great enjoyment in not being able to recenter our bodies, as long as it only occurs for brief moments, in peaks and dips dispersed throughout the narrative.

When the Bat-Pod is introduced in *The Dark Knight Rises*, it is in a traveling shot from behind and below Batman while Lower Wacker Drive is cast in darkness, so only a very slight silhouette of the vehicle can be seen. As the lights come back on, Batman slows the Bat-Pod to a halt as we pull up behind him. Starting up again, the film cuts to a close-up of the front of Batman from below as he starts driving, cutting to a shot from below and behind him, which then cuts to a reverse shot of his front from below. All these shots are traveling shots moving at high velocity with the Bat-Pod closing in. Shot from below, Batman towers over us as the Bat-Pod either closes in on us or moves away from us. The kinetics are clear: Batman is in complete control of his vehicle and the film is in complete control of us. We are pulled along the mounted camera with a smooth, self-assured confidence in the motion, although the objects flying past us left and right make us truly apprehensive. These vehicle-mount shots remain stable, smooth, fluid and balanced, which ends up infusing us with the same sensations. Although the scene is tense, Batman exudes intense confidence being in control, and by extension so do we. This is a body that can do anything. (*See Figure 3.1 in the insert.*)

Christopher Nolan's Batman trilogy is interesting in the landscape of superhero movies precisely because of this self-assured cinematic body. While all superhero movies show superhuman deeds performed by the characters, Nolan's movies are the only ones shot in the IMAX format, which makes the cinematic body super-cinematic in comparison. Despite the bulkiness of IMAX cameras, Nolan decided to strap them on a Steadicam rig and use them for the biggest action sequences. Providing a deeper and more intense experience, the detail and sharpness of the image is not entirely lost despite the necessity of reducing the film to 35mm in most cinemas. The action sequences of *The Dark Knight* and *The Dark Knight Rises* are thus not only superhuman performances, they are also cinematically superior: sharper, deeper, richer, they present a cinematic body that is beyond the capacity of other superhero movies.

At the same time, Matthias Stork's two-part video essay "Chaos Cinema" argues for a new style of blockbuster film-making which throws classical continuity style editing, and even Bordwell's intensified continuity, out the window in favor of excess, exaggeration and overindulgence.[21] Spatial coherence is lost; camera movements are no longer motivated; editing speed picks up for no reason; framing is tighter; and focus is usually shallow. Often the same event will be shown from different angles in order to intensify the moment. Many critics have picked up on this notion of a decrease in narrative coherence in favor of audiovisual intensity. At almost the same time as Stork, Steven Shaviro proposed post-continuity as a different term for much the same development, although Shaviro's term aligns with the tradition of continuity editing and the post-classical tradition. Speaking specifically of *Gamer*, Shaviro defines post-continuity as

> a continual cinematic barrage, with no respite. It is filled with shots from handheld cameras, lurching camera movements, extreme angles, violent jump cuts, cutting so rapid as to induce vertigo, extreme closeups, a deliberately ugly color palette, video glitches, and so on. The combat scenes in Slayer, in particular, are edited behavioristically more than spatially. That is to say, the frequent cuts and jolting shifts of angle have less to do with orienting us towards action in space, than with setting off autonomic responses in the viewer".[22]

Nolan's Batman movies are more restrained than that, even if some of the action scenes do have a rapid editing pace. Favoring the Steadicam over the handheld camera, the Batman movies move at a breakneck pace but rarely completely break continuity style. Instead, Nolan's trilogy gives us surprisingly fluid, assured and self-contained movements when Batman is in his different vehicles, despite the superhuman movements these vehicles perform. This is in contrast to the barrage Shaviro identifies in *Gamer*, *Domino* (Tony Scott 2005) and other movies. Where *Gamer* is jerky, nervous and turbulent, the Batman movies are fluid, assured and stable. Furthermore, although neither Stork nor Shaviro really go into detail with this issue, there is also the fact that these post-continuity scenes are moments of spectacle rather than narrative. Continuity editing is traditionally employed to articulate narrative and coherent space, and Nolan remains within the narrative tradition in his trilogy, except for the action sequences, where he is willing to move into a form of superhuman spectacle, making us feel what it is like to be Batman in his vehicles.

This superhuman sensation is one of the biggest attractions of Nolan's movies and is most fully experienced in the flight sequence with the Bat. As the Bat descends to pursue Bane's minions in both the truck and the stolen Tumbler, the camera movement is again smooth and continuous. The kinetics of the movie plunges us into a headlong pursuit of these vehicles. Parallel editing is used to alternate between the Bat pursuit, Catwoman's pursuit on the Bat-Pod and the confrontation between Blake and the police officers, ratcheting up the tension. The Bat shots are always assured and smooth, even when dodging missiles or buildings, moving in long traveling shots or weaving between buildings, exploiting the vertical axis in a total mastery of space. In contrast to this are the shots from inside the pursued vehicles, where Miranda, Gordon and other characters are shaken and jolted while their vehicles lurch and tilt. The kinetics could not be any more different: The Bat is in control (and, parenthetically, so is Catwoman on the Bat-Pod), while the regular humans are very much out of control. Considering the extreme vehicular movements, the smooth motion of Nolan's IMAX images provide a sumptuous contrast; we are pulled along by the movie but always feel in control, never destabilized, and so we are content to leave our bodies in the hands of the movie, much like we leave our bodies to roller-coasters. The alternating shots between Batman and Catwoman and the regular humans clearly align us with the superheroes – those are the shots where we feel safest, and by extension, where we feel at home in the zone created between camera and viewer. We are Batman in those shots: self-assured, in control and courageous. (*See Figure 3.2 in the insert.*)

The superhuman control we feel in these situations comes from the use of nonhuman camera point-of-view's performed by vehicle-mounts and digital effects. Through extreme spectacle, combined with balanced, authoritative kinetics, sensations flow through us that we could never otherwise feel. As Barker beautifully puts it, speaking of contemporary action films in general: "By alternating shots taken from inside vehicles with those taken from cameras mounted on them, these films force us into movements that aren't meant for humans, only for machines. In these moments, we go where not even fearless drivers and pilots would dare to go; we are riding without seat belts, without windshields, without any protection at all. The film throws us out and gives us nothing to hang onto."[23]

Yet I do believe that the scenes in *The Dark Knight Rises* gives us something to hold on to: Batman. He is constantly cool and collected, and his self-assured embodiment counters the disorienting and vertiginous shots that do appear in the films. Furthermore, as Barker herself points out, the shots alternate between inside and outside, which means that we do get some respite from the out of control sensation of being outside the vehicle. Also, this description is in sharp contrast to the one that Stork gives of the "crash-cam" style that we shall explore in the next section on the *Bourne* films. In the Bourne films, we are constantly placed in precarious positions *inside* vehicles only, which produces a vulnerable sensation. By contrast, Batman makes us feel superhuman, able to go where no one else can go, in possession of a body that can do anything.

To boldly go where no one has gone before is the premise of super-hero movies and provides a spectacle that is very literally out of this world. We relish these moments of sheer, delightful terror, because there is something to hold onto: the superhuman cinematic body. Barker is right when she argues that we go where no driver or pilot would ever go; that is why we watch these movies. The fascination of feeling more than oneself, to be taken beyond (but not out of) one's body for a little while, while still safely in one's seat, is the adrenaline rush of the twenty-first century. Nolan's Batman films, for all their spectacular excesses, remain restrained enough when compared to other contemporary action films, and in many ways they must, considering their function and position within a larger action cinema culture: to bring Batman back to the box office forefront.

Superhero films can succeed precisely in the way that they gener-ate superhuman sensations in us. Yet, at the same time, this convention becomes a limitation, a line they cannot cross. This convention constrains their narrative form as much as the shape of their movements: we know that the superhero will triumph, and we know that we are safe in their hands. While Batman generally works through vehicles and prosthetic extensions, this still maintains a clear division between human and non-human, where the human body is obviously in control. Extensions allow for extending our sensations, but it is with the vulnerable body that move-ments can take on far more disorienting swerves.

The Frantic Camera: The Bourne Sequence

Kinetics can also be produced through camerawork and editing, rather than movement within the frame. Some of the most notorious examples of cam-era kinetics are Paul Greengrass' contributions to the Jason Bourne series. A spy-thriller action series based on three books by Robert Ludlum, which are sometimes called the Jason Bourne Trilogy, the Jason Bourne films consist of four films so far: *The Bourne Identity* (Doug Liman 2002), *The Bourne Supremacy* (Paul Greengrass 2004), *The Bourne Ultimatum* (Paul

Greengrass 2007), and *The Bourne Legacy* (Tony Gilroy 2012). *The Bourne Legacy* notably does not feature Jason Bourne (Matt Damon) but instead focuses on Aaron Cross (Jeremy Renner), another agent working for the clandestine Treadstone Project. A fifth film, reuniting Matt Damon and Paul Greengrass, has been announced, alongside a sixth film featuring Aaron Cross. Clearly a popular series, the basic premise is that Jason Bourne is a government assassin working for Operation Treadstone who suffers amnesia during his last mission. Trying to recover his true identity is his primary objective in the films, alongside exposing Operation Treadstone and returning to a life of normalcy. Having accomplished this at the end of the third film, the fourth film reveals more programs like Treadstone, in which agents are treated with viral drugs to make them better killers.

The signature visual style for the Bourne series is the shaky camera, the run-and-gun style, the off-center framing and unstable composition of the two Greengrass films. Although initially criticized, when Greengrass left the series for Gilroy to take over, critics missed the frantic camerawork. Rather than debate the relative merits of Greengrass' visual style, I would like to draw attention to the way the two films produce kinetics that often place us directly in harm's way while also disorienting us and forcing us to stretch our perception in order to keep pace with the film. There are many scenes in Greengrass' two films in which Bourne is out of control and only manages to survive through sheer luck. These scenes where Bourne teeters on the brink of death are usually done in a frenetic jumble of images, but in fact we find the entire audiovisual style of the films to be busy and disordered. Even dialog scenes are kept fast-paced through jittery camerawork and stressful editing.

Greengrass' style, which prompted David Bordwell to refer to the Bourne films as the "Unsteadicam chronicles," seeks out energy at every turn through "fast cutting, arcing camera movements, sudden frame entrances, the nervousness of the handheld shot."[24] Such energy is directed straight at us, making us feel the full assault of the audiovisuals. Significantly, there is no unilateral direction of the motion in any of these shots, which is one of the reasons they come off as queasy and unsettling: we have no way of knowing in which direction the action will move, and this induces a loss of equilibrium and a sensation of vertigo. Feeling out of control comes from our eye movement being constantly forced to move horizontally across the screen in a manner that resembles scanning, although faster and more incessant. Such involuntary lateral scanning sometimes induces motion sickness, which is why some viewers will feel a sense of nausea at watching such jerky sequences.

A significant example, early in *The Bourne Supremacy*, comes as Bourne enjoys life in Goa with Marie (Franka Potente) and a Russian oligarch attempts to frame him for stealing the Neski files, which document a $20 million theft seven years earlier. Kirill (Karl Urban) attempts to kill Bourne, which results in a car chase. While the chase scene is brief compared to that film's climactic car chase, tension and stress are triggered through jouncy camera movements moving in all directions along with the cinematic body. Framing is decentered, and rack-focus disturbs our depth of field, as do several axial cuts. For instance, we see Marie running towards the car to screen left in a medium straight angle shot cut to a medium low angle shot from the other side of the car, then Marie running towards screen right. The direction of movement shifts 180 degrees, colliding the two trajectories. Add to this the bumpy handheld shot, which produces micro-movements up-down and left-right, and space is fragmented as lines of movement cross and collide.

Such fragmentation of space is what I call a *crash cut*, following Geoff King's notion of action cinema's impact effects and explosive editing, as well as Shaviro's broader concept of post-continuity.[25] Shaviro identifies a stylistics of post-continuity, in which "a preoccupation with immediate effects trumps any concern for broader continuity – whether on the immediate shot-by-shot level, or on that of the overall narrative."[26] As is evident from Shaviro's further discussion, post-continuity is not solely a matter of editing but is a much larger system. Conversely, King suggests that "explosive editing provides a powerful source of impact that fits with the continued desire of Hollywood to offer large-scale spectacle to draw audiences to the cinema."[27] Both Shaviro and King – despite a decade between their two works – locate in action cinema the central preoccupation of immediate effects that work directly on the viewer. King picks up Sergei Eisenstein's old phrase of cinema as "a series of blows to the consciousness and emotions of the audience" as indicative of the work done to the audience by action films.[28]

Crash cutting is thus a matter of impacting the viewer's body directly through sheer speed of editing. This is often achieved by cutting between opposite movements, so that a movement from left to right is joined to a movement from right to left. This jarring experience forces us to recalibrate trajectories and sacrifices spatial orientation in favor of bodily motility and muscular apprehension. Related to the smash cut, although not joining two distinct scenes, the crash cut is the impact of two or more lines of movement crashing into each other. In this way, the movement of objects and camera movements crash into/against one another simultaneously in the crash cut, a process which I will refer to as concussive editing. We become kinetically disoriented as the motion of bodies and the forces acting on them collide. Concussive editing becomes another way for producing more energy, while using that energy to unsettle our spatial orientation.

While the score does help to smooth out this disorientation, it is worth noting that the music itself is fast-paced and jagged, with almost stinger-like violins. These high-pitched strings jolt our nerves, and although they do provide a sense of continuity, they also induce the stressful sensation of motion that pushes us forward, making us impatient with the sometimes reluctant Marie. The score produces another trajectory, another line of force that generates energy and a stressful need for movement. The intimate bodily correlation between musical beats and heart beats also works in scenes like this to induce a sense of restlessness, the urge to move even if we are not exactly sure in which direction. The score, then, as much as the images, works to preaccelerate us, inciting a sense of the necessity of motion, any motion, in any direction.

Even non-action scenes can employ concussive editing to increase the tension of an otherwise stale scene. Consider the scene where Pamela Landy (Joan Allen) is given access to the Treadstone files, goes to the archive room and browses through them. While this scene could have easily been shot in a medium shot, with a few close-ups to reveal the pertinent information, and accompanied by dramatic score to produce the necessary tension and suspense, we instead get a frazzled scene with an average shot length of 1.4 seconds, with 30 shots in about 40 seconds. The editing pace here is faster than most action film set pieces, yet the information being conveyed is that Bourne is a rogue agent with amnesia and deceased Agent

Conklin (Chris Cooper) is somehow involved. Kept in the same jumbled, handheld style, the shot pans throughout the scene, while switching intermittently between low angles and straight angles. The movement pattern is: camera moves down – sideways shot – static handheld – down. This patterns runs in a continual loop. Even though Bordwell is right to argue that we can cope with the information being dispersed here, because it is one piece of information per shot and there is plenty of restating of what we have just seen (folders, papers, photos of the same people over and over again), and because we know this type of scene from similar films and even the first Bourne film, the effect remains jolting, and we lose our sense of orientation.[29] Despite the simplicity of the scene, tension and suspense are racked up immensely. In fact, it is precisely because the scene is so simple and minimalist that we can cope with the jumble of images, losing only our spatial orientation and not our narrative orientation as well.

The overall strategy of the film replicates the above scene's incessant disorientation with a breathtaking pace that gives us no respite in its churn of constant motion. Interestingly, Bordwell agrees with this line of argument when he states that "the style achieves a visceral impact," although his normative desire for traditional filmmaking forces him to continue, "but at the cost of coherence and spatial orientation."[30] As Shaviro shows at length, coherence and spatial orientation are no longer important in a post-cinema much more interested in immediate payoffs and visceral impact. Whether or not one believes that films such as *The Bourne Ultimatum* reveal a decline in contemporary filmmaking, a lack of attention to detail and clarity of spatial articulation, the fact remains that most of the films that reign at the box office employ such concussive devices. Attention is given to movement and energies, rather than spatial clarity and a sense of detail.

The final show-down in *The Bourne Supremacy* reveals this preoccupation with energies and movement. The kinetics of the scene constantly shift and morph, incessantly throwing us into precarious positions and near misses. Bleeding and injured, Bourne is on the run from Kirill and steals a taxi to get away. Kirill steals another car, and a hectic five-minute car chase concludes the much longer pursuit sequence. The lead-in is filmed in the run-and-gun style from both character perspectives, Bourne moving through a grocery store while scanning for anything that might help, and Kirill following the trail of blood the injured Bourne leaves behind. The constant straight angle shots tilting down to spot the blood interrupt the lateral trajectory that Kirill otherwise follows, making his shots bumpy.

Bourne gets into the taxi and drives off at high speed. He attempts to navigate the road while also looking at a map and pouring vodka on his gunshot wound. The camera bounces around inside the car trying to show all these actions, yet primarily produces a blur of indecipherable motion. The dragging streaks of color from the too fast swoosh pans disorient us as we hear Bourne's ragged breathing. However, what truly unsettles us are the whooshes of cars going by and the near-misses with parked cars. Due to the blur of the jittery camera, we cannot tell exactly what happens, which adds to the stress and confusion. Everything adds up to a sense that things are going haywire, completely spinning out of control. Unlike Nolan's Batman films, here we are given nothing to hold on to, continuously being hurtled around inside the car while the few master shots give us little sense of orientation, although these shots do reveal that police cars are chasing Bourne.

With no warning, a car crashes into the driver side; shot in a medium close-up from inside the car as Bourne is pushed to the side, it then cuts to a low-angle shot with glass spraying all over the car. *(See Figure 3.3 in the insert.)* A brief shot from above shows us the police car spinning around and Bourne's taxi veering off to screen right. Then we are back inside the car with Bourne as he tries to bring the car back under control. Extreme close-ups of his hand gripping the gear shift and his feet working the pedals provide only the barest minimum of spatial orientation, because we recognize the layout of a car, but these shots simultaneously keep us from actually seeing what is going on outside the car. This is what Matthias Stork calls the "crash-cam": "Objects move towards the camera, at a high pace, and penetrate, indeed fracture, both the (intra-diegetic) camera apparatus and the screen, crossing the invisible dividing line between spectacle and audience, thereby intruding upon the viewer's personal space."[31] Rather than being placed in a safe third-person position, we are instead placed as the target of objects crashing towards and even into us. The crash-cam is a good indicator of the changes action cinema is currently undergoing, allowing for shots and edits that break the classical continuity system and the stable production of time and space. The crash-cam also shows the extent to which we are placed in vulnerable positions and denied access to a clear orientation that would provide a sense of comfort and safety.

There are a few more examples of the crash-cam in the chase sequence, but it only ever happens with Bourne: there is never a crash-cam shot from either Kirill's or any of the police officers' point of view. A few times we also see the crash from outside the car, only then to cut back inside to see Bourne's face spin around with sprays of glass and the sound of metal bending. As the car is spinning, this motion further unsettles our experience, but it also brings in a brief moment of authenticity and anchoring, since the shot is performed by Matt Damon, not a stunt man. These reaction shots thus further the sense of precarious sensation and vulnerability: not so much because we think that Damon is in any danger, but more because we get to see the body that we are generally aligned with throughout the films being right in the middle of danger. The high-speed impact of the cars makes these shots moments of vulnerability, although to a lesser extent than actually seeing the collision with another car or truck head-on would. The very fact that the crash-cam has been employed relatively rarely still makes this a novel experience, although I do not think we can ever exactly grow comfortable with it. It remains the closest approximation to being in a car crash that we can get, without actually being in a car crash.

Throughout the car chase, the overall impression of the camerawork is jumbled, as if we were right in the middle of the action. Although it comes across as a point of view shot, it never actually is, since it never occupies the same space as Bourne. We often see his face, his shoulder or other parts of his body indicating where he is. Instead, these shots are what we can call *participatory shots*, shots that for better or worse make us feel as if we are right next to Bourne. There are enough shots from outside the car, or inside Kirill's car, that this effect never becomes dominant, but it is strong enough that we feel vulnerable and out of control. Unlike Bourne, who always knows what to do and always make things work out, we are never able to act. In fact, we are generally not allowed to share in Bourne's embodiment in the way we often are with action protagonists, as in the Batman films. Instead, Bourne moves too fast, too unexpectedly and almost too erratically for us to keep up. While there are plenty of scenes that provide a sense of physical empowerment, we are usually left just off to the side of those, never clearly aligned with the action.

With the concussive editing, the crash-cam and the participatory shots, we get a cinematic body that constantly puts our body at risk. Keeling, swerving and teetering on the edge, the flurry of sound-images keeps us off balance. Everything moves kinetically, but we are pinned in place, stunned by the multitude of trajectories that collide and crash into each other. Concussive rather than forceful and powerful, the Bourne sequence is an exercise in visceral impact that threatens to extirpate us. This elicits an intense state of awareness, in which we are constantly on the look-out for new threats and dangers. Although Bourne is haunted by his past, it is always through an unknown future danger that this haunting occurs. Because of his amnesia, his past is futural, always still to come back to him. His past manifests in the form of a threat, indicating a generalized fear of the future in the Bourne films.

Yet there are other ways of using the flurry of images. In an impressive scene in *The Bourne Ultimatum*, Bourne meets up with reporter Simon Ross (Paddy Considine), who is writing a series of expose articles on Bourne, Treadstone and Blackbriar in an attempt to expose the government's assassins. Taking place at London's Waterloo Station, Bourne has to speak with Ross without the CIA listening in or anyone being able to stop or catch him. Employing a burner phone, Bourne directs Ross around the busy terminal, dodging agents and avoiding surveillance cameras as the same time. The scene is constructed in a clear pattern, crosscutting between Bourne and Ross navigating the terminal and the CIA surveillance room in the US, where agents are trying to figure out who Ross is talking to and where he is going. We are also introduced to Paz (Edgar Ramirez), a Blackbriar assassin, who takes off from a hotel room to kill Bourne.

Shot in the by-now familiar handheld style filled with participatory shots, swoosh pans and jittery rhythms, the scene thrusts us into trying to keep track of all the things that are going on. Even the shots in the CIA operations room are filmed in the frantic handheld style, with lots of low angle shots, reframing and zoom shots. Furthermore, the operations room is also filled with big screen TVs and computer monitors that we never focus on but that insert more motion into the shots. At the terminal, most of the shots are medium close-ups, kept close to the faces of Bourne and Ross always looking out of frame at some possible assailant. The few master shots we get are brief, often pans or tracks, swooshing from one person to another person. The crowd in the terminal scatters movement across the frame, obscuring most shots and blocking clear views of where we are. Similarly, there are plenty of shots restating the action, but rather than providing clarity, they provide more motion and more confusion, since these shots are kept in tight framing. Our eyes cannot help but catch the movement of all the people, making perception difficult.

Once again, we are never given access to Bourne's actions or knowledge; instead he directs Ross by saying "turn right", "go into the liquor store", and only then do we see the store or what awaits when Ross turns. This use of restricted narration and point of view keeps us engaged in what is happening, trying to second-guess Bourne while being kept on the edge of our seat worrying about an agent catching up with Bourne, since there are several blind angles in these shots. This driving sense of tension is amplified by the fast-paced score, which employs brief staccato strings and kettle drums to set a blistering pace. Here again space becomes vectorized as trajectories of motion that cross and double over each other constantly. Everyone looks offscreen; the ambient noise is high in the mix adding more chaos, and everything happens suddenly when a new movement enters the frame.

Bourne abruptly steps close to Ross in a tunnel, which cuts the score off, providing a calming moment in the eye of the storm, when even the cameras slow down to give us a conventional shot reverse shot rhythm for the duration of their talk. Ross provides the crucial piece of information that Bourne needs: that Blackbriar is a Treadstone update, that Bourne is still the agency's dirty little secret, providing enough new information that Bourne can continue in his quest for discovering who he is. Then they have to split up, and the faster-paced rhythm picks up again. Fear makes Ross step into the line of sight of the surveillance cameras, and immediately the agents swarm toward him. Bourne directs Ross into another tunnel with the agents following him. As the agents are about to get Ross, Bourne unexpectedly jumps from a side corridor and punches one of them.

A brief fight ensues, showcasing the way these fights are choreographed. They primarily consist of brief bursts of one-punch shots, where one character throws a punch, kick or similar before the shot cuts. Combined with the shaky handheld camera, the fight is more a blur than a clear expression of force. With one punch per shot, the sequence is easily assembled into a fast-paced fight which covers up the fact that the actors are not skilled martial artists. Contrary to the Hong Kong style of shooting action films, which I discuss in further detail in the next chapter, the Bourne series favors close framings which reveal that it is in fact Matt Damon fighting. Most of the shots have his face in them, thus providing the same sense of authenticity that we find in the crash-cam shots. Yet this authenticity comes at the expense of full-on bodily mastery. Instead, the kinetics of the participatory shots must stand in for the masterful bodily display of physical empowerment. The film's impact comes not through human bodily mastery and physical power, but instead through the frenetic body of the film. The shots still utilize concussive editing in the way motion flicks back and forth at odd angles.

After the brutal fight, Ross and Bourne split up again, Bourne promising to get Ross out alive. The following sequence at the CIA operations room has Noah Vosen (David Strathairn) saying at they should both be killed. This sequence is shot in a calmer style than the frantic pacing we found there earlier, when they were trying to locate Ross. Clearly, the cameras must be calm to ensure that we register this significant piece of information. The last section of the scene in the train station also has the one conventionally constructed instance of suspense. We see Paz, the assassin, getting ready to shoot and are given a subjective view through the scope towards the door Ross is hiding behind. We thus know, when he says he can get to the exit, that he will be killed if he does not listen to Bourne and wait. Ross runs out the door and gets shot. Bourne rushes over, grabs something and runs off. We switch to Paz's perspective and see him trying to get a clear shot at Bourne, but when he sees the Bobbies chasing Bourne, he packs up and leaves. Bourne rushes out of the terminal, and this concludes the scene.

The primary function of this scene in terms of plot is to have Bourne learn of Blackbriar and his own central role in the whole Treadstone affair. This allows him to continue unravelling the agency. In terms of mood, it is a tense and suspense-filled scene. The mood is achieved primarily through camerawork and the kinetics that constantly move offscreen into unknown space. The moving crowd plays a large part in this, because its constant motion, which has little to do with the actual action and movement of the characters, prompts a saccadic eye response. In brief, a saccade is the quick, simultaneous movement of both eyes when scanning. A completely normal physiological response, voluntary saccades occur constantly when we look at objects and our surroundings. What happens, however, in the Waterloo station scene is that reflexive saccades are produced involuntarily in response to movement. Simply put: We are trying to keep an eye on everyone in the terminal because they are moving, and we have been primed by the film to see every single instance of motion as a potential threat. Clearly, we are not able to do this, nor is it necessary to understanding the narrative action. It is an involuntary response, but one that elicits stress and anxiety because there are so many lines of movement. Once again, there is a similar response to the jittery, staccato rhythm of the score, which incessantly drives on. All in all, although little violence occurs in this scene, it remains incredibly busy and overwhelming.

A general trait for all the Bourne films, but especially the ones that Greengrass directed, is that we are pushed into haywire movement and action, never fully in control. The precarious positioning of Bourne, and often us right next to him, is overwhelming much of the time. The narration demands that the camera jitter stops when important information is given, but it immediately picks up again once the information has been established. Kinetic perception is necessary to keep up with the cinematic body, the stressful and restless motion that constantly careens all around us. With an almost constant presence of threat, we are forced to develop hyper-awareness for the duration of the film, in which we constantly scan the entire frame for any unexpected movement or objects hurtling towards us.

Obviously there are stable and calm sequences in the films, otherwise they would be nigh unwatchable. However, what matters is that we are consistently placed in positions of vulnerability, able only to scan around for movement. Such unsteadiness makes for a highly uncomfortable embodiment throughout the films, since we are rarely given pause for any long period of time. Vulnerable and shaky, the experience of watching the Bourne films is one of ceaseless awareness and an unstable sense of space and embodiment. In many ways, all the Bourne films are extended chase sequences, where even the dialog-driven narrative moments are filled with nervous anxiety that goes beyond the conventional suspense of knowing more than the characters. Rather, the restricted narration alongside the restricted camerawork produces constant surprise and tension, a sense of having no idea where events are going to go next or where we are going to end up next. What we are primed to recognize is that there are always future threats and only constant readiness and hyper-awareness can keep us safe. The embodiment established in these films moves from human to cinematic and renders a culture of fear palpable through a system of signification that conditions lived experience, as Anderson terms it.[32] That is to say, the Bourne series expresses our culture of fear, but it also modulates us through fear.

In this way, we see how affective modulation works as a force that produces ideology. On the face of it, the Bourne series is critical of intelligence operations and the brutal and amoral world of spies and assassins. Yet the film can easily accommodate such apparent ideological resistance because its primary effect is bodily tension. Whether or not we agree with the film's surface critique of intelligence operations, we cannot help but feel unsettled and anxious by the end of the film. The film produces the very structure that it apparently critiques, not through ideological obfuscation but rather through affective modulation and entrainment.

Such a move is doubly pacifying. First, we are led to embody the very ideological structure we think we are critiquing. Second, we are presented with a narrative that leads us to think we are rejecting the critique we in fact are led to embody. This is the very heart of the *pharmakon* at work here. All the Bourne films openly decry and denounce the use of assassinations, the use of torture and the inefficiency and cruelty of what is in essence a symbolic substitute for the war on terror. Yet not only do the films always push Bourne to kill and torture in order to stop murder and torture, we are also left in an embodied state of frantic anxiety that ends up necessitating Bourne's actions. We are left ideologically pacified, with no other option than to accept the necessities of the means of the war on terror; but we are also left bodily pacified, which necessitates other bodies standing in for us, performing the very actions that we do not wish performed.

A bitter pill to swallow, surely, but one that has the sweet, charming performance of Matt Damon to help the medicine go down. Bourne's shocked rejection of his own, earlier actions is convincingly portrayed by the affable nature of Damon's performance and helped by his star image as do-gooder for a progressive America. This is clearly one reason why *The Bourne Legacy* was less successful; Jeremy Renner's lacks Damon's cuddly warmth. It also gives the lie to Damon's own denouncement of James Bond as an imperialist misogynist. While an entirely accurate description of

Bond, Damon's statement overlooks the fact that Bourne is simply a hawk-ish neocon in a Snuggie.

Audiovisual Mayhem: *Mad Max: Fury Road*

Production of energy does not happen solely through frantic camera work, jumbled composition and concussive editing. George Miller's action extravaganza *Mad Max: Fury Road* provides an astounding clarity of the movement of characters, vehicles and objects in the frame, and utilizes negative parallax of movement towards the audience to great effect, but in a radically different manner from the crash-cam in the Bourne sequence. Rather than the precarious positioning of Bourne's participatory shots, *Fury Road* provides an emboldening sense of control and power in its articulation of space. 3D effects play a major role in this enactment of physical empowerment, but due to the film's exceptional and unusual narrative form, we do not find a straightforward embodiment of a singularly strong, capable protagonist.

Mad Max: Fury Road tells the story of Imperator Furiosa (Charlize Theron), a lieutenant in the service of the despot Immortan Joe, as she tries to escape with Joe's five breeder wives, hoping to get to "the Green Place," the only lush place left in the post-apocalyptic wasteland. Along the way, she joins forces with Max Rockatansky (Tom Hardy) to fight off Joe's pursuing war boy forces. Furiosa, the five escapee women and Max drive across infested mudflats to encounter the Vuvalini. This encounter reveals that Furiosa's green place is now the festering mudflats they just drove across. Max persuades the despondent Furiosa to return to Joe's citadel and take it from him. After a furious battle against Joe and his war boys, Furiosa manages to kill Joe and claim the citadel as a free place.

Mad Max: Fury Road is the fourth installment in a series begun in 1979 with *Mad Max*, followed by *Mad Max 2: The Road Warrior* (1981) and *Mad Max Beyond Thunderdome* (1985), all films directed by George Miller. The series evolves from a dystopic thriller to a post-apocalyptic action film, all held together rather unevenly by Mad Max's exploits in this world. What changes with *Fury Road* is that the perspective shifts from Mad Max to Furiosa, casting Max as helper rather than hero. What has not changed is the baroque style of the world, a bricolage of wasteland punk, people dressed in fetish gear for the apocalypse, and an abundance of rusty machinery. Like most good science fiction, a larger world is alluded to rather than explained in great detail, suggesting a mythology based around guzzoline, guns and a Valhalla for warriors. The central question is who killed the world, and it is evident that *Fury Road* carries an ecological message not present in the earlier films, which instead focused on a nuclear apocalypse suited to the Cold War rhetoric of its time. As McKenzie Wark points out, however, there is no escape to the green place, giving us the sense that the environmental disaster is total.[33] While *Fury Road* in no way feels like the Bourne sequence, it shares with those films the structure of being essentially one long chase sequence. Rushing away from the war boys towards the green place only to reverse direction and return to the citadel reveals the crucial fact that there is no escape. Unlike Bourne who always leaves for another place at the end of each film, Furiosa and the women have no choice but to take back the world they can get, rather than the world they want.

As a 3D film there is a predictable emphasis on negative parallax movement. Although only rarely employed in conventional 2D cinema, because it breaks the perceptual realism of the cinematic frame, 3D cinema is designed to take advantage of objects and characters bulging out towards the viewer. Due to the requirement of two images projected simultaneously, 3D cinema is also sometimes termed stereoscopy, a technique for enhancing the illusion of depth in images. The traditional cinematic screen is referred to as the stereo plane, the focal point of which has zero parallax. When objects or characters move toward the background, they move into positive parallax, essentially what conventional cinema terms depth of field. However, 3D cinema can also successfully move an object towards the viewer, producing the sensation that the object is closer to the viewer than the screen is. This movement is called negative parallax and moves into what is called audience space, as distinct from screen space, which is the space behind the screen.[34]

As is to be expected, the primary function of making a film 3D, whether by shooting in stereo (i.e. with two cameras) or converting a 2D image in post-production, is to engage with the audience space to create a more tactile, immersive sensation. *Fury Road* is no exception, opening on a 3D sequence that establishes the stereoscopic effect and returning to it particularly in its frenzied chase scenes. After the opening voice-over, which provides a mixture of exposition and introduction to Max and the setting, Max drives off into the desert, and with no sound to announce them, war boys throttle past from behind us. Their vehicles emerge on screen left and screen right, as if we were standing in the middle of the action. A gorgeous, sweeping extreme-wide-shot pan articulates the spatial relations between Max's car and the war boys following him. As Max crashes and pulls himself out of the car, we get flashbacks to his daughter being run over by a car. In a brief frontal shot, the car careens straight into us before the shot cuts back to Max. In this way, the 3D nature of the film is announced.

Interestingly, it is also worth pointing out that the film opens with a shot almost identical to the crash-cam of the Bourne films. However, the use of negative parallax does not necessarily induce the same vulnerable effect found in Bourne's crash-cam scenes. In fact, *Fury Road* distinguishes itself by providing a very stable sense of embodied space. We are clear about the visual choreography but also given access to a more empowered embodiment of the characters. This does not prevent the film from employing elastic special effects, or what Yvonne Spielmann has dubbed "spatials," since they "aim at a spectacular expansion of spatial dimensions."[35] While one might think that 3D cinema's preeminent function would be to render perspectival space more realistically, we should keep in mind that perspectival space is in itself a special effect: the ability to evoke three dimensions through two dimensions. Rather, 3D cinema is meant to evoke voluminous space, and not necessarily realistically. *Fury Road* employs a number of shots that produce paradoxical space, a space that cannot exist, much like the mirror space in *Sucker Punch*.

Fury Road gets much of its force from the lateral shots of trucks and cars driving across a gorgeous, vibrant auburn landscape. These traveling shots articulate a sense of speed and momentum while still giving clear access to actions and positions. The clarity of the horizontal trajectory, as well as the predominantly flat landscape, provides a superb backdrop for movement in other directions, which generates torque, a twisting of the line of force that speeds directly ahead. The war rig that Furiosa commands becomes both a line of flight, in its literal attempt at escaping Immortan Joe, and a vector, which must be stopped by the war boys. The very kinetics of the war rig and the film's driving energy are parallel to the narrative momentum. The escape scene in which Immortan Joe realizes that Furiosa is leaving with his wives exemplifies this tension between forward momentum and disruptive forces quite well.

With Joe's war boys bearing down on them, Furiosa and her party are also being chased by a band of Buzzards, Russian desert pirates driving spiked vehicles. As the three lines of force converge, a feverish battle ensues between Furiosa's unwitting war boy crew, the Buzzards and the pursuing war boys, who know that Furiosa is trying to escape. Although the action is fast-paced, with lots of kinetic movement, the film keeps everything clear is through its tight use of continuity editing. As Furiosa's party try to outrun the Buzzards, a trap-line lifts from the sand, making a war boy car crash. Shot frontally in a wide shot, we see the car flip, but then we cut to a lateral shot from the side, providing a clear view of how the car flips on its own axis and catapults a war boy out of the back seat. We then cut back to a frontal shot of Furiosa's war rig veering off screen left, the car still flipping on the screen plane and the war boy flying directly into audience space in a blur. The war boy tumbles over the camera and out of frame as we cut to a reverse shot that shows him falling into the sand, Furiosa's war rig thundering past screen right. Although hectic and fast-paced, the spatial relations are clear; we understand where every object is in relation to each other, and even when the direction is reversed, objects remain within a coherent space. (*See Figure 3.4 in the insert.*)

There are three trajectories at play here: the war rig, the flipping car and the flying war boy. The war rig produces a line of force that induces energy but is not at risk of hitting us. The flipping car also produces motion energy without our being placed at risk. Lastly, the war boy flies directly towards us, but above our heads, suggesting that the reverse shot is us spinning to see where he goes. Contrast this with the crash-cam in *The Bourne Supremacy*, which maintained the frontal shot *while* the crash occurred and after, thus suggesting that we are inside the event. In *Fury Road*, we are kept safely between the events, although there are more lines of force at work. Furthermore, the static, stable shots also extend our sense of clarity and safety. Yet at the same time everything moves quickly, giving us little time to fully orient ourselves. The use of focus is telling here. Rather than shooting in deep focus, the shots are kept relatively shallow, forcing a specific point of attention: the flipping car. That makes the two other trajectories come off as faster, particularly the flying war boy, whose trajectory appears as a kind of motion blur due to his heading straight for us. Speed is induced through these multiple trajectories and motion blurs, making it difficult to absorb every single action.

Indeed, there are several times when realistic spatial relations are sacrificed for a more visceral, bodily assault. We find several near misses of objects flying off screen right or screen left. When a Buzzard drives into a war boy on a motor cycle, he is catapulted straight into the camera's focal point, and we get a zoom effect straight onto his face and into his eyes, indicating that we are hit by the war boy. The way the film maintains continuity and coherent space here is by employing a match cut to Furiosa's head, so that the graphic matching subsumes the cut in action, which is otherwise spatially incoherent. Furthermore, the sheer speed at which the war boy is catapulted towards us ensures that one can only really see, with any degree of clarity, the way his face rams into the audience space by doing frame-by-frame progression on one's home media player. In the theater, the line of force would be swallowed by the sheer speed of the images. Similarly, when a war boy is shot by arrows and sacrifices himself for the rest, he jumps off his car onto the Buzzard car in a slow-motion wide shot that clearly establishes spatial relations before he rams into the car with his explosive javelins and a fireball blasts just screen right of Max, who is tied to the prow of another war boy's car. This speed-ramping provides the ground on which the blast can accelerate without loss of orientation.

Another strategy for generating movement energy comes in the fast-motion push-in and pull-out shots. A push-in shot is where the camera is pushed closer to the subject, as a pull-out shot is where the camera is pulled further away from the subject. If done slowly, the effect is mostly one of paying more attention to the subject or the background, as the case may be. With fast-motion shots, however, there is a physical jolt, a sudden movement towards or away from the subject. Used often in *Fury Road*, we could call this *space-ramping*, because the sensation is such a jolt that it inevitably makes us shift bodily. Primarily used to punctuate jumps, crashes or swerves in *Fury Road*, the effect is not unlike the crash-cam, except that we never actually crash. Instead, there is a sudden burst of energy catapulted at us, another example of an audiovisual affectile that kinetically engages us bodily. While space-ramping feels like an involuntary spasm, there is not the same sense of trepidation as in *The Bourne Supremacy*, though there is a distinctive bodily rush of energy. And although they are also refram-ing shots, these shots move beyond mere reframing: the purpose is not to produce a new composition but simply to jolt us awake with unexpected movement in an unexpected direction. While such shots are in no way new, they are intensified through *Fury Road's* stereoscopic images, because the push or pull moves directly into the audience space. The effect is clearly immersive and haptic, the rendering of short, affectile punches that inten-sify the generation of energy and speed.

While the film mainly develops a rhythm of shots that clearly estab-lish space either right before or right after an explosion or crash, several moments in the film produce a jerky, uneven motion that comes simply from speeding up the images. In the spectacular final chase scene, all tricks are used to induce sensations of speed. The use of 3D images allows for a greater sensation of space and so for a greater experience of the rush of trajectories, since the bulging nature of 3D gives direct access to move-ments in parallax, as opposed to our having to infer them from perspec-tival images. Our perceptual machinery thus skips a part of the normal process of cinema due to the felt sensation of space. Yet with the flickering, jouncy images in this final chase, we also experience these trajectories in an unsettling, stable orientation.

We find this particularly in crash shots where objects fly in either nega-tive or positive parallax, such as when the side of Furiosa's war rig is torn off by a hook. The impact causes one of the old women to jerk forward, while the side of the rig itself is pulled away in the next shot. Both shots ramp the image up slightly, making it faster and producing a jittery sen-sation that corresponds to the shock of the punch and pull of the hook. Similarly, when Max cuts a chain hooked to the rig, the chain flies through the windshield of a war boy's car. Shot inside the car with the war boy in front of us, the speed-ramping jitters the image in one of the film's few examples of crash-cam shots.

We also experience all three dimensions of space, with the vertical axis added by the long, jouncy poles attached to the war boy's cars, which allow them to swoop down on the war rig. The best example is when a war boy is

85

filmed from below in a jump cut sequence as he swings down to grab Toast the Knowing (Zoë Kravitz). The negative parallax movement as he falls straight into the camera cuts to a high angle shot of his arms reaching out toward Toast from screen right and screen left. We are literally placed just below the war boy's head. Then we cut to a low angle shot again as the war boy lifts Toast up and pulls her back as he flicks back to his car. The positive parallax of Toast being pulled away is an effective use of 3D imagery to intensify the experience of losing Toast.

By contrast, the subsequent sequence is of Max almost falling off the rig but being saved by Furiosa's hydraulic arm. We see Max's fall in a horizontal shot, followed by a low angle shot from below Max, shooting upward and providing a terrifying position for Max and us. Stabbed in the side by a war boy, Furiosa cannot hold on to Max for long. A war boy speeds up his car to ram Max, but Furiosa smashes her rig into the car. The car flips over, a zoom shot moving into the car and onto the war boy's face. Nux, the same war boy onto whose car Max was tied, comes out from under the rig and kicks Max onto The People Eater's truck (John Howard). Utilizing the downward trajectory of his fall and then letting Max hang helpless for several shots as cars and trucks careen around him produces a sensation of helplessness in us that is different from the vulnerability of the Bourne films, although clearly related.

As Max jumps off the truck onto the war rig, he is grabbed by another pole-swaying war boy, and they are pulled up by the pole as they wrestle. In a traveling lateral shot, the couple swings to the other side of the car, coming very close to slamming into the ground. The war boy pushes Max's head toward the ground in a low shot that shows how close he is to it. Max manages to push off the war boy, who then tumbles under the wheels of another truck as we see the People Eater's truck explodes in an imposing fireball. We see the fireball first in a side shot, then a low angle frontal shot, with Max close to the ground, and finally a high angle shot of Max flinging across the screen and the entire fleet of vehicles, all forward trajectories as the fireball throws several war boys and expands towards the sides of the screen from its center position. *(See Figure 3.5 in the insert.)* This sequence instills us with an enormous sense of physical empowerment centered on Max's body and his muscular experience of being thrown all around the screen. One of the most imposing sequences in the entire film, the vertical

Figure 2.1 *Iron Man 3*: One of the suits is reassembling itself, having just disposed of several Extremis-infected villains.

Figure 2.2 *Iron Man 2*: The nonhuman vectors of desire created by dancing bodies and metal suit.

Figure 2.3 *Sucker Punch*: This top image is the beginning of the tracking shot, while the bottom one is near the end of the shot, which becomes the new physical space.

Figure 2.4 *Sucker Punch*: See above caption.

Figure 2.5 *Sucker Punch*: The smooth space of Babydoll gliding towards a killer robot.

Figure 3.1 *The Dark Knight Rises*: Batman in superhuman control on his Bat-Pod.

Figure 3.2 *The Dark Knight Rises*: Batman glides in superhuman control in his Bat.

Figure 3.3 *The Bourne Supremacy*: A close-up of Matt Damon as the truck crashes into his car in a crash-cam shot.

Figure 3.4 *Mad Max: Fury Road*: Clear articulation of space, as a war boy flies towards us.

Figure 3.5 *Mad Max: Fury Road*: A fireball explosion with Max pivoting screen right on the pole.

Figure 4.1 *Crank: High Voltage*: Above, we see Chev being jumpstarted and below is the supercinematic zoom onto his artificial heart.

Figure 4.2 *Crank: High Voltage*: See above caption.

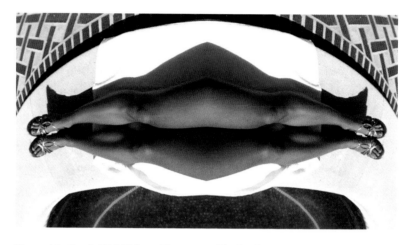

Figure 4.3 *Crank: High Voltage*: The mirrored body of a woman, reduced to only legs.

Figure 4.4 *Jupiter Ascending*: Caine being hurled towards a glass roof in a continuous shot.

Figure 4.5 *Jupiter Ascending*: Jupiter and Caine are reduced to tiny dots against the sublime spectacle of destruction.

Figure 5.1 *Real Steel*: Synchronous movement of Charlie and Atom.

Figure 5.2 *Avatar*: Movement into audience space, threatened by the predator beast.

Figure 5.3 *Avatar*: The mighty Toruk being dominated from above by Jake.

Figure 6.1 *Transformers: Dark of the Moon*: A soldier falls to the ground in a continuous shot.

Figure 6.2 *Transformers: Dark of the Moon*: The Driller and Shockwave.

Figure 6.3 *Transformers: Dark of the Moon*: A Decepticon leaps over Bumblebee in a sonic null extension.

Figure 6.4 *Battle Los Angeles*: The underwhelming explosion of the alien craft, otherwise expressed through sound.

Figure 6.5 *The Hurt Locker*: Stillness through close-up, dust and a crawling fly.

Figure 6.6 *The Hurt Locker*: Tight framing produces intimacy and tension in the car bomb scene.

axis is utilized to great effect here, inducing sensations that would be hard to otherwise elicit.

The vertical axis is established as a threat, in contrast to the horizontal axis of the lines of force. Without wanting to push the analogy too far, the vertical threat of the war boys becomes parallel to the hierarchical threat of Immortan Joe. Both the opening and closing scenes of the citadel reveal a clear hierarchy established in part by the use of the vertical axis. The imposing height of Joe's plateau makes him hover above his minions, who all literally look up to him. Much of the film's horizontal trajectory can be said to be an attempt at torpedoing this vertical axis, instead seeking a more level hierarchy. Yet this reading is problematized by Furiosa's ride up in the lift at the end of the film. Whether this shot is meant to indicate a warning that hierarchical power will always re-assert itself or to signal a change in power structures is hard to say.

The immense physical empowerment that *Fury Road* so depends on comes from the combination of vehicle and driver, symbolized in Furiosa's hydraulic left arm. Although she and Immortan Joe are both literal cyborgs in the film, every scene of intense bodily sensation is in fact contingent on a combination of human and machine. Deeply machinic in nature, all the sensations are thus intensified by this combination. And just as the spectacular scenes depend on machine-human hybrids, the protagonists in this film are far more dependent on each other than is conventional.

Typically, action films are centered on one protagonist, who often has a sidekick that might also serve as the object that needs protection. Consider Kyle Reese (Michael Biehn) in *The Terminator* (James Cameron 1984), who must protect Sarah Connor (Linda Hamilton). Alternatively, the buddy movie may provide two protagonists, although one is usually cast as secondary comic relief, such as *Lethal Weapon* (Richard Donner 1987), where Martin Riggs (Mel Gibson) serves as the primary protagonist and Roger Murtaugh (Danny Glover) complements him, thus completing the pair. While Murtaugh is mostly comic relief in the sequels, the structure still holds in films such as *48 Hrs.* (Walter Hill 1982), where Nick Nolte is the action star and Eddie Murphy provides comic relief.

By contrast, *Fury Road* clearly has two primary protagonists in Furiosa and Max, but the five women serve as more than mere damsels in distress to be saved. They participate in the fight sequences, as

87

do the Vuvalani crones. Although it is not unusual for the supporting roles to help the protagonist every so often, such as in *Die Hard* (John McTiernan 1988), when Sergeant Al Powell (Reginald VelJohnson) shoots the terrorist Karl (Alexander Godunov) to save John McClane's life (Bruce Willis), the sheer number of times that characters help each other in *Fury Road* is highly unusual. The added fact that by far most of these are woman, several of them old women, makes for an exceptional use of embodiment. There are countless examples where one character assists another, such as when one of the Vuvalani holds onto Max so he can reach down and unhook the chains on the rig, or when a Vuvalani stands up to beat the war boy who is strangling Furiosa with a garrote, when Cheedo the Fragile (Courtney Eaton) helps Furiosa get on to Joe's war rig, or when Toast steers the rig after Furiosa has pulled Joe's face off. But there are also other examples earlier in the film, such as when the group is caught in the midlands with their rig and the Bullet Farmer (Richard Carter) is gaining on them. Max shoots at the searchlight but misses. While he is taking aim again, Furiosa comes up behind Max and he gives her the rifle, letting her rest it on his shoulder. Literally lending her his body in this sequence, it is only through this sense of shared bodily capability that they are able to shoot out the searchlight and blind the Bullet Farmer.

The physical empowerment that we feel during the film does not originate from only one or two main characters but from a whole host of bodies that all contribute. Many of these instances are not minimal actions but surprisingly forceful ones, such as when one of the Vuvalani smashes a bullet into a war boy's head, killing him instantly. The bodily alignment and empowerment becomes distributed and underscores the group effort it takes to vanquish Immortan Joe. In that sense, we are exposed to a network of affects and sensations, which also help to reduce the singular sensations so often attributed to only white, male protagonists. Our attention and bodily awareness is stretched in a way that perfectly aligns with how Max is not the hero in this film, despite his clear status as protagonist in the first trilogy. Presumably, this is also why the film caused such an uproar among pathetic "men's rights" viewers, who seemed unable to stomach that anyone other than a man could perform spectacular feats without becoming masculinized in the process.[36] What matters to me is not only the fact that so much of the action is undertaken by women but also that there is no central embodied character. We desire to put ourselves in the positions of several different characters in order to satisfy the most experiences, as Whitehead would have it. For me, that is the film's most astounding success.

What *Mad Max: Fury Road* accomplishes is to produce a multitude of sensations that pull us in different directions due to the use of several characters' spectacular actions, but also due to the enormous amount of trajectories put into motion. The spare use of dialog, along with the fact that most of the action takes place at high speed, forces us to fully engage with the lines of force that the sound-images relentlessly pump out. The pure utilization of kinetics makes the film one of the most engrossing action films ever produced, in part because of the clarity of the camerawork and the velocities at which everything moves. In this way, the film manages to be both hyperactive and situationally clear, which is an impressive feat.

The film also manages to subvert and negotiate the singularly masculine embodiment of most actions films. Important not only from a gender politics point of view, this affective entrainment of a collective embodiment disrupts the generic articulation of narrative force and allows for multiple engagements that are exceedingly rare in action films. *Fury Road* stands at the apex of action cinema's subversive potentialities, as one of the clearest examples of Miriam Hansen's argument that mimetic innervation may produce the energy that affords us the energies to disrupt conventional lines of articulation. This realization also puts us in a position to consider the film's preference for horizontality as opposed to verticality. Precisely because our embodiment is distributed across several characters, that embodiment does not stand as singular and individual. More than anything, the success of Furiosa and her party is a group effort and not the result of one person. Because Max is not positioned as the great white male savior, the only way to fully enjoy the film is to align ourselves bodily with women and men, people of color and old people; people of all kinds are part of bringing down the singular white male that is Immortan Joe. *Mad Max: Fury Road* is thus miles apart from the predominance of contemporary action films.

Hyper-Perception

The films I have discussed here are all instances of extreme deployments of movement within and of the cinematic frame. The kinetics produced by the rapid up-down movements, sweeping camera tracks and pans, and fast-paced editing are not stable spaces that we can easily orient ourselves within. Instead, they are intensive lines of force that perform rather than represent the world we currently live in. On a sensorial level, then, we engage with these films in what Miriam Hansen terms a play-form of second nature. Characters' stunts and uninhibited movements in all three dimensions produce a kind of counter to the violence of ideology otherwise perpetrated by the films. We find a tension that cannot easily be resolved or answered. These films activate the individual viewer's experience, affectivity and memory, while also depending on the audience as "a heterogenous, volatile social collective."[37] We are tied into a larger collective whole through these films, suggesting that our enjoyment is always shared and social. As evidenced by *Fury Road*, however, subversion and affective intervention can also be made available as bodily resources for a different kind of collective.

Through sheer intensity and excess of motion, these films produce what Steven Shaviro has termed a "possibility space", which traces the forces that shape the world and tries to locate "its sticking points, its intermittencies and interruptions."[38] In other words, the films enact both the forces that work upon us and the lines of flight. While Miriam Hansen and Shaviro would not agree on the liberating nature of these possibility spaces, it is clear that the possibility spaces are the same as what Hansen refers to as play-forms of the image/body-space of cinema.[39] That intense motion along all axes has increased as cinema technologies become lighter and more advanced also produces a new state of attention, a new mass production of the senses which emphasizes kinesthesia over visual perception.

In these moments, our perception is stretched across multiple points of attention, what Wood calls "distributed attention".[40] Keeping in mind that perception here should not be understood as cognitive or conscious, it is better to recognize that kinetics demand we discard a unifocal gaze in favor of a multifocal scanning, which allows us to encompass all the moving elements within the cinematic space, including that of screen perspective. In other words, it is better to consider perception ecological than somehow residing singularly in us. Films such as *Fury Road* constantly and consistently push at the limits of our perception, moving too fast, with too many objects and vectors at work simultaneously. We feel ourselves traversed by kinetics, and the only reason we feel comfortable is that the film consistently brings the spatial morphs back to the mastery of the characters. Editing plays a large part in this process, since it typically matches on characters, grounding the velocity of images in the human body. Yet as I have shown, there is a tension between the superhuman movements of the characters and the nonhuman movements of the camera, and much of our experience is bound up in the nonhuman movements. That some films never dare to fully dissolve us into nonhuman worlding is more a matter of the film's narrative conservatism than it is determined by the limits of technology.

Scott Bukatman's influential proposition of cinema's kaleidoscopic perception is, then, replaced by a hyper-perception, which favors motion, kinetics and energies: all sensations that stave off paralysis. As evidenced by *Fury Road* in particular, sensation and perception become stretched, distributed and even strained by the vectoral power of the images. Taken together, these films suggest a vectoral cinema that bends human perception by exploding stable conventions of movement, opening instead the nonhuman and making it perceptible in human perception. Such adaptation is precisely aesthetic: it is a matter of *aisthesis*, a matter of augmenting and transforming the way we perceive the world. Vectoral cinema inaugurates a new audio-vision that is not only haptic and tactile but also plural and dispersed.

By *plural* and *dispersed*, I mean the multiple, heterogenous perceptions that interweave between the viewer's body and the cinematic body, the traversal of perceptions spilling across each other. We encounter a kind of ambient perception. Deleuze posits Dziga Vertov's concept of gaseous perception as what a nonhuman perception might be like; no longer a solid state that cannot move, perception instead becomes a state of free movement.[41] This gaseous perception has been associated with the American experimental cinema of Stan Brakhage and Michael Snow, for instance, and predominantly figures in the use of "hyper-rapid montage: extraction of a point of inversion or transformation (for the correlation of immobilisation of the image is the extreme mobility of the support, and the photogramme acts as the differential element producing refulgence and great haste)."[42] Yet as we have seen, montage, or editing, is not necessarily the predominant mode employed in the films I have discussed, though all of them engage with nonhuman perception. We do find rapid editing, to be sure, but also rapid camerawork and a flurry of fast-moving objects within the frame.

William Brown similarly picks up on gaseous perception in his *Supercinema*, pointing out that ultra-fast camera movements and extreme zooms or tracking shots can work as a kind of gaseous perception.[43] However, I would argue that hyper-perception is a better term for the effect of contemporary action cinema, in which a perception develops that stretches across an environment or milieu with multiple focal points. In this way, our perception is retooled or repurposed by the integration of new image technologies, not unlike how Jay David Bolter and Richard Grusin define hypermediacy in their book *Remediation*: "The logic of hypermediacy multiplies the signs of mediation and in this way tries to reproduce the rich sensorium of human experience."[44] In much the same way, our perception is multiplied into hyper-perception.

Hyper-perception becomes a matter of managing kinetics. It suggests an exceeding of perception due to the acceleration of action cinema's audiovisuals. Hyper-perception is thus both faster than normal perception and contingent on more than one type of perception, i.e. it involves a kind of nonhuman perception because trajectories and velocities disperse aperspectivly across the cinematic screen, even into audience space in the case of 3D films. That is to say, the kinetics of these films do not converge on a focal point of the screen but across several points at the same time. Indeed, I would argue that the films I have discussed are not satisfied with merely reproducing human experience but desire to augment and supplement human experience with a nonhuman one.

Thus hyper-perception is precisely an ecological perception, embedded in a larger spatial network. Hyper-perception becomes flexible, adapting to the new post-cinematic image regime that puts new pressures and limitations on us. I outlined previously how often we are placed in a position of danger, having to keep an eye out for too many lines of movement. At the same time, enormous amounts of energy are released to overcome our state of paralysis within the culture of fear. The plural, distributed nature of perception affords new powerful forms of embodiment rendered though the films. Action films' mimetic force allows for bodily reassurance and affective comfort through the production of new powerful embodiments. These embodiments incorporate nonhuman capacities and so bolster us against a human fear.

Action films fill us with embodied sensations of potency in order to dispel that fear. As we saw in this chapter, this is primarily achieved through the production of energy and lines of force. Kinetics becomes a way for us to understand how the transformation set about by the vector takes on direction and articulation. Kinetics thus comes after the vector's line of force, but it guides and limits the ways the vector can move. At the same time, kinetics is about bodies and how bodies react and articulate to transfer of energy. We can see the extent to which kinetics always combines with embodiment in one way or another, which makes it more important to understand exactly how bodies respond to the vectors of affect and kinetics of energy. This becomes the guiding question for the next chapter.

4

Volatility and Flexible Bodies

We have already seen how much contemporary action cinema depends on eliciting bodily sensations and engaging our perception in new ways. The result is a different sense of embodiment, a topic I have already begun to broach in earlier chapters. My basic contention is that we allow ourselves to step not only into the embodiment of the characters in these films but also into the cinematic body itself. Such contiguity is extended, as I have tried to show, by the incorporation of new and nonhuman modes of camera movements, but also by an ensuing shift in the correlation of the cinematic body with the actor's body. The characters and actors' bodies in contemporary action cinema must likewise be extended. That is to say, action cinema begins to depend on bodies that can move and act in ways that human bodies cannot. Bodies become volatile in the encounter with vectors of affect and kinetics of energy, so we may begin to register the effects of vectors and kinetics on the bodies themselves: of characters, films and viewers.

Many action films have pushed human capabilities to their limits. One defining example is the *Matrix* series, with its trademarked bullet-time effects, which show off a control of time and space no human could ever accomplish. Hong Kong cinema's long history of *wuxia* films, with their use of wire-frames in addition to hyper-skilled martial artists and actors – films such as *Crouching Tiger, Hidden Dragon* (Ang Lee 2000), *Hero* (Yimou Zhang 2002) and others in the regrettably brief cycle of Hong Kong films that became prominent in US markets – present another example. Even if traditional *wuxia* films never established a foothold in Hollywood, they surely inspired later Hollywood films such as the Wachowskis' *Jupiter Ascending* (2015). Similarly, while many examples of the French action film tradition, films like *Banlieue 13* (English title *District B13*, Pierre Morel 2004), only became lackluster remakes (*Brick Mansions*, Camille Delaware 2014), their use of parkour was assimilated into films such as the Daniel Craig Bond-cycle (*Casino Royale* 2006, *Quantum of Solace* 2008 and *Skyfall* 2012). Clearly, there is great hunger for superhuman bodies in contemporary culture.

Contrasted with the classic 1980s action films, where actors like Arnold Schwarzenegger and Sylvester Stallone became machinic through bodybuilding, in newer action films we find a form of assemblage embodiment that moves between human body and technological body. If the action heroes of the 1980s were "hard bodies," recuperating a sense of lost masculinity, contemporary action heroes are "flexible bodies," capable of movements that go beyond human capacity through the use of wire-frames, compositing and digital effects.[1] Furthermore, Hollywood's fascination with technology has also meant that instead of employing actors that are skilled in martial arts and capable of sustaining the choreographed fight ballets that Bordwell dissects in *Planet Hollywood*, the emphasis has shifted to favor fast-paced editing and computer-generated imagery to produce a post-cinematic body that induces sensations of extreme volatility.

I think of this concept as *volatility* because it suggests both flying (from the Latin *volare*) and changeability. Action heroes suggest flexible adaptation to any situation or event. Contemporary action heroes must be flexible bodies, then, because they must take on any necessary shape, perform any necessary action. The concept of physical empowerment through martial arts is well-documented in action film studies. In his article "Kinesthesia in Martial Arts Films" (1998), Aaron Anderson discusses an early example of the use of fight choreography and the kinesthesia developed from the bodily action of martial artists. Similarly, Man-Fung Yip discusses sensory realism in his article "In the Realm of the Senses," (2014) a term which he connects closely to the physical capacity of the star. Most persistent in this thought is Lisa Purse, who both in her excellent article "Gestures and Postures of Mastery" and throughout her book, *Contemporary Action Cinema*, outlines the sensations of "becoming-powerful" through the protagonist's body.

However, rather than argue for the undeniable truth of the sensory realism, kinesthesia and the process of "becoming-powerful," I wish to point to the fact that contemporary action cinema does not, in fact, depend overly much on the physical capacity of the star's body, for the very simple reason that they, generally speaking, are not excellent martial artists. While undoubtedly well-trained – or at least well-toned – actors such as Channing Tatum, Tom Cruise, Matt Damon, Tom Hardy and others are no martial artists. And even when they are, for instance Jason Statham, these abilities are never displayed in the same way as with Bruce Lee, Jet Li or Cynthia Rothrock. Even in films that pit Asian actors against European actors, such as *War* (Philip G. Atwell 2007), where Statham faces off against Li, there is no climactic showdown between them to display their abilities. Instead, the physical capacities of the Asian actor are always introduced early on as a threat, only later to be vanquished by other means, such as in *Lethal Weapon 4* (Richard Donner 1998), where Wah Sing Ku (Jet Li) is shot dead by Martin Riggs. In other words, the volatility of contemporary action bodies emerges from the use of affective vectors and energetic kinetics developed in the two previous chapters.

Indeed, the fascination with augmenting the human body through post-cinematic means is evidenced in films like *300* (Zack Snyder 2006) and *300: Rise of an Empire* (Noam Murro 2014), wherein the imposing chest muscles of the Spartans are in fact makeup effects later enhanced digitally in post-production. What matters, then, are the kinds of sensations elicited by this nonhuman, supercinematic body, which can pull us in new and different directions.[2] The films I deal with here have a keen desire for a nonhuman body, with capacities beyond human ones, although in the end these bodies must be made available for human consumption as the elicitation of sensation. This desire questions the body's role and deconstructs the body as an individual, unified entity in favor of a body assemblage.

The Wired Body: *Crank: High Voltage*

A man has his heart replaced with an artificial one, loses its battery pack and refuels it with a car's jumpstart pack, after which he runs down the street at a breakneck pace. This scene indicates the bodily logic found in *Crank: High Voltage*, by the director duo consisting of Mark Neveldine and Brian Taylor called Neveldine/Taylor. This is a sequel to the 2006 *Crank*, by the same directors and continues exactly where the first film left off. Both *Crank* films are more interested in the sheer adrenaline rush of visual kinetics and an outrageous embodiment, than coherent stories with logically unfolding narratives.

Purse's argument about the action hero's body-in-motion centers on the idea that an actual pro-filmic event intensifies the viewer's experience, as opposed to the flattening of affect that occurs with computer-generated animation and digital bodies. She argues that excessive computer-generated imagery can "actually work against an embodied engagement with the action body."[3] Yet it seems to me that Purse's emphasis lies too heavily on a human-centered notion of becoming, and that she insists too much on the superiority of a phenomenological articulation of the human body as eliciting sensations recognizable to us. Counter to this argument, I believe that some actions films are entirely happy with eliciting nonhuman sensations and engaging with a nonhuman embodiment. These volatile action films engage an embodiment that is not simply superhuman, as in exceeding the human body in degree, but is fully nonhuman and exceeds the human body *in kind*. In other words, these films produce sensations and experiences that suggest a broader realm of embodiment.

In the first *Crank* film, we meet Chev Chelios (Jason Statham) as he wakes up, after being poisoned for having killed a Chinese crime boss, a murder we later learn he did not commit. Trying at first to find an antidote, Chev later resigns himself to simply exact his revenge before his own inevitable demise. Adrenaline being the only thing that can keep him alive, Chev constantly needs to perform extreme acts to keep himself alive. Eventually, this revenge mission leads him to confront his own boss, after which he is thrown out of a helicopter and dies when he hits the road. Although nominally a remake of *D.O.A.* (Rudolph Maté 1950), there is little except the setup that binds the two films together. *Crank: High Voltage* begins with

Chev being literally shoveled off the road and taken to an operating room. Here, Chev's heart is removed to be transplanted into Poon Dong (David Carradine). Learning that Poon Dong intends to keep him alive and harvest his organs as necessary, Chev breaks free in order to keep his big English cock. This sends Chev on another rampage through LA's streets as he tries to find Johnny Vang (Art Hsu) and recover his heart. The chase climaxes at the home of the brother of two gangsters Chev killed in the first film. To recharge his heart, Chev grabs on to high voltage cables that sets him on fire. Burning, he beats the gangster El Huron (Clifton Collins Jr.) to death and collapses, hallucinating a re-union with his love, Eve (Amy Smart). In a blurry credit scene, we see Eve and Chev's doctor, Miles (Dwight Yoakam), attempt to resuscitate Chev but then give up. After they have left, however, a completely bandaged Chev opens his eyes, ready for another sequel.

While in the first film Chev is kept going mostly on drugs, in the second he literally becomes a cyborg, a human-machine hybrid, when his heart is exchanged for an artificial one. Suitable for a film that is incredibly more outrageous than the first one, the artificial heart opens up new avenues of obtaining energy. Chev needs electricity and regularly electrocutes himself, on stun guns, switch boxes and anything else that will jolt him. In the cartoon world of *Crank*, this both recharges his heart and makes him stronger, increasing his power the more electricity he is subjected to. The first time we see this in action is after Chev has crashed his car and as a consequence destroyed his battery pack. He asks a couple of drivers to give him a jump and they hook a car jumper to their car and Chev hooks one clamp on his nipple and the second on his tongue. As they gun the car, Chev screams and the camera jerks around his face in a close-up, alternating between a high-angle shot, a lateral extreme close-up on his tongue and a low angle shot with plenty of lens flare. The colors invert and mismatch as individual frames also go off-center, in some of which he is almost out-of-frame. With the crackle of electricity sparking in the soundtrack, we are also jolted out of a stable experience. The camera tracks down to Chev's chest and zooms into his chest cavity, showing the artificial heart pumping faster and faster. We zoom out of the chest cavity to find Chev sprinting frantically down the road. *(See Figures 4.1 and 4.2 in the insert.)*

This brief, initial charge sequence indicates the film's emphasis on spasmodic camerawork to suggest Chev's physical state of being. Primarily employed in shots that feature Chev rather than other characters, and particularly prominent in shots immediately following a major injection, this technique become a signature style for the entire film. While many of these shots would also fit well in the earlier *Crank*, or other Neveldine/Taylor films for that matter, some of the formal properties are pushed even further in *Crank: High Voltage*. I have already discussed the machinic sensations instilled by the camera moving in ways that are humanly impossible, in what Brown calls supercinematic shots, and here again we quite clearly find those sensations operating at the heart of the matter. The digitally rendered shots of Chev's artificial heart are against a black backdrop, not the viscera that we would actually find inside his chest.

What happens in this moment is the breach of any possible embodied engagement with the image, because the non-diegetic camera moves in a way that is physically impossible. This discorrelates us from the images, as Shane Denson has argued, because we are shifted out of the structural homology that Vivian Sobchack identified in her classic work *The Address of the Eye*. In other words, even though the camera does not always function as a character, the camera has traditionally been put in a place where the viewer could be, given the affordances of the camera. Thus, even crane shots and helicopter shots are shots that imitate what it would be like for us on that crane or in that helicopter. When the camera zooms into Chev's body, even leaving out all the intestines inside him, there is no way that we could ever move like that. We thus lose our sense of embodiment and find ourselves instead in what Denson calls a processual field.[4] Already in this sequence, we begin to get a sense of Chev's flexible body, a body that the camera can zoom through, but also a body that is happy to accommodate clamps and electricity shooting through it. There is no relevant dividing line between human body and electronic devices; everything works through a transfer of energies.

Yet while there are several shots of Chev's stuttering heart, these brief instances are not enough for us to lose our sense of embodiment for the entirety of the film. One might easily argue that these shots work more like inserts or brief orientation shots and are, on the whole, easily assimilated by the viewer. But there are a plethora of devices at work to discorrelate our embodiment. Chev's charging down the street right after being jumped by the car is one such instance. Not only is the sound-track blaring fast-paced punk-rock style music, as is to be expected, but the images deploy several key devices that unsettle our experience. The first shot is a jittery shot using an out-of-phase shutter that produces a peculiar, almost stop-motion-like judder of the images, what we could call a *flutter shot*. Fish-eye lenses are employed on moving camera rigs to shoot Chev frontally and high-angle while he is running. Further sensory distortion comes from shooting laterally on Chev's head and then cutting to his feet pounding on the asphalt, then to a shot straight down on Chev's bald pate from above. To compound all of this, freeze frames are interspersed into the moving images, producing small sudden jolts of inaction that contrast with the frenetic speed of the out-of-phase images, which have further been convoluted in post-production to add stretched lines of motion blur.

Compounding the fast-paced editing, the speed of the sound-images suggests a strange torsion of embodiment here. On the one hand, as I have argued in earlier chapters, we find vectoral forces and kinetics applied across the images, suggesting a powerful line of force which induces intense sensations. On the other, we find stops, starts and spurts that fragment and shatter our bodily engagement with the images. Constant commutation of perspectives induces an almost strobe-like effect that runs counter to a sensation of powerful physical empowerment. While the film's generally tumultuous velocity might be a way to align us with Chev's desperation and anger, scenes like Chev running down the street work to distance us from his movement and what Purse refers to as his gestures. The best way to think about the shutter-motions of this sequence is as a form of frac-tured embodiment that does not align with a fully human bodily experi-ence. Here, our bodies must begin to take on the flexible and volatile nature of Chev's body in order to align with the intensity of the sound-images. The audiovisual acceleration pushes our correlated embodiment to the brink, stretching our limits.

From a theoretical standpoint, we find a clash between a body-centered film phenomenology and a nonhuman, affect-based film process phi-losophy. The invaluable insights that film phenomenology have given us into how we align ourselves with the film's body, how the film's sensuous nature draws us in and expands our embodied experience, are overtaken here by a cinema that no longer cares about human embodiment, not even superhuman embodiment. Sobchack's structural homology splinters as bodily continuity dissolves into a motion blur. Speed blurs out our body, stretching it and making it volatile, outside of our control. This explains, as Denson also notes, why critics like Jim Emerson dislike such volatile films, noting that "the reason they don't work for many of us is because, in reality, they give us nothing to respond to – just a blur of incomprehensible images and sounds, without spatial context or allowing for emotional investment."[5] But who wants emotional investment when you can get pure sensation?

Emerson himself goes on to note that he dislikes high beats-per-minute EDM, yet surely this says more about him than it does EDM. Yes, the rhythms of volatile films like *Crank: High Voltage* are very different from beautifully embodied, choreographed *wuxia* films, but they are meant to be. And when Emerson argues that there can be no crescendos in such films, because those rhythms are unsustainable, he once again mistakes the cinematic body for a human body. Crescendos can last a long time.

While film phenomenology emphasizes the flow-like experience of films, these films instead come off as crackling bursts that are not articulable as flow. As such, these films do not attempt to engage with a sensuous, bodily consciousness but instead attempt to work directly on the nervous system. That is why affect is a better approach to these films than emotion-oriented phenomenology, simply because volatile films do not attempt to produce fully fleshed-out emotions or characters. Both *Crank* films joke with this notion in their reference – both overtly in the titles and also once in each film in Chev's dialogue – to poor quality methamphetamine, a drug that also works directly on the nervous system. Such a nervous system must be adaptable and flexible to accommodate the constant trajectory shifts of the film's discorrelated sound-images.

Similarly, in the final big shoot-out, we also find this discorrelated embodiment. Everything comes to a head as Chev is brought to El Huron (Clifton Collins Jr.), who wants revenge on him for killing his brothers in the first *Crank* film. As Venus (Efren Ramirez), Orlando (Reno Wilson) and Ria (Bai Ling) all show up with friends, a ridiculous over-the-top gunfight ensues. Spatial orientation is sacrificed in favor of an emphasis on ludicrous shooting, filmed with plenty of swoosh pans, canted angles and fast-paced editing, such as when Ria guns down the gardener and all the statues. The scene is constructed conventionally enough in terms of seeing who shoots whom and what, but little effort is made to orient us spatially. Instead, the scene consists mostly of a string of encounters and conclusions to the plot lines laid out during the film.

Venus faces off against the people who killed his brother in the first film. In a scene that is a clear reference to martial arts films, and especially Bruce Lee, Venus displays his prowess with nunchucks. This seems to follow Purse's concept of a posture of mastery, where "these postures signal the limitless potential of the body ready for action, a symbol of about-to-be-demonstrated potency."[6] Indeed, Venus whirls the nunchucks in a deadly display, filmed from a flurry of angles. Yet again the freeze frames insert themselves, breaking the posture of mastery and the ensuing gestures of lethal skill into a weird, jerky jumble. The sense of mastery is further undercut as Venus proceeds to beat up the moogs only to stumble and fall because of his full body Tourette's syndrome, which makes him jerk and twitch uncontrollably. While clearly an example of acknowledging the convention of gestures of mastery through irony, the freeze frames inevitably function to produce the same torsion as we saw in Chev's running scene. Once again, what is meant to be a virtuoso display of physical empowerment becomes a staticky, jerky, helter-skelter movement that both acknowledges physical power and denies unmitigated access to it.

A non-action centered example in the same scene is its establishing shots. Opening with the *Crank* films' usual introductory shorthand of using a Google Earth zoom into a location, they illustrate the typical shots of a gangster's den: a pool, thugs with guns and gold chains, tan women in bikinis and so forth. However, a few of the shots of female bodies are disruptive in that they are not only shot with a fisheye lens but also mirrored, producing an image that consists of two halves of a body doubled over itself. *(See Figure 4.3 in the insert.)* There is no particular reason for this mirroring other than a sheer excess of the visual. Yet the effect is another version of discorrelation, because it ruptures the way we can position ourselves in perspectival space. We are forced instead to engage the image as something flat, which cannot reproduce a pro-filmic event but instead produces a form of Linda Williams' "frenzy of the visible," a concept that she develops in her book *Hard Core*, stating that "the direct human vision of events, places, and bodies began to be mediated by an optical apparatus that sees in place of the 'naked eye'."[7] We are confronted with images that are not results of human vision but instead a different form of mediation. In this case, particularly because it is a naked woman, the mirrored fish-eye shots take on even more significance as we become infatuated with the process of mediation itself, rather than what is being mediated. Although initially eliciting sexual desire, this desire is shifted onto the process of hypermediation itself. What is fetishized is not the naked female form, but instead cinema's capacity to produce flexible, volatile bodies; bodies that cannot exist outside of moving image media, yet are deeply fascinating.

This is true for most of the other shots in *Crank: High Voltage* and begins to explain the erratic, idiosyncratic style of Neveldine/Taylor: they care little about showing the world and even less about three-act structures and character development. What they care about is sensory overload and the volatility of their shots. Jerky, helter-skelter camerawork does not hide or obscure the pro-filmic events but displays and fetishizes the cinematic medium *as medium*, rather than as transparent channel. Their emphasis on hypermediacy is evident in their disregard for cinematic conventions and their blatant use of nonsensical devices, such as when Chev is being chased by police early in the film and we see an intertitle stating, "9 seconds later". The absurdity serves its own purpose.

Similarly, when Chev grabs the high voltage cables, bursts into flame and is catapulted away, then returns to beat El Huron and save Venus, the punch is a freeze frame that zooms in. Reminiscent most of all of the K.O. cut-scene in martial arts games, flow is again disrupted in favor of stutters. However, for volatile films we are wrong to try to find a sense of flow in the bodies of the characters and actors. Rather, what *Crank: High Voltage* shows us is that the physical empowerment we find in these films is that of the cinematic body, a body that is no longer based on a human model of movement nor occupies logical perspectives. This is why Chev's body is a volatile, flexible body, and why our bodies must be as well, if we are to fully appreciate the intensities of *Crank: High Voltage*. This is a visceral, rather than optical, cinematic body. Of course Neveldine/Taylor's films are as audiovisual as any, but they do not favor a visual regime or a visual transfer point of knowledge, power and pleasure. A visceral cinema is one that we can feel more than see. This is why they can mix the poor resolution Google Earth images with regular cinematic images, why the 8-bit animation of the opening titles displaying Chev falling from the helicopter works, and why they can employ the supercinematic zooms going into Chev's body and displaying the artificial heart. Realistic, visual reproduction is irrelevant to the ecstatic rendering of volatile bodies.

And they are not alone in emphasizing pure visceral display over logical, coherent perspectival images. Joseph Kahn's *Torque* takes an identical approach, pushing what is otherwise a mediocre motorcycle rip-off of *The Fast and the Furious* series and turning it into a delirious cinematic trip of wide shots zooming into the engine cylinders of the motorcycles and similar cartoon-like shots. While Stork argues that films like these push into abstraction, it seems to me that they push into hypermediacy. Here there is a flow that is masterful, and it comes in the form of the post-cinematic body's production of pure sensation at any cost. Action films have their own logic and have always had leeway to push into sound-images of pure sensation, as long as it likewise elicited sensation in the audience. But this hypermediated flow of sensation cannot be articulated by a human body, and it cannot be replicated by human bodies; but crucially it can be experienced by human bodies. This is what Bolter and Grusin mean when they argue that hypermediacy is another strategy for engaging with our desire for immediacy, since sensory overload is also a form of immediacy. Such immediacy connects to micro-perceptual bursts and pulses that go below conscious perception in what amounts to a rendering of the volatile body.

I previously argued that contemporary action cinema stretches our perception, engaging it not through depth but laterally, requiring a mode of hyper-perception to keep pace with these cinematic speed machines. In *Crank: High Voltage* our sensations, not just our perception, are stretched. We must accommodate new intensities constantly throughout the film, requiring a flexible embodiment that can adapt to any event, any necessary action. We can see here how we are given a break, a relief, in not having to understand where everything is or how to orient ourselves in space. There is no space; there is only the pure production of sensation, and it teeters, because of that, on the nonhuman. Such intensity lies in sub-perceptual matter and impacts and modulates our pre-personal embodiment. That is to say, the films move too fast and are too fragmented for us to perceive them: we feel them. *Crank: High Voltage* displays a powerful cinematic body, capable of moving and turning in ways that we could never do. Surely this is one of the attractions of, as well as aversions to, these films. Bordwell and Emerson may well dislike what they perceive to be the poor craftsmanship of Neveldine/Taylor, but they are missing the point: this is not choreography or ballet; this is sheer mayhem and volatile exuberance, and the films are better for it. Films like *Crank* also begin to suggest the allure of the nonhuman, the weird, vivid pulses that are articulated through the intense post-cinematic body. Volatility is a way to embody the vectors and kinetics that are too intense for human bodies.

Smooth Movements: *Jupiter Ascending*

Not all films that articulate volatility are as relentless in their audiovisual expression as Neveldine/Taylor's films. Films such as *Wanted* (Timur Bekmambetov 2008), *Max Payne* (John Moore 2008) and *Sherlock Holmes* (Guy Ritchie 2009) slow down time to a crawl through superslow sequences, while superhero films like *The Incredible Hulk* (Louis Leterrier 2008) and *The Amazing Spider-Man* (Marc Webb 2012) show radical physical comportments, all aimed at astonishing us and impacting our bodies in ways that go beyond our physical capacity for movement. The Wachowskis' *Jupiter Ascending* (2015) is a recent addition to these films and employs stunning sequences of volatility.

In this film, the bodily mastery of traditional action films merges with that of a post-cinematic body generated by computer-generated images. Unlike the hypermediated images of *Crank: High Voltage*, where the volatility comes from the disparity of individual elements and the choppy nature of different images and visual perspectives jumbled together, *Jupiter Ascending* has the feeling of flow. With emphasis placed squarely on digital imaging, the sound-images achieve a smoothness that is almost the exact opposite of *Crank: High Voltage* and several of the other films I have discussed so far. Yet the intensity of these computer-generated sequences is such that they push a state of volatility on us.

Jupiter Ascending tells the story of Jupiter Jones (Mila Kunis), who grows up an illegal Russian immigrant in Chicago but comes to learn that she is in fact heiress to the Abrasax galactic dynasty through genetic rebirth. Hunted by the agents of Balem (Eddie Redmayne), Jupiter is saved by Caine Wise (Channing Tatum), although she is still brought to a distant planet. Here, Balem's brother Titus (Douglas Booth) tricks Jupiter into marrying him in order to wrest the inheritance of planet Earth from Balem. He almost succeeds, but Caine shows up in the nick of time to prevent the wedding. At the same time, Balem has captured Jupiter's family in his refinery on planet Jupiter and demands she sign Earth over to him in exchange for her family's safety. Balem would then be able to harvest Earth for the youth serum that they all crave. Jupiter refuses, defeats Balem, and is rescued off the planet by Caine. Jupiter happily returns to her cleaning job.

It should be noted that the planet Jupiter in the film is closer to Edgar Rice Burroughs' Mars in his *A Princess of Mars* and similar early pulp space operas than the actual planet Jupiter. While planet Jupiter remains a gas giant, there are also structures on it and a somewhat amicable atmosphere. Similarly, warp drives enable people to travel at the blink of an eye, and Caine manages to survive in space for several minutes simply by holding his breath. The film makes no concessions to any form of realism but is an unapologetic space opera, interested only in unique vistas, the vastness of space and exotic species and fashions. In much the same way, the film employs a variety of unusual spatials and impressive kinetic battle scenes between starships. Computer-generated imagery is used to produce immense wide shots of impossibly large scales, reducing humans to tiny pinpricks, thus indicating the sublime nature of the universe. *Jupiter Ascending* is a film interested in size and grandeur, and the same goes for its special effects, which then render the film volatile.

We find the first example of volatility when Jupiter goes to a clinic to sell her eggs in exchange for money to buy a telescope. Salem's agents attempt to kill her there, but Caine arrives to help. As Jupiter hovers over the bed, slowly being choked to death, Caine comes running in and shoots the fake medical staff. In the first shots it seems he simply runs across the room, but in the next medium panning shot, we see Caine leap up into the upper corner of the room and hang there, aiming his gun. Flitting down in a smooth camera movement, Caine blocks shots with his shield as one of the aliens jumps up into the corner. More aliens come at Caine from the ceiling as he jumps around, floating and hovering. The camera pans around but remains stable, emphasizing Caine's spectacular movements: he walks backwards up the cupboards in the room, spinning around to defeat an alien. The editing is fast-paced but adheres to the continuity system, producing a clear and coherent space, although Caine's body moves in less stable ways. His gravity-defying stunts are unusual, not because he moves in ways that we cannot but because of the *way* he moves. Caine's movements are fluid, and although they are forceful, they do not have the jerky quality of jumping around frantically, which dominated Chev's movements. Instead, Caine seems as if he can move in any direction at will, having complete mastery over space. The camerawork supports this sensation with its steady, stable fast shots.

We find in this sequence an impulse similar to the ballet-like martial arts sequences that Hong Kong action cinema employs so well. Bordwell emphasizes the fascinating movement of human bodies in continuous takes that overwhelm and delight us in martial arts films.[8] He terms this "a strategy of expressive amplification" and locates much of its strategy in a "pause/burst/pause pattern," in which the actor's gestures and movements are clearly legible.[9] These fight scenes are affective thrusts that are located squarely in the body of the performer. For this reason, Yip refers to the sensation as sensory realism, which "builds on correspondences between a film's perceptual and visceral sensations and the viewer's real-life sense experiences."[10] Caine's movements are overwhelming examples of physical empowerment, because I recognize from my own sense experiences that I could never move like that. But *Jupiter Ascending* exceeds the burst-based technique of Hong Kong martial arts cinema in that it refuses to pause. We do get a few instances of Caine pausing in a posture of mastery, but these moments are exceedingly brief. Rather than a pause/burst/pause pattern, *Jupiter Ascending's* pattern is one of solid movement, a flurry that suggests smoothness because there are no breaks.

The Wachowskis are well-versed in Hong Kong cinema, something that was evident from their first foray into action cinema with *The Matrix*. However, they have also always been interested in moving beyond the techniques of Hong Kong cinema, and *Jupiter Ascending* expresses that desire in the way that Caine moves. Rather than the superhuman physical mastery of the Hong Kong *wuxia* films, here we find a compressed version of it, a version that is accelerated and more contingent on digital imaging. First,

107

the flurry of the camerawork's panning is opposite to the wide shots often used in *wuxia* to ground the spectacular bodily movement. Second, while *wuxia* also depends on the actual physical abilities of the actors, *Jupiter Ascending* is resolutely placed in the digital realm, with Tatum's body digitally enhanced, partly by removing the wire-frames that hold him in place but more significantly because he is fighting digital animations.

The weird, atrophied bodies of the aliens are fully digital and so enable a different sense of embodiment. We find that embodiment expressed primarily in the use of the vertical axis. The aliens attack Caine from all angles, doubling the sense of flurry to include bodies as well. This angular vector of attack suggests a friction-filled torsion between the steady shots and the flurry of alien bodies. In a sense, the unusual positioning of the bodies – both Caine's and the aliens' – require low angle shots that then pan and swoosh. In this torsion the homology between camera and human body breaks down. The camera moves in acrobatic ways and employs unusual compositions, such as focusing on Caine's feet as he walks backwards up the cupboards. Of course, this composition reveals Caine's abilities, but the general thrust of the camerawork still unseats us, despite the fact that the shots are stable. Once again we see how in contemporary action films the fascination shifts from human bodies to that of the post-cinematic body itself. Rather than being awed and impressed with the bodies of the performers, we are instead impressed with the post-cinematic body, and the way it opens cinematic space in new ways, eliciting new forms of sensation.

Here movement becomes entirely smooth and fluid, a continuous flow that can be traversed in ways that go beyond human embodiment. Take for instance Caine's gliding descent to the planet after Jupiter has been kidnapped. Caine rushes to the starship and hangs on to a low-hanging rudder. First, there is an impressive tracking shot of the starship descending to the planet's surface and the imposing colorful vista. We cut to see Caine hanging on to the lower rudder, getting a sense of his physical power from his ability to hang on to a ship that has just traveled through space. He looks down on the planet in a low angle shot that emphasizes the power and readiness of his body. Finally, he lets go and falls down in a continuous shot over a waterfall, engaging his gravity boots to glide across the lake and towards the city, the camera tracking him but not zooming in, thus giving us full view of the city, the water and his silhouette becoming smaller as he glides into the city.

At some point, computer-generated animation takes over, and Caine's body becomes entirely digital. There is no way for us to tell exactly when this happens. Instead, we experience the majestic glide as one continuous imposing movement, especially because the shot does not follow Caine but allows us to take in the size and scope of everything as he disappears. This shot is an example of what Brown calls digital cinema's conquest of space, "a mastery of space that is beyond the abilities of the analogue camera alone."[11] The continuous movement of Caine's body can only exist as continuous in a digital cinema, and no matter the athletic abilities of the performer, the experience would never be the same in a sequence of shots. In this way, the shot works perfectly for a space opera far more interested in grandeur than in realism. Bodies move across vast vistas in exuberant ways precisely to induce sensations of grandeur and the sublime. Purse's idea of becoming-powerful is here supplanted by a becoming-nonhuman, a move into scales beyond the human.

Grandeur and scale are also vital components of the final battle of the film, around which the Abrasax refinery collapses into the planet Jupiter. Jupiter has refused Balem, while Caine fights one of Balem's henchmen. Both of these sequences have interesting spatials. Jupiter's scene focuses on the sensation of falling and downward movement, while Caine's scene focuses on continuous and supercinematic articulations of space. Crosscutting allows both scenes to feed intensity from each other. Jupiter falls through a long tunnel with Balem. Constantly at risk from flying debris, she is consistently shot falling down from screen left toward screen right, as is Balem, thus producing a clear spatial orientation. Dodging the debris, Jupiter falls for several shots, suggesting a long, fast fall. We see Balem grab hold of some railing while Jupiter falls past him, only to grab a cable and fling herself onto a platform. The daring physical stunt is clearly visible, the angle shifting to shoot from below as Jupiter swings to safety, but otherwise we are generally in a position of safety, allowing for a thrilling engagement with the action. But it remains safe, and we are not placed in any risky positions.

Caine's fight is somewhat different, however, as he twists and turns to fight the lizard-like, winged henchman. They fly through space but constantly tumble and fall and drop, the camera swirling around them as our sense of gravity is challenged. Alternating between close-ups that show the fight and medium shots that orient us in space, the vertical construction of the refinery adds a sense of the vertical axis but also helps to accelerate the pace of their tumbling bodies. Caine manages to get on top of the lizard and forces him to the ground. They crash through a glass ceiling and slam into the floor. Their fight is shot in slow-motion, with Caine doing spin kicks and the camera panning and moving to give us full access to his movements. Then the lizard grabs Caine as he is on the ground, the camera swoops around him in a half-circle. It travels up to shoot the lizard frontally at chest height as he jumps high into the air; the camera tracks back and pans up as the lizard swings Caine into the glass ceiling, and we are now straight below Caine, where we see cracks and fissures in the glass before the shot cuts to a slightly tighter shot of Caine's face. *(See Figure 4.4 in the insert.)*

This dramatic, continuous slow-motion shot becomes an impressive and imposing articulation of space, which is once again contingent on digital imagery. The smooth movement of the camera from behind Caine to its final position below him is intense in its own right and adds the final flourish of shock when Caine actually crashes into the glass above us rather than having cut to a safer position. Much like the crash-cam discussed in the previous chapter, this shot places us in the middle of the action, although in a slightly less vulnerable position. Instead, the contorting movement of the camera is what induces the most intense sensation, both in terms of the position we are placed in and the smoothness of the motion. This smoothness of motion produces a sense of mastery, but it is a mastery located in the post-cinematic shots, not human movement. The shot itself is constructed by compositing several shots into one seemingly continuous shot; our alignment and engagement shift onto the post-cinematic body and the machinic sensations that accompany it.

The entire climactic scene employs a similar smooth sensation of space, one that constantly moves, pans and tracks across all axes. Balem, Jupiter and Caine all fall several times but also spend much of their time climbing, japing and flying. The post-cinematic body of these grand expanses of space in all directions make for a scale that moves beyond immediate human comprehension, positioning human bodies as small and vulnerable against the enormity of planet Jupiter. There is another shot of Caine, having jumped through an access port, in which he glides away against endless vistas of destruction and flame, again shot in a continuous shot that brings us from a medium close-up of Caine to an extreme wide shot where he vanishes off in the horizon. Similarly, when Jupiter falls toward her death, we see her recede against the bottom, before cutting to an upward shot in which she is small and growing bigger as she approaches us; then Caine catches her, after which the scene cuts to another shot of him gliding past buildings exploding. These shots are always placed against enormous scales of destruction, expansive horizons of nothing but flame and other views of human bodies dwarfed by the magnitude of space around them. Yet even against such scale, there is a sense of continuity and smoothness of motion. In itself, this vastness traversed by the human bodies produces a sense of mastery, suggesting that scales beyond the human can be brought into contact with and conquered by the human. *(See Figure 4.5 in the insert.)*

Thus, there is a tension between the sensations that come from inherently nonhuman smoothness and scale and the way that these shots still work to locate us in the human, insisting that humans can indeed master them. Although the film ends ambiguously, the conclusion itself is conventional, with Jupiter and Caine playing around at flying, him now with wings and her with the gravity boots, the credits sequence functions as a cosmic zoom, cutting from an epic shot of the Chicago skyline to one of a solar system with star nebulas behind it in the far reaches of space. We zoom out as planets zoom past us and bands of alien hieroglyphics form circles around the planets and tie solar systems together in circles. The further out we zoom, the more we recognize that these circles form helixes that resemble DNA strings. While the grand scale matches the rest of the film, we can argue two interpretations of the cosmic zoom. One would be that DNA helixes are the fractal building blocks of everything, no matter how big or small. This argument dissolves scale into one of relation: everything binds together in similar patterns. The human being is simply one instance of a universal pattern. The other argument would be that everything has been ordered and patterned by the Abrasax dynasty and others like them for easy harvesting. This suggests that humans control and dominate all of creation, everything is there for our taking. In either case, scale, and the smoothness of that scale as a continuity rather than a hierarchical space, is what matters.

Jupiter Ascending is volatile for the complete opposite reason *Crank: High Voltage* is volatile: for its smooth and continuous shots, the way it employs unusual spatials to engage and draw us in. This insistence on fluidity and flow pushes the film beyond the structural homology between human and cinematic body. What this shows us is that the structural homology can also be breached by shots that are overly smooth and overly continuous, not only frenetically rapid-fire shots whose celerity overpowers us. That is to say, speed and velocity can be attained through continuous shots that move in ways that we cannot emulate. This is so because the spatials used in *Jupiter Ascending* intensify our perception of space in that they constantly move in ways that go beyond our embodiment.

The sensations we experience through those shots and the resonance between the post-cinematic shots and those of the more conventional action shots, such as the various chase sequences I've discussed, are at the crux of these films. These sensations produce volatility in us, the physical sensorial shocks that every film depends on but in *Jupiter Ascending* attempt to wrest us out of our regular assumption about our bodies. There is a resonance here between the cinematic body and our bodies, in that as its body grows increasingly volatile, so do ours. Most of the post-cinematic shots in the film center on bodies and their movement through space. However, unlike *Crank: High Voltage*, where bodies and the cinematic body are constantly fragmented, the post-cinematic body of *Jupiter Ascending* is a smooth structure that refuses to hierarchize between objects, instead it suggests that everything is in relation to everything else through the use of continuous shots. This is also shown over and over again in the way that scale is used to allow characters to master space in smooth ways. Bodies are not articulated in *Jupiter Ascending* but are instead pure lines of force that cut across anything.

This is also Jupiter's lesson: she might be the heiress to the entire Earth, but she is happier with her dysfunctional family, cutting across the hierarchy of power. Also for this reason, the film ends with her learning how to use the gravity boots and Caine regaining his wings. Not only can he be a literal angel for Jupiter, but he can also move unfettered across space again. The smoothness of the shots become a smoothness of experience, an articulation so smooth that it goes beyond human embodiment. Our embodiment is always riddled with stops, starts and skips that register as cracks in our experience. By contrast, Caine's embodiment (and the concomitant post-cinematic embodiment) is so smooth and assured that such mastery is clearly beyond us.

We find again, in *Jupiter Ascending*, this notion that bodily comportment and mimetic innervation are ways of resisting and subverting hierarchy, both for the protagonists and in turn the viewers, who are innervated in ways that go beyond the norm, opened up to new sensations, which then allow for a broadening of experience. While such a broadening of experience may not seem political or ideological, the sensation of how bodies elide structures of containment and produce lines of flight can suggest an overturning of embedded power structures. The freedom of movement located in the body, as well as the exuberance of that same movement, allows for moments that challenge conventional structures of feeling. It's all the more disappointing, then, that the narrative closure of *Jupiter Ascending* is so regressive: Jupiter accepts a heterosexual union, makes peace with her family and realizes that she enjoys her low-paid job. While one might argue that the film eschews the triumphalism of a fairy-tale ending, the appeal to a romanticized working class ideal is equally noxious. Yet of course, this discrepancy might well chafe viewers who have just been innervated to exuberant new heights, and so the film might produce resistance to its own ideological closure.

Body Assemblages

The emphatic shift that contemporary action cinema has undergone towards the post-cinematic audiovisual body and away from the structural homology of the human body and the cinematic body is best viewed as an attempt to engage the viewer in new and more immersive ways. A faster-paced, more volatile mode of expression is then one way of pulling the viewer further into the film, suggesting energy through relatively straightforward means. In this process, the haptic participation of action films reaches further into our body and works on our nervous system. Whether or not this happens directly is a complicated question to answer. As I have shown action films today are highly mediated, deploying a

113

barrage of different devices that engage us through hypermediacy rather than an attempt at producing transparency. Clearly, such hypermediation would appear to not work directly on our nervous system. Yet from a different perspective, they do indeed work directly on us, because the intensity of the sound-images is so great that their affective energies burrow beneath our conscious perception. Therefore, what we consider to be "us" occurs *after* and *as a result of* these intensities.

We must recognize, then, that whether or not we enjoy these films, our bodies throb with the beat of their rhythms. They impact us at a level on which we cannot resist or reject them, and through this process our bodies become volatile, a rhythmic combination of themselves and the post-cinematic body, what Virilio terms an "intraorganic intrusion of technology and its micromachines into the heart of the living."[12] We should not take this to mean a literal, material prosthetic relation, in the way it has been presented in the two films I have dealt with here, but only that when our nervous systems are stimulated by these cinematic speed machines, our sensations and perceptions are restructured. And so, subsequently, is our embodiment, because our embodiment is contingent on our sensory relation to the surrounding world. We emerge from and through that world via the many different connections and relations we enter into inside it.

In such a view, there is no way to define a body proper or a world proper; there are only intermixings and hybrids. Because of this state of intermingling, there is no way to talk about the body in the singular either. Instead, as Arthur Kroker has suggested, we occupy a multiplicity of bodies, and these bodies are constantly "inflected, intermediated, complicated."[13] We can think of everyday situations in which our bodies are inflected by the caffeine we consume to feel sharper; in the same way, films inflect our bodies through affective entrainment. When our bodies become volatile, it is because we desire to become an assemblage to produce better, or more suitable, sensations. This desire is affective, a precognitive machinic sensation wherein bodies reach for each other, grasping for connection, because the more articulated a body can be, the more successful it will be.

Crucially, then, our bodies are not containers but agents in a larger environment in which they attempt to adapt and emerge more successful. Virilio sees this as part of the third revolution, the "transplant revolution," which obliterates the useful distinction between the human body and technology.[14] The film's body becomes the crux of our engagement with the film. These films are not only contingent on issues of narrative and characterization, like all narrative films, but also engage directly and haptically with our senses and nervous system and refuse to distinguish between the two. The discorrelation between the post-cinematic sound-images and our bodies does not mean that we are somehow disembodied or that we cannot engage with the films. On the contrary, we are engrossed more deeply into these films because of their post-cinematic articulations of our sensations. Contemporary action cinema's rhythms and energies engage us in new ways simply because we are not yet accustomed to these discorrelated images.

Therefore, the films often come off as distancing, as in the case of *Crank: High Voltage*, where the volatile nature of the film pushes us out of our comfort zone. But as in the case of *Jupiter Ascending*, the volatile relation can emerge just as much through the nonhuman, smooth spatial articulation of the film. In either case, our bodies must open themselves to the new foldings of the films in order to let us feel the sensations pulsed our way. This is what Whitehead calls the "'satisfaction' of the completed subject."[15] To put this another way, the process of experience is the integration of several disparate processes into one stable experience. Once that experience has been expressed and finished, it moves on to the next, and so on. As our sensations and perceptions are interpellated by cinematic machines, our bodies are similarly interpellated. The cinematic body participates in our experience of the film, and as it becomes increasingly hypermediated, so our experience becomes increasingly hypermediated, in what I termed hyper-perception in the previous chapter. As Susan Buck-Morss points out, "the nervous system is not contained within the body's limits. The circuit from sense-perception to motor response begins and ends in the world."[16] When the world changes, so too do our sense-perceptions and our bodily responses; as our sense-perceptions and bodily responses are reconfigured by new sound-image technologies, we then experience the world differently.

For Virilio, this hypermediation of our bodies expresses the ultimate degradation of humanity and is essentially the tragedy of our culture. However, instead of accepting such an inherent negative relation with technology, we should consider the ways in which aesthetic modes and forms broaden and expand our embodied relation to the world. Whitehead's concept of satisfaction through integration is crucial in this respect. Whitehead views all experience as a constant, unfolding process, without distinguishing between entities. In this way, the encounter between film and viewer necessarily transforms our relation to the world, but this same encounter also transforms our being-in-the-world, i.e. our embodiment. Borrowing from Mark B.N. Hansen, new aesthetic forms offer "new sensory affordances for us to enframe through our embodiment."[17] The intensity of film exists as an affectile that ruptures our stable sense of embodiment and gives birth to new sensations and new bodily comportments. As Hansen expresses this relation, it is a heterogenesis of "the interface between human being and sensory environment."[18] We experience through film, as it were, a new mode of sensing the world. We understand our bodily capacities differently when these films push and disrupt our stable sense of embodiment through sheer speed and intensity. We must recognize that when relations change, that is to say when acceleration occurs, we change as a result.

This change occurs because we must satisfy, in at least some way, the sensate feelings the film encounter elicits. But this satisfaction, which is what Whitehead refers to, does not necessarily imply something agreeable or pleasant. Rather, satisfaction means something closer to achievement, the moment when two elements integrate in whatever way available to them. Such satisfaction may just as easily be unpleasant, but it is the element of experience from which new sensations come, "the advance from disjunction to conjunction."[19] This is how, for Whitehead, "the many become one, and are increased by one," a process that describes how different elements unify into a larger assemblage.[20] In the experience of contemporary action films, formal properties are pushed to extremes, articulating sensations that have never been articulated in this way before. Yet as the cinematic body becomes ever more articulated, so too do our bodies; the interface between our bodies and the surrounding environment converge in new forms of heterogenesis. All this is to say that as films express new experiences for us through their post-cinematic bodies, we are consequently opened up to new sensations and experiences, because our bodies work as connectors, attempting to satisfy or achieve the feelings that films produce.

We might lament the neglect of earlier, more clearly articulated forms of embodiment, as we might prefer the exuberant physically empowering embodiments of Hong Kong *wuxia* films, and we might therefore be left cold when "satisfying" the sensations of a film like *Crank: High Voltage;* but we cannot ignore that the aesthetic innovations and achievements of these films represent a different engagement with film. By expanding beyond human physical comportment, these films ask us to step into a volatile bodily relation with them, a relation that can either feel jagged or smooth but in all cases produces new sensate intensities. These films make our bodies throb in beat to the machinic sensations they articulate. In other words, like earlier shock rhythms of modernity, these films produce new rhythms, what I will call the drone rhythms of contemporary action cinema. We must recognize that there is no useful distinction between human embodiment and cinematic forms in regards to what film does. What film does is engage our bodies in a complex thrum of rhythms, and these rhythms constantly and consistently evolve, transform and change in response to the surrounding media ecology.

In precisely this way, volatility names a relation in which we can be recompensed from fear by stepping into a body assemblage. Our bodies can be bolstered to withstand the paralysis of fear through affective modulation. We are entrained to accept and enjoy bodily amplification and connection, because volatility functions as a reprieve. Volatility dangles a lure for our bodies in the same reciprocal relationship as that between wasp and orchid, one based on beneficial exchange. These reverberations remain ecological vibrations, ways that bodies move in and out of sync with a culture of fear, irrespective of their individual articulations. The openings of our bodies to multiple connections become what William Connolly has dubbed "somatic markers," moments in which we filter experience bodily rather than cognitively.[21] Somatic markers are similar to priming in that they provide non-cognitive assistance, in which bodily reactions supersede conscious control. Whereas priming elicits judgments and affects, somatic markers work at the level of sensations, where our bodies react without our conscious participation. We reflexively reach out to connect to other bodies because they offer safety and reprieve from fear. To do so without wanting to, without being aware, is a somatic marker of life in a culture of fear.

Action films thus function as bodily proxies for new sensations and affects, and through this relationship, our bodies turn volatile and

117

must become flexible to accommodate these new sensations and affects. Made flexible by the vectors and kinetics that the films generate, our embodiment transforms into a heterogenesis of sensations. Our bodies are shielded from the culture of fear's incessant dread while we step into these assemblages of volatility, potency and mastery. Similarly, our bodily relations stretch and become flexible in new ways, and we recognize that our bodies do not stop at our skin. Rather, our bodies connect to other bodies in machinic assemblages. One of the dominant assemblages has become the drone body, a corporeal projection that is becoming more popular in action cinema today, and to which I will turn now. The corporeal projection is thus volatility and flexibility pushed to new extremes.

5

Corporeal Projections and Drone Bodies

With action cinema's emphasis on physical empowerment and ability, power becomes a central concern. I have already shown several ways in which post-cinematic bodies express power and render forces across and with our bodies. These lines of force are articulated through cinematic means, but contemporary action cinema has also moved beyond traditional cinematic means to develop new techniques for the expression of power. A number of films have likewise picked up on a furthering of this central concern in the drone age: the expression of power at a distance. Typically, these films employ what are best termed drone bodies. The films depict scenarios in which characters remotely control human or humanoid bodies as replacements or substitutes for their own bodies. While *Surrogates* (Jonathan Mostow 2009), where drone bodies are used to provide people with a better, more idealized version of themselves, stands out in its function as an allegory for the narcissism of a social media society in which we can project any kind of idealized version of ourselves; I am much more interested in the somewhat different relationship to drone bodies depicted in two other films. *Real Steel* (Shawn Levy 2011) produces a tension between the human body's capabilities and those of the robot fighters that humans operate. To a large extent, the human body wins out. This scenario is seen differently in *Avatar* (James Cameron 2009), where the drone

119

body becomes a form of transcendence, not only for the paraplegic Marine but also as a form of evolution to a better stage of humanity. In *Avatar's* scenario, the drone body wins. The corporeal projection of the drone body builds on the volatility and flexibility of the post-cinematic body by using motion capture technologies, and so pushes embodiment further into a machinic assemblage. Rather than bodily mastery, drone bodies project power at a distance, literally going further than the volatile body.

Although seemingly very different, these two films focus on the notions of power and vulnerability and their complicated relationship. This is telling, for, as drone theorist Grégoire Chamayou points out, the main difference and main advantage of drones are not so much that they are unmanned as that they allow for the projection of power without projecting vulnerability.[1] Whereas the films I have dealt with so far present physical empowerment as a function of the human body – even when it is augmented or amplified – these films instead present a scenario of power and agency at a distance. In fact, in many ways this corporeal projection is presented as preferable to that of conventional human embodiment. The films argue for a drone embodiment that disperses and distributes the projection of power across multiple agents. Both films present scenarios in which the narrative resolution can only be achieved by extending the human body through means other than the human. That is to say, the protagonists, although clearly human, can only hope to triumph by allowing themselves to be extended by the nonhuman.

These films thus revolve around the concepts of teleaction and telepresence, notions that are central to Virilio's conception of media, in which he has persistently argued that the energy of audiovisual media will inevitably render us inert.[2] Technologies of presence and perception will render human movement unnecessary, because machines can perform movement for us. As Chamayou points out, one of the radical aspects of the drone is that it disrupts established categories, confusing and obfuscating issues such as location, ethics and – I would argue – embodiment. That drone embodiment is complicated is evident in Chamayou's concept of telechiric machines, a concept he borrows from J.W. Clark, in which "the machine may be thought of as an alter ego for the man who operates it."[3] Virilio would agree with this concept, and has himself described something like it under the term, teleoperation, a process dependent on telematics: "the technologies and services using both information technology and tel-ecommunications for collecting, storing, processing and communicating information."[4]

Yet if the machine is the alter ego of the teleoperator, who performs the action in question? The machine or the operator? I propose the term *teleso-matics* for the blurry body boundary that the drone bodies articulate in the following films. Primarily employed in medical anthropology, the idea of telesomatics refers to the sensation of another body within one's own body, rather than on the body surface.[5] Here, the sensations are experienced not exactly as one's own but also not as other or alien; they occupy a pecu-liar liminal zone. These sensations are felt, but their origins are obscured or confused in much the same way the sensations from teleoperating a machine are obfuscated. What Virilio sees as the dissolution of the human body becomes a sensory extension of the drone body assemblage. Rather than the flexibility of the volatile body, telesomatics extends the body's pro-jection of power.

Drone body assemblage is the situation in both films, although the exact nature of how these sensations are articulated and what they mean are different. However, I would like to suggest that both of them participate in an affective entrainment of telesomatics. These films articulate our sen-sorium in such as manner as to be primed into acting at a distance through somatic markers of body connectivity. Particularily, in the case of *Avatar*, such affective entrainment is constructed through the use of stereoscopic immersion, alongside a distinct emphasis on volatile bodies, expressing the idea that we can do more when we engage with a multitude of bodies. We learn how to cede autonomy to other bodies and across other trajectories.

Impact Capture: *Real Steel*

The introduction of motion capture technologies has allowed for a broader range of expression of the human body. On a relatively banal level, motion capture has allowed filmmakers to produce ever more spectacular sequences that go far beyond what the human body could ever achieve, while at the same time maintaining a connection, however tenuous, to the human body. As such, motion capture sequences are part of the notion of vectors that I discussed in the first chapter, although they occupy a special area due to their blurring of bodily boundaries: not solely human performer and not solely computer-generated animation, they create instead an assemblage.

Much like computer-generated animation, motion capture is a form of image production without a traditional camera. Significantly, motion capture technologies record movements rather than images. When we view bodies as vectors of movement, we recognize that, in fact, there is little difference between motion capture sequences and photographically recorded movements in terms of the affects and sensations we encounter. The sound-images have impact, whatever their referentiality. Thus, the assemblage of motion capture sequences does not hinder our sensory experience of the film, but instead opens up new modes of movement and sensation. Motion capture becomes a matter not only of capturing the movements of a motion capture actor, but also of capturing the motion of bodies on screen and the motion of the camera's trajectories in order to render our embodiment differently.

Real Steel encapsulates this motion capture aesthetic perfectly, mirroring the motion capture process in the character-robot relationship. Set in a future where robot boxing has replaced human boxing, Charlie Kenton (Hugh Jackman) must learn to operate a robot as well as he operates his own body in order to win back the respect of his son Max Kenton (Dakota Goyo). Based on the short story "Steel" by Richard Matheson, the film jettisons the short story's allegory of blue collar workers trying to survive in a post-industrial rust belt in favor of a father-and-son story, with a love interest put into the mix. What the film keeps is the tension between human embodiment and technological embodiment. Clearly paradoxical for a film that not only centers on the use of robots as boxers, but is also so embedded in a digital imaging production process, we find here an expression that appears to favor human embodiment but in fact prefers nonhuman embodiment.

The film's fascination comes from a fetishistic covering of its own ultimate logic. While the narrative suggests that technology can never beat real human relations, the film's appeal comes from its deployment of digital, substitute bodies to produce exhilarating spectacle. Although certainly the narrative carries its own pleasures, they are fairly generic and trivial in this case. The father-son story becomes a predictable family triangle with the introduction of Bailey Tallet (Evangeline Lilly). While Charlie does not actually defeat the ultimate robot Zeus, his brawn and resilience make him the "People's Champion," suggesting a tension between the people and huge corporations. In any case, as Charlie realizes, he has won the far more important fight for his son's heart and love. This is the narrative trajectory, or the emotional movement, of the film, its sentimental stance allowing for an engrossing tale of how a father found his way back to his son.

But there is also another trajectory, not associated directly with narrative or character engagement. We could call this trajectory the bodily movement, in which the fights become central to our experience of the film. The fights clearly function as somatic markers of narrative progression, and in this way, *Real Steel* is like *Rocky* and other boxing films where the protagonist must train to overcome adversity. Of course, for *Real Steel*, this trope exists in combination with those of vehicle films, such as *Days of Thunder*, where the protagonist must fix a vehicle in order to win the final contest. For *Real Steel*, the central concern is how to move the somatic markers from human to nonhuman: Charlie has to learn to robot box as well as he boxed with his own body. That is to say, although it appears as though Charlie has to learn how to be a better robot boxer, in fact he has to learn how to box like a robot.

In the early fights, we are clearly aligned with Charlie as he works on the robots to make them better and hopes to move on to the higher ranks, getting better fights. The story, focusing on the father-son relationship and Charlie's possible relationship with Bailey, help with this. Also, these early robot fights, such as the first fight featuring Noisy Boy, focus primarily on Charlie, rather than the robots. Having repaired Noisy Boy, Charlie takes on a fight against the robot Midas. During the fight, the majority of shots are of Charlie looking at the fight and controlling Noisy Boy. There is also plenty of interaction between Charlie and Max. Charlie's embodiment is restrained and restricted. He mostly speaks into a microphone and when things start to go bad, he uses the tablet to make the robot perform new moves. Charlie's own body, however, moves very little. The shots of the fight remain engaging, but they are generally shot from outside the ring in medium wide shots. The close-ups are almost always shot with the ringside ropes between us and the robots. We are quite literally spatially cut off from the robots and are presented instead with access to Charlie and his increasing failure to win the fight. Rather than elicit tense sensations of the fight, the scene is quite conventional and is more likely to elicit sympathy for Charlie and Max than any bodily engagement with the fighting. In this way, the film places the emphasis squarely on the relationship between people in the opening scenes.

However, when Max discovers Atom, things begin to change. The film shifts focus to Max and his relationship with Atom, who comes across as far more human than any of the other robots so far. Not only is Atom's design less outlandish than the other robots, but the way Atom moves in response to Max makes Atom feel more like a pet. This mimicked movement of bodies is central for our engagement with the characters. While the earlier robots move in stilted, overly powerful ways, there is a sense of smoothness and human articulation to Atom's comportment. That he moves along to a child's movements also makes him less alien and induces us with a sense of bodily alignment that we never get with any of the other robots. In this way, the distinction between bodies begins to break down.

In fact, we can argue for a certain sense of entwining between Max and Atom, and further, that since we have aligned ourselves bodily with Max through the film, we also begin to align ourselves with Atom. That we are slowly invited to align ourselves with Atom is significant, because it eases us into the transition of embodying a motion capture character. While this may at first seem trivial, it matters, because, as Vivian Sobchack has argued, "each technology not only differently *mediates* our figurations of bodily existence but also *constitutes* them."[6] That is to say, every technology affords us new experiences, but it does so by radically reconfiguring our bodily engagement with our environment. So, even though motion capture images may look like regular cinematic images, they are in fact different and do afford us new sensations.

Motion capture technologies present new ways for recording the movements of bodies, primarily with the purpose of layering a different, digital body onto those movements. Motion capture cameras record movements but not appearances through the use of what is known as cloud marks, tiny dots on the actor's body. These dots provide a wire-frame mesh that reproduces the body's movements but is easily mapped onto a different, digitally animated body. The advantage to motion capture is that it speeds up animation while also infusing the movements with a supposedly more human-looking motion.

While digital technologies are traditionally regarded as absorbing presence in favor of distance, in the case of motion capture this distance is both foreshortened and increased. On the one hand, the motion capture camera foreshortens the physical distance in relation to the motion capture actor, since the cloud marks are placed directly on the body. On the other hand, distance increases because of the dispersal of the resulting character's body over motion capture camera, motion capture actors, virtual cameras, simulcams, computer rendering and animation and similar mediating instances. In both regards, however, the camera-actor relation intensifies the transfer of energy. Tanine Allison has argued that motion capture should be understood as a form of translation, in the original sense, in which "translation was originally used to signify the conveyance of people or objects from one place to another, as well as the change in substance from one thing to another."[7] This argument is parallel to the one I have made earlier about the vectorized affects of contemporary action cinema, although in the case of motion capture, we are not talking about a purely digital process but a hybrid process of human and digital performance.

Motion capture technologies are processes in which information is translated from the human body to a digital body solely through movement. Crucially, energy is translated as well as information. The purpose of motion capture technologies is not simply to turn human bodily motion into digital motion, it is to capture the energies of that motion in order to project them at us. This produces, in effect, what Drew Ayers has called bilocation, the extension of presence into more than one location.[8] For me, the significance is that this is a two-way street. Not only do we sense a residual effect of the motion actor's energetic presence but these motion capture sequences also afford us new engagements with the energies produced by these sequences. It becomes easier for us to immerse ourselves into these sequences because of their intensity. This is true because motion capture technologies produce a presence of movement that extends beyond any kind of digital referentiality, effecting what is, in Allison's argument, an act of translation.

As Massumi has argued, the digital must always be converted back into analog for it to be accessible to us.[9] Digital images are rendered visually as analog images, since we would never be able to read the ASCII code of a computer-generated animation. This is why, as I argued earlier, the referentiality of digital images does not matter, only the way they present themselves to us. Ayers' phenomenological schema for what he calls "technologies of presence" is thus correct; we are presented with presence, even if it originates in discrete digital code.[10] Yet Ayers is only correct up to a point, because even the phenomenologically accessible images that motion capture sequences eventually end up as are never purified of their digital origins. There is a digital remainder that may not be perceptible but still impacts us and our experience. I have argued so far for how every single new imaging technology begins as a radically new, nonhuman experience beyond our bodily scope and is then slowly integrated into our bodily experience through affective entrainment: the new becomes conventional only to fade into oblivion.

That there is a productive torsion, however, in this encounter with the digital remainder becomes evident in the climactic battle between robots: Atom facing off against Zeus. The fight starts out not too dissimilar from the earlier fights, in which we are mostly aligned with Charlie and Max and the shots of the robots are further away, typically outside the ring. Yet as Atom is beaten more and more, we move closer in on the fight until we are inside the ring with the robots. We still get reaction shots from Charlie and Max, but we are generally placed alongside Atom. Furthermore, there is an interesting discrepancy between the two robots and their controllers. For Atom, it is Charlie who gives voice commands. For Zeus, however, it is a host of controllers and operators in front of a multitude of screens, so that Zeus is only nominally controlled by Tak Mashido (Karl Yune). We see here how the film locates agency idealistically in one human body, since there is a distinct sense of Mashido cheating by operating Zeus with a whole crew.

Then, Atom's sound receiver breaks, and he can no longer be voice controlled. Instead, Charlie has to engage shadow mode, which is the way Atom mimics human movement. Filled with self-doubt, Charlie says he is unable to face boxing again, but Max insists that he can, which suggests a primordial relation between father-son-robot, in which the artificial robot ends up facilitating a very real bond between father and son. The artificial is what allows human beings to come closer together and form natural bonds. From a formal standpoint, the scene is a complex motion capture sequence in which the human body is slowly elided. First, human motion capture actors play out the fight between Atom and Zeus, shot from a total of seventy cameras to form a fully rendered 3D environment. After that, director Shawn Levy operates a virtual camera through that 3D environment to produce a previsualization of what the final scene will look like. A physical camera is set up to perform match moving, i.e. moving along the same trajectory in real space that the virtual camera tracked in simulated space. Then the scene is shot with the match moving camera and a so-called simulcam, which inserts a rough animation on the camera monitors. The simulcam is used so that the cinematographer and director can see if the physical performers interact properly with the motion capture ones.

Match-moving cameras have been used for a long time in filmmaking and are one of the foundations of the integration of miniatures with performers, as well as the integration of computer-generated imagery with live-action footage. However, traditionally, the live-action footage has been shot first and then match moving has been employed to produce either a miniature shot or, later, a virtual camera trajectory for computer-generated imagery or animation shots. What happened with *Real Steel* was that the supplement overtook the live-action footage. Motion capture sequences were shot first, and only then the live-action sequences were shot to obey the previsualization.

Narratively, when we see Jackman perform boxing moves that Atom replicates in the ring to almost defeat Zeus, we are being told the human is superior: only a real human boxer can defeat the automaton before him. However, on a production level, the situation is reversed, and the human body must comply with the digital bodies. Jackman, then, dances to the movement of the motion capture, rather than the reverse. *(See Figure 5.1 in the insert.)* Movement comes before acting, and Jackman transforms into a puppet, just as the robots work through telemetry. Here we begin to see how motion capture technologies work not simply as tools but rather as machines that reconfigure the human sensorium. If, as Patricia Clough argues, the human eye and the moving camera are linked and inseparable, then motion capture cameras, virtual cameras and simulcams are similarly inseparable from the human body.[11] With the shift to motion capture technologies, which record movements rather than images, we find a transition from film as a primarily ocular medium to film as a haptic medium, contingent on motion and motility. Rather than producing images for the viewer, these films attempt to induce motion in the viewer's body.[12] This machinic assemblage produces different experiences than those of the moving camera, making the human body simply one body among others in a network of vectors.

We find a peculiar doubled sensation of feeling both aligned with Jackman's body and with Atom's. For both bodies, the film employs a range of techniques in terms of how the motion capture works as well as how the camera moves, pulling us into the middle of the fights and providing access to wins and defeats in terms of reaction shots. However, the most spectacular and intense movements come from the motion capture technologies in conjunction with digital animation. These sequences allow for movements that go beyond normal bodily experience, and so intensify our experience of the film. This experience is one that follows Ayers' logic of bilocation. The motion capture technologies have fragmented the body of the performer and then assembled it again differently. The body fragments to produce a new whole through computer-generated animation, which "translates and extends the movements and material 'weight' and presence of the actor into a different space, allowing for the multilocality – in both time and space – of the actor's body."[13] However, the process of translation and extension also indicates change. Indeed, new media technologies translate our experience into new forms.[14] So, while *Real Steel* may at first glance come off as entirely traditional in its audiovisual expression, the fact that its post-cinematic body has been thoroughly translated through a digital process means that it contorts the traditional experience of fight sequences into new forms.

Tele-technologies push perception beyond the human body, and while Virilio remains within the field of telesthesia, perception at a distance, we find in *Real Steel* an increase in the telesomatic relation of action and power at a distance. Motion capture technologies are not about the reproduction of images but about the intensification of images, achieved through the paradoxical obliteration of the image into pure motion. The film attempts to gloss over the way digital bodies swallow human ones by use of narrative means. The story of *Real Steel* reinforces the human element as central in that only a human boxer can truly defeat the emotionless other of the machine. Surely this is also why the human owner of the champion boxer Zeus is coded as Asian, so as to intensify Zeus' associations of otherness. However, the experience of *Real Steel* is entirely different, contingent as it is on the utilization of motion capture technologies. The most intense moments of the film are centered on the telesomatics of experiencing through Atom as well as Charlie. The film would not be as successful without those sequences, nor would the sequences be as intense had they used other cinematic devices. Only the distributed embodiment of the film can encompass our telesomatic relation to it.

Real Steel is a double articulation of embodiment; on the one hand, we align ourselves traditionally and conventionally with the human bodies and characters. The star power of Hugh Jackman functions as what we can think of as an attractor: the vehicle through which we have learned to watch and engage with films. On the other hand, the more the film progresses, the more we are aligned with Atom, who is conversely humanized for us. Significantly, the more we wish to engage in the intensity of the fights, the more we have to switch our embodiment to Atom to do so. As the story progresses, Atom's body, despite being clearly nonhuman, becomes the primary attractor for our embodiment. There is a folding into each other in terms of actor, character and robot bodies, what I earlier called an entwining.

In *Real Steel*, embodiment is extended and shared between two bodies on screen, but this on-screen relationship becomes emblematic for the way that we are invited to join the dance of bodies. The early scenes slowly work their way under our skin and into our muscular, proprioceptive relations with the screen, to the extent that we feel the movement of other bodies in ours. As our bodies engage with the screen bodies, the relations change; we engage in the film, our bodies participating in the movements on screen. This movement in fact parallels the narrative action on screen as well, even as it is ideologically obfuscated. We recognize cognitively that Charlie must step in and take over the match, because nothing substitutes for real human action, yet what we feel is different. Our sensory engagement is with the drone body, and to fully realize the excitement of the film, that is precisely the position we must step into. The sensory realism we find in *Real Steel* is now a digital realism, though still bodily. When new technologies affectively entrain our bodily responses, inevitably this leads to a situation in which we are primed for action through means other than our own bodies. We are entrained to accept inert behavior and static motility in exchange for sensory intensity.

Richness of Motion: *Avatar*

Full-bodied movement and richness of motion are central sensations for James Cameron's *Avatar*, and the film attempts to elicit as many sensations of movement as it can from its viewer. Its deployment of 3D effects, as well as movement across all three axes, focuses on this singular goal. As such, it is hard to not read the film as an allegory for the transition to 3D cinema, perhaps even as an elegy for 2D cinema. Jake Sully (Sam Worthington) is a Marine who due to an injury is now paraplegic, and the story centers, in part, on him moving through space in a wholly new way, just as the 3D audience is invited to engage fully with the stereoscopic film and therefore learn a new way of experiencing films. Filmed with groundbreaking 3D camera rigs, called the Fusion Camera System or, humbly, the Reality Camera System 1, *Avatar* also used motion capture, performance capture and extended sequences of computer-generated animations. The intention was to make as immersive an environment as possible while also making all shots appear similar, such that motion capture, conventional photography and animation would all have the same feel and texture.

The story of *Avatar* is Sully's encounter with the natives of Pandora, the Na'vi. Jake is on a mission to learn as much as he can about their culture and possibly convince a clan of Na'vi to move away from their ancestral home. The Resources Development Administration (RDA) wants to gain access to unobtanium, a rare mineral that will solve Earth's energy crisis. Jake works with a group of scientists led by Dr. Grace Augustine (Sigourney Weaver) to learn more about the Na'vi culture, while also overcoming his paralyzing injury. Since Pandora's atmosphere is poisonous for humans, human-Na'vi hybrids, called avatars, are used to explore the planet. Humans connect via teletechnologies to these avatar bodies and have full sensory experience of their avatar's bodies. Jake encounters Neytiri (Zoe Saldana), a Na'vi, and inevitably falls in love with her. Realizing that the Na'vi will never leave their home, Jake tries to convince Colonel Miles Quaritch (Stephen Lang) that they should give up. Instead, Quaritch orders the Na'vi home destroyed. Jake's only option is to convince the Na'vi to follow his lead and gather all the Na'vi tribes to retaliate and defend Pandora. Having been successful, Jake's essence is then transferred into his Na'vi avatar body, leaving his own crippled body behind in exchange for a glorious life on Pandora.

Clearly a body normative film, *Avatar* makes much of the Na'vi's natural and ecologically balanced life as contrasted to the metal-and-oil lives of humans. Everything on Pandora is connected in a vast neural network, which has more connections than the human brain and shows the interrelatedness of all living things. This ecological message is brought home by the wonderful capacities for movement that Pandora offers. Not unlike *Real Steel*, the way that our embodiment can be amplified through access to a better body is central. For this reason, it is imperative that the viewer be as engrossed as possible in the film's environment, even more so than in the film's narrative. A lot of time is spent in the first half of the film introducing us to the wonders of Pandora, most of which includes movement in one way or the other, and movement is also central to Jake's eventual victory against a technologically superior force.

Just as *Real Steel* suggests that with motion capture technologies we shift to a bodily connection between film and us, a fleshing out of our experience, as Sobchack calls it, so too does *Avatar*.[15] Yet this fleshing out is far more precarious and thrilling than what was achieved in *Real Steel*. With *Real Steel*, the fights and the motion capture sequences were kept within the boxing ring, but in *Avatar* we find a vast world of new and threatening experiences ready to be explored. Jake's first encounter with Pandora is grim and hectic. On a scouting expedition, he encounters a predator beast and is chased through the jungle. Shot predominantly from the front, there is a lot of movement into negative parallax, as is to be expected for a stereoscopic film. In contrast to the more spatially clear lateral shots, which are occasionally cut to provide orientation, the frontal shots constantly push the threat of the predator into the audience space. We, as much as Jake, are assaulted by the predator's lunges.

While the frontal shots are relatively stable and have a comparatively slow editing rhythm, the camerawork becomes significantly more jumbled when Jake tries to hide in a little hole under a tree. Here the camera judders around while the predator lunges for Jake. We move from inside the hole to outside and back in. The camera tumbles around frantically, producing claustrophobic feelings of capture and of space being too tight for comfort. This tension is countered by a boundless leap into space. Jake sprints from the little hole, runs to the edge of a cliff and jumps. However, because of the vegetation, we are surprised by the sudden opening onto a huge waterfall, especially because of the tight framing, which restricts our vision.

When Jake leaps into empty space, the film alternates between high angle shots that emphasize height and vertigo and low angle shots that show where the predator is in relation to him. *(See Figure 5.2 in the insert.)* Both shots orient us in space but also induce tension, the height of the fall, the closeness of the predator. Spatial relations are clearly articulated here precisely because they induce intense sensations, as well as a sense of awe and thrill at the scale. Here, the continuity of space in 3D cinema is central. We follow Jake down in an assemblage of shots, but the fullest and most surprising articulation of space is when Jake hits the water and, in a continuous shot, moves below it. The lack of a cut when Jake hits the water is surprising because of the duration of the shot, which follows Jake from high above the water. The smoothness of the animation is a sensation of physical control in itself, a sensation that runs counter to Jake's frazzled and out of control movements. This tension between two different bodies is interesting because it mirrors Jake trying to learn to adapt to and control his avatar body. In much the same way, we are adapting to the mobility and continuous movement of the stereoscopic body. The attraction of 3D cinema comes from such moments of unexpected new ways of moving, the safe threat of dangers moving into audience space and the new ways we have to learn how to articulate and embody cinematic space.

Avatar, as conceived and shot in 3D, as opposed to converted to 3D in post-production, makes extensive use of embodiment in three dimensions. While it may seem counterintuitive, since we live our lives in three dimensions, stereoscopic films articulate cinematic space differently than reality, and we experience it differently, simply because we have been conditioned to understand and perceive cinematic space as the representation of three dimensions in two dimensions. As Miriam Ross points out regarding *Avatar*, 3D cinema constructs a fractured statement by refusing to position clear signs and relations between objects on its surface, which in turn draws attention to the images' textured and tactile quality. The screen speaks out to the audience and invites participation by showing and frustrating our understanding of its content, in this way drawing us closer to its surface.[16]

Traditional cinema has by necessity employed perspectival space and made the third dimension expressive, either through deep space and depth of field, where elements are unified, or through shallow space, where our attention and focus are directly and concretely manipulated and modulated. Three dimensional space, by contrast, suggests a more full-bodied experience, where ideally we can orient our bodies in different ways. The vectors of action and movement guide and constrain our attention, but our immersion is different, and again as a result of these different image technologies, our embodied experience of the films is different. Until stereoscopic cinema becomes second nature, that is to say, transparent through conditioning and convention, the 3D experience remains different.[17]

The continuous shot of Jake falling into the water and swimming below the surface emphasizes the new forms of experience that stereoscopic cinema wants us to engage in. As in *Jupiter Ascending*, the imposing smoothness of the shot, the unhindered movement through the water surface, is a felt shock to our system. Such continuous shots allow for new embodied experiences, and so allow new forms of mastery. Significantly, then, Jake is consistently out of control on his first night in Pandora's jungles, while the stereoscopic body itself is very much in control, producing spectacular movements and swoops which make us align with that stereoscopic body in order to satisfy those new feelings. This is entirely parallel to the experience of Jake and his two bodies: paraplegic and avatar. To step into another body, *Avatar* tells us, is to step into a richer, fuller sensorium. This is what Miriam Ross has termed hyperhaptic qualities of stereoscopic cinema, emphasizing that "the underlying hyperhaptic qualities of the stereoscopic effect mean that complex viewer positions are produced in relation to the content that is made visible in the field screen."[18]

This emphasis on new bodily comportments is evident in the way that Jake has to learn to think differently while on Pandora. The full utilization of all three dimensions, especially the vertical axis, is crucial for Jake's success against the RDA. Jake must dominate the fearsome dragon-like Toruk in order to have a fearsome weapon against the RDA, but also to convince the other Na'vi that he is worthy to follow into combat. Although we never actually see how Jake bests the beast, we learn his plan is to fly higher than the dragon, since it would have no reason to look up, being the most dangerous animal around. In other words, vertical dominance must be asserted, and this can only be done through a breakneck dive towards the dragon. *(See Figure 5.3 in the insert.)* The dive is the last shot we get of Jake until later, when he returns with the dragon under his control. While we never see the fight, we understand that vertical dominance has been asserted. Thus, Jake is successful in thinking of verticality differently, using verticality as a technique of control.

Movement in ways that we are not accustomed to once again becomes central for the film here. Kristen Whissel has mapped this sense of up/down movement onto what she refers to as cinema's new verticality.[19] Associating the inevitability and inertia of history with the forces of down, as in *Titanic* (James Cameron 1997), and the escape from tradition in upwards movement, as in *Crouching Tiger, Hidden Dragon* (Ang Lee 2000), Whissel sets up an easy dialectic of up-good, down-bad. Whissel's argument about verticality holds true here, to the extent that whoever can go higher is the more powerful one. However, the direction of down is more complicated, since it is fraught with danger while at the same time being the key to success.[20] Verticality is better seen in terms of Sara Ross' powerful sensations of mastery through space: "Soaring through space, by contrast, has historically been associated with progress and mastery, both literally and metaphorically, and thus can be used to structure the overall journey of a heroic protagonist."[21] In *Avatar*, then, Jake has to learn how to move in new ways, ways that are not even humanly possible but possible only through his avatar body and its augmenting capacities. The hair of the Na'vi works as a connector that allows for a shared embodiment between beings, whether between the horse-like creatures or the dangerous dragon. Although presented in the film as a natural and deep connection, this shared embodiment is entirely congruent with the shared embodiment humans use for their avatar bodies. The only discrepancy is that the human connectors are technological, while the Na'vi connection is organic. In either scenario, however, the idea is that a shared embodiment grants access to a fuller and richer experience. In other words, our world can be fleshed out in new ways through a shared embodiment.

Both forms of connections are seen as unmediated and completely transparent. There is no lag, no glitch, no signal distortion in Jake's avatar embodiment, nor is there in his connection to the flying lizards or the dragon. Similarly, the film's deployment of hyperhaptic images is an attempt at inducing a likewise unmediated experience. As Ross points out, "the flight sequence has been a favorite vehicle for displaying the potential of cinematic technology to produce a spectacular illusion of unmediated spectator participation."[22] The hyperhaptic images that move into a space we are not used to having filled suggest immediate, unmediated experience. Parallax movement becomes the second axis of control and dominance in *Avatar*, but this time directed at us. We are assaulted by these protruding, disruptive images.

Humans are generally cast as immobile in the film, which is significant. Most of the human characters move around inside buildings, steadily walking through somber blue-grey interiors across a horizontal plane. Or they are inside vehicles, often cast in shadow. By contrast, the Na'vi and the avatar bodies roam through a vibrant, lush world, moving unfettered in all directions. A complicated mix of sensations combining thrill, danger and release suggest a kind of bodily frontier experience, where life on Pandora is richer and fuller, even if it is also more dangerous and risky. All human bodies, and not solely Jake's, are seen as deficient, lacking a primal connection to nature. Such a deficiency can only be overcome through the intensity of living life precariously. Danger is the price you pay for the wonders of full-bodied immersion and the sensations of unhindered spatial movement. Fear can be dispelled through bodily immersion into other bodies, whether the avatar bodies or other creatures' bodies.

Yet at the same time, of course, all of these full-bodied experiences are rendered through a telesomatic relation. Jake does not feel any reduction or loss of transmission in the connection to his avatar body. The fantasy of *Avatar*, then, is also that we can move beyond mediation and achieve full-blown transparency. Yet this transparency, this intense condition of immediacy, can only be expressed through advanced media technologies.

On the narrative level, the human-Na'vi hybrid avatar bodies are made through the most advanced technologies available, while, on a production level, transparency is made available by the Reality Camera System 1. More importantly, the film's audiovisual expression constantly works to engage us at a distance. All films do this, but the ways in which *Avatar* does it is crucial, because engagement at a distance is embedded in the narrative level, suggesting that Jake's experience of Pandora is meant to be a parallel to our experience of *Avatar*.

But *Avatar* is not only a 3D film, it is also an animated motion capture film, which complicates our sense of embodiment even further. During the final battle, when we see Jake fly the dragon and leap onto one of the gunships, we are given an incredibly complicated sequence that involves a host of imaging technologies to produce the final result. In this way, the body we see jumping onto a gunship is itself a dense assemblage: motion capture actor, who is not always Sam Worthington but sometimes a stunt performer; performance capture cameras, which capture Worthington's acting performance and distorts his face to a Na'vi face; animation to produce a Na'vi body, as well as the dragon's body instead of the rig the performer jumps from. Despite the camera system being called Reality Camera System 1, we must recognize the incredibly mediated process necessary to produce a sense of continuous space and movement. The spectacular attraction of the parallax effect is meant to cover up this mediated process with the sensation of unmediated experience. We find, therefore, the paradox that Bolter and Grusin locate in hypermediation: the desire for immediacy through means other than transparency. To put it slightly differently, more mediation, not less, is *Avatar's* method for producing immediacy. This is a form of sensory assault, in which the speed of hyperhaptic images pursues an aggressive strategy of pumping out spectacular sequences in the hope that this will overwhelm us so much that it feels immediate and authentic. In fact, of course, this sense of authenticity is achievable only through highly artificial means. Yet the end result is one of sensory impacts that manifest as authenticity because our sensations and affects are real.

What *Avatar* shows us is that there is a wonderful world out there, and it is best experienced through magnificent 3D cinema, in which we can truly feel the intensity of movement. Similarly, our bodies need amplification to fully sense all the exuberant energies of Pandora. Jake leaves his human body behind in order to escape the curse of immobility, which is presented as the ultimate form of lack in the film. Movement in an immersive space is therefore exalted, the ultimate freedom. Much like Jake, who must learn to master verticality in order to defeat the moribund humans, we must allow the film to take over our bodies, to relinquish ourselves to the film's parallax vectors of intensity. In doing so, we learn how to let bodies other than our own articulate our experiences. For *Avatar* that is the only real way to live: through a shared embodiment.

Both on a narrative and a formal level, shared embodiment allows for a richer sensory experience. While there is a tension between the technological embodiment of the avatar bodies and that of the organic connection between Na'vi and Pandora fauna, it is glossed over by the intensity of the stereoscopic images. The cinematic experience of *Avatar* is thus one where hypermediation masks as transparency to lure us into a new and broader sensorium. The majestic, and even sublime, sensations of Pandora are accessible only if we allow ourselves to step into this shared and amplified embodiment. Going by the number of so-called post-*Avatar* depressions, stepping into such an amplified, shared embodiment was not a problem for most audiences.[23] Yet *Avatar* also remains the most singularly astounding example of Virilio's concept of polar inertia: intense sensations of movement despite remaining entirely immobile.[24] The full-bodied sense of immersion that the film facilitates encourages this telesomatic engagement.

Yet we should also recognize that the shared embodiment produced by *Avatar* is far from the distributed embodiment of *Mad Max: Fury Road*. *Avatar* comes off far more regressive and conservative in its body ideals of moving bodies and the singularity of the strong, capable white male. Although Jake might be blue, due to his avatar body, he is in fact white, male and militaristic. So capable is this white male that he can easily best Na'vi riders and warriors who grew up on Pandora. This fact is what gives lie to *Avatar*'s apparent message of ecology and tolerance. While the film might seem to criticize the military-industrial complex, it does so by substituting it with the military-entertainment complex. Although the weapons of RDA seem colonialist, the audiovisual weapons of *Avatar*'s sound-images similarly colonize our sensorium, hijacking them for the production of a sensory immediacy, and an overpowering one at that. The ideology of technology has never been more prominently displayed.

Telesomatics

What we find in the two films is an emphasis on the doubling of bodies through the intensity of movement. As such, embodiment is no longer unitary but rather a distributed phenomenon. Of course, this in no way signals an end to embodiment, but is instead a change of relations between bodily elements. No longer is our embodiment a static entity; it is now an active agent that participates across a field of energies and flows. We engage with the bodies on screen but also the cinematic body itself, a body that has been reconfigured by the use of motion capture technologies. Our embodiment is therefore not a unitary object in our possession or control, but is best understood as emerging through qualities of interaction with other bodies. As we saw in the case of *Avatar*, distributed embodiment can also work as a controlling modulation that favors certain forms and modes of embodiment over others.

By being part of these processes, embodiment is also subject to modulation and control within its larger environment. These motion capture technologies present a telesomatic relation, wherein our relation to the screen image refers primarily to an attempt at capturing us as vectors of affective movement. Identification is no longer a matter of empathic recognition of actor performance, but instead a matter of us aligning with the movement of the motion capture character. While this may sound like a prosthetic relationship, one wherein we act through extensions of ourselves, that is not the case. A prosthetic relationship suggests a one-directional movement and control: we control our prostheses. This is not the case here. Here there is a trade-off in terms of affective engagement and modulation. We can only affectively engage with the stereoscopic images and motion captures sequences if we are willing to let those same images overwhelm us, if, as it were, we relinquish sensory control.

We can refer to this telesomatic relation as a tension between dispersed agencies, wherein we are not fully in control, and pluralized efficacies, through which we can do more things and engage in more actions if we allow the images to fold into us. This blurring is what Virilio finds deeply disturbing and calls the law of proximity: distance becomes reconfigured and trivial with the use of teletechnologies. These films show how distance is not just extensive but also intensive: things are not far away if their sensations are intense. We are dealing with a reconfiguration of human agency, one in which we willingly cede autonomy to a range of technologies and which results in dispersed agency and pluralized efficacies. Things go wild as we go inert, satisfied with a sense of action at a distance.

I have already argued that motion capture and animation technologies exist on the same plane of operation as the human body, emphasizing vectorized movements as forms of telesomatics. Virilio suggests that the mobile human will increasingly become a motile human, our mental imagery dominated by inner feelings of action.[25] The drone is the perfect figure for these inner feelings of action being expressed at a distance. Motion capture technologies function as the exteriorization of this interior state, as long as we acknowledge that the interior state is produced by this process of exteriorization through enfolding the heterogenous assemblage of materials, or what Bennett calls an interfolding of the human and the nonhuman.[26] There is no functional difference between interior and exterior sensations, they are produced in the same process of concrescence; that is, in the integration of separate elements into one through conjunction.

Human embodiment, then, is increasingly recognized not as unitary but as a conjunctive node in a larger environmental process. If, as Shaviro argues, affects are adverbs, expressing the quality of experiences and how entities relate to each other, sensations are conjunctions, the integration of more than one action or instance simultaneously.[27] Jake is human *and* Na'vi *and* dragon at the same time. Charlie is himself *and* Atom at the same time. We are ourselves *and* film, our bodies *and* cinematic body at the same time. The sensations of stereoscopic images simply keep adding to the assemblage: motion capture *and* animation *and* performance capture and so on. There is no limit to the number of integrations that can be made. All that is required, as Virilio points out, is a surplus of excitement, or energy, so that our passivity, or inertia, can be overcome *through intense sensation* rather than extensive movement.[28] As I have argued throughout this book, contemporary action cinema is rife with such energy. In fact, it is the primary purpose to produce such energies in us through audiovisual intensity.

139

This intensity of contemporary action cinema's sound-images is what Virilio terms media proximity: being made to feel close to things that are in fact far. Motion capture's distributed embodiment is another turn of this screw and suggests that we may lose a distinction between inside and outside as egocentration overtakes exocentration.[29] We have already seen that contemporary action cinema does not privilege spatial orientation, what we can consider cinema's version of exocentration, favoring instead a kind of egocentration in the production of sensations and affects. We should not concern ourselves too much with egocentration as a psychoanalytic term. Rather, we should think about it as a shift of orientation from spatial location to affective location: we are where the affect is.

It is in this way that we establish a telesomatic relation to the surrounding environment, allowing for the protrusion and projection of technologies as a substitute or shared embodiment. We allow technologies to be projections in both directions, moving into the environment and folding back into us. Entirely correlate to the situations of both *Real Steel* and *Avatar*, this experience also finds a correlate in their use of motion capture and 3D images. Relinquishing control to the sensory modulations of these technologies is the only way to receive and feel their intense sensations, the only way to reach their lures for feeling. And so audiovisual technologies, "universally and remotely, control today's culture and its inhabitants from within themselves."[30]

Films are not literal drones, but they are projections of power nonetheless. Our assumptions about movement are reconfigured when audiovisual vehicles can perform movements for us. Our actions are reconfigured. Our actions are only ours nominally, but they are still substitute embodiments as long as they induce energy, or affect. Animation is no longer connected to the human or animal body, but now to something that also occurs in non-organic life. These films, then, come alive, crackling with intense energies that allow us to move without moving. Our bodily preacceleration becomes enough, a preferred, safe and controllable experience. Yet in letting ourselves be affected by these sound-images, we also allow for modulations of our bodily states. Bodies other than our own work for us constantly, and cinema is no exception.

As projections of power, films flesh out our bodies in ways that we cannot predict or fully control. There is a necessary component of submission to any cinematic experience, a willingness to immerse in the sound-images in ways that go beyond conscious assimilation. This is simply the *aisthesis* of film, the way that our senses are always articulated through an aesthetic encounter, the integration of multiple sensations into one subject. Yet this subject is contingent on these sensations and the accompanying modulation; the subject only emerges as a function of these sensations and modulations. A film, like all forms of culture, projects power into us, although we only exist as us after having felt it, however minimally the subsequent change.

But we can only emerge as satisfied or achieved subjects if we step into the cinematic experience. In doing so, we accept a telesomatic relationship and in fact are entrained to appreciate the dispersed agencies and pluralized efficacies of these intensive sound-images. Or, to phrase it slightly differently, our worldly sensibility is articulated in a way that regards intensive sensation as similar to extensive action. In fact, we are primed or preaccelerated for extensive actions undertaken by bodies other than our own in exchange for intensive sensations. Our affects are tied up with the actions of other bodies, no matter the status of those bodies, i.e. technological or otherwise. We are, in other words, primed to be embodied through a complex interaction of human and nonhuman agencies, all distributed within a larger media ecology.

Through this interaction, our embodiment is bolstered, rendered free from fear. The *aisthetic* relation allows for an integration of multiple bodies to induce more movement, and so offers a reprieve from paralysis. Although we are rendered inert through teletechnologies, telesomatics allow for a larger embodiment, which does not weigh us down but induces more energy in us – more affective entrainment through integration of several bodies to avoid fear. Telesomatics is thus a furthering of somatic markers, a specific articulation of bodily connections that generate new, nonhuman capacities. Here we see how vectors and kinetics converge through the flexible, volatile body and accelerate into a corporeal projection of power. Projecting power without projecting vulnerability is the primary function of these films, generating the sensation that we act from a position of safety. Yet as we have also seen, these films overtake our embodiment and entrain us to a condition of proxy actions. We distribute our embodiment to let other appendages act for us. At the same time, this produces us as passive subjects, subjects happy to let objects act and enjoy the exhilarating vector of affects, much as I argued in "Vectors and the Transfer of Affect." The effect of such vectors, kinetics, volatilities and projections of power on our consciousness is what I will turn to in the next chapter on droning and audiovisual stunning.

6

Droning and Audiovisual Stun Mode

As I have argued, contemporary action cinema has become a full frontal sensory assault. The immensity of audiovisual spectacles is geared to
produce overwhelming sensations, to suffuse and even dominate our perception. I have outlined several ways in which contemporary action cinema functions as sensory assault, distending perception through vectoral
images, kinetics, body volatility and a telesomatic relation to the world.
Here, I wish instead to investigate the production of a drone subject. I will
do this by turning to two other formal functions: editing and sound. These
two aspects suggest the ways in which these films become exhausting to
watch through their sheer overpowering intensity. We are inundated with
cataclysmic spectacles of destruction and mayhem, all of which suggest a
revision of Virilio's concept of cinema as, "I fly," to cinema as, "I destroy".
What these intense audiovisual affectiles do is to articulate experience in a
highly specific form, what I believe can best be understood as *droning*. In
the previous chapter I argued that our interior state is produced by exterior
relations, and this interior state thus becomes the focus of this chapter.

Music philosopher Robin James' work on drone sound suggests a process of droning that disrupts and distorts perception by obscuring some
modes of perception while amplifying others.[1] Her argument resides in
the primarily sonic experience of drone tones, which works "by creating a

consistent psychological timbre or pitch–terror".[2] Droning, then, becomes a way to suffuse us with a mood that rivets us to the audiovisual spectacle. This mood is first a bodily condition, instilled, in the case of film, by the haptic effects of both editing and the particularly turbulent sound of drone tones; droning "is a *condition* of being terrorized, a condition that impacts everything you do."[3] As should be evident, James' concept of droning runs parallel to the concepts of modulation, entrainment and priming that I have employed so far. We find here a blurring of the line between form and affect: drone tones are sonic forms, but they induce a pre-subjective state that is best understood as itself a drone, a monotonous, non-distinct feeling, which does not distinguish between visual or aural sensorial impressions. Instead, droning suggests a haptic cluster of sensations that exist outside of and cannot easily be integrated into our conscious experience, because the cluster is not cognitive but bodily, made up of vibrations induced by the impact of droning sound-images. These vibrations modulate, prime and entrain the subject condition that follows, and should thus be seen as the ground from which our consciousness arises.

Two examples in contemporary action cinema stand out in terms of the drone of sound-images: Michael Bay's Transformers series and Jonathan Liebesman's *Battle: Los Angeles* (2011). Together, these films showcase the shock-and-awe aesthetics of contemporary action cinema, hurling us into the middle of the action as a means of droning out perceptual reflection and cognition. Yet sound design and the drone of sound-images can also function in resistant and subversive ways. Kathryn Bigelow's *The Hurt Locker* (2008) presents us with an example of how the drone of a film's sound-images works to unsettle us, to place us outside ourselves in order to question dominant sensations and experiences. In all three cases, the films enact a distinctive rhythm that may be at odds with our own bodily rhythm.

For this reason, I intend to draw on what Michel Chion has termed the *superfield*: "the space created, in multitrack films, by ambient natural sounds, city noises, music, and all sorts of rustlings that surround the visual space and that can issue from loudspeakers outside the physical boundaries of the screen."[4] For Chion, the superfield is associated with sound but also modifies "the structure of editing and scene construction."[5] Sound makes it possible to suggest continuity and cohesion while joining shots that are otherwise not necessarily spatially cogent. Sound design thus takes on more significance in these cases. Within contemporary cinema, we find growing attention paid to sound design, particularly sound design that no longer fits into neat diegetic sound versus non-diegetic musical score categories. Made possible by various technological advances such as Dolby Surround and multi-speaker systems, as well as digital audio workflows, sound has taken on a far more impressionistic role in contemporary action cinema. Traditionally, diegetic sound has worked to induce a sense of realism into the image, while the non-diegetic musical score has functioned as intensifier or atmospheric addition to the existing image. In that tradition, sound is subordinate to the image, serving only to bolster and amplify the expression of the image in what Michel Chion has dubbed "unification" and "synchresis".[6] Yet the superfield has expanded in the age of digital sound production to include sound as music and music as sound, as K.J. Donnelly has suggested.[7] In this expanded superfield, we find rather a form of *turbulent sound*, sound that is not only asynchretic but in fact produces an intensity in addition to that of the image, amplifying the image by creating a sonic field of its own. Turbulent sound produces a sonic space that does not follow the spatiotemporal logic of the image. As such, turbulent sound is post-synchretic, not aligned with the image track but preoccupied with its own form of sensorial impact.

Appetite for Destruction: *Transformers*

I know no better example of the sensory overload of sound-images than Michael Bay's Transformers series. Currently consisting of four films – *Transformers* (2007), *Transformers: Revenge of the Fallen* (2009), *Transformers: Dark of the Moon* (2011) and *Transformers: Age of Extinction* (2014) – a fifth installment is in development, slated for release in 2017. The toy-franchise-turned-billion-dollar-movie-franchise stands at the apex of the blockbuster food chain. The success of these films is most likely found in the franchise's innovative approach to keeping the narrative structure clear and familiar, thus allowing for maximum excess and pyrotechnic "Bayhem" throughout the films. All the films are variations of the millennial battle between the friendly Autobots and the nefarious Decepticons, with humanity caught in the middle. The Autobots, led by

Optimus Prime, selflessly defend humans despite humanity's acrimonious acts against the alien robots. Conversely, Megatron incessantly leads the Decepticons against the Autobots to win domination of the universe. This basic structure is simple, yet flexible enough to allow the introduction of new alien robots in each installment without confusing the fundamental Manichean struggle.

Against this epic backdrop of good versus evil unfolds a baffling sequence of kinetic action set pieces, all designed for maximum spectacular impact. There is a sense in which this frenzy of the sensible is entirely pornographic: every single aspect of each film converges to elicit bodily responses from us. Narrative is kept to a bare minimum, while also intensified in its continuity to keep the narrative structure lucid. However, due to the films' repetitive narrative form, established in the first film, the narrative really only functions as what Miriam Hansen defines as a scaffold "that allows for a wide range of aesthetic effects and experiences".[8] Narrative is what allows all the spectacular sequences to take place within a coherent framework, providing an excuse for unleashing a maximum overdrive of excessive effects.

Several of the actors themselves have commented on the aggressive nature of the first *Transformers*, with Megan Fox saying "it made me feel very masculine and aggressive, like you want to just punch someone," while Julie White pointed out that "it's huge, it's concussive, it hurts your head." Similarly, Michael Bay is entirely aware that he punishes the audience's sense of time and space. In the extras for *Transformers: Age of Extinction* Bay expounds on his visual style and how he deliberately employs unique camera positions with movement along several axes, because such a setup warps the audience's experience of time and space. Bay enjoys cutting from epic wide shots to extreme close-ups, once again wrenching stable time and space perception from the audience.

We might question the wisdom of a director who deliberately destroys and distorts the audience's sense of time and space, since conventional wisdom argues that the audience is far more likely to engage with films that provide clear and stable articulations of time and space, simply because it means we can understand the cinematic space.[9] Yet as the box office shows, contemporary audiences appear less worried about spatiotemporal stability than film critics. As long as we accept King and Shaviro's earlier argument that contemporary action cinema is about immediate impact, then Bay's decisions make sense and in fact place him at the very center of action cinema today. MUBI, a streaming and film criticism site, clearly agrees, featuring several articles on Michael Bay's *Transformers* in the wake of *Age of Extinction*. All these articles point out the spectacular display, the sensory abstraction and the delight in Bay's perceptual stun mode.[10]

I am interested here exactly in this perceptual stun mode, particularly its audiovisual construction. Of particular interest is how sound and image work together as a means of producing the most intense experience possible. Considering the lengthy nature of the franchise, it is not possible to deal in-depth with all the films, so instead I will allow a few examples to metonymically stand in for the franchise as a whole. As I am particularly interested in the extremity of spectacle used, I have chosen a scene from *Dark of the Moon* where the climactic battle over Chicago functions as the clearest expression of Bay's stun mode. My argument is that this stun mode is more than simply a matter of audiovisual attraction; in fact, it pushes the boundaries of what we can perceive.

In *Dark of the Moon*, it is revealed that humans went to the Moon to investigate the crash of the Ark, a spacecraft from Cybertron, the home of all the Transformers. In the present day, the Autobots learn of the existence of the Ark, as well as that of Sentinel Prime, their previous leader and Optimus' mentor. Yet the Autobots are led into a trap when they bring the Ark back to Earth, since Sentinel made a deal with Megatron to save the Transformers from extinction. Everything comes to a head over Chicago, where the Decepticons attempt to bring Cybertron into the Milky Way to enslave humanity. The Autobots succeed in defeating the Decepticons and destroying the Space Bridge, which also destroys their home planet Cybertron in the process. Victorious, the Autobots must accept the fact that they now live on Earth.

The battle of Chicago is a 40-minute, protracted series of images of destruction and chaos. As is usual in the films, several of the scenes are solely composed of Transformers battling each other, which means that computer-generated animation once again takes pride of place. However, Bay is intelligent enough to intersperse human action in order to make it easier for us to engage with and follow the narrative. This is done in one of two ways. The first, and easiest, solution is to place humans in direct danger of the robot battles. To stay safe, the human characters must constantly run and hide. This provides the option of giving us reaction shots of scared humans, enforcing the dangerous nature of the battle. The second strategy is to have human characters be directly attacked by Decepticons, which is of course far more dangerous for the humans but allows for less robot spectacle.

One of the pinnacle sequences takes place in a broken skyscraper that leans at a precarious angle. The Decepticons blast the building with the aim of stopping Sam, Carly and the unit of soldiers trying to prevent the Space Bridge from being erected. The slant of the skyscraper makes all the objects in the room fall to one side, producing a lot of lateral movement. As Shockwave approaches the building, it shifts more, and the humans hide as Shockwave jumps into it. Hiding behind pillars, the humans nervously wait while Shockwave scans the room. Employing several tracking shots, the editing suggests movement counter to Shockwave's arm-cannon, producing a more dynamic shot, with movement along several axes. When discovered, all the humans race for the windows, and we cut to the outside, where we see the soldiers breaking through the glass in slow-motion. The editing overlaps and shows the jump from two different angles: first from the side, and then from above, with the soldiers shooting down. Then we get another lateral shot of Sam and Carly as they jump after the soldiers. The interspersed shot from above breaks the continuity rule of only showing an event once, but adds to the kaleidoscopic sense of movement in the jump segment. We cut to a shot of the soldiers landing on the slanted windows of the building shot at canted angle, with a swoosh pan moving counter to the soldiers' fall. The shot pans back down keeping the soldiers, Sam and Carly in the frame, then cuts to a low angle reaction shot of Sam screaming. This cuts to a wide crane shot that lifts up and tilts down towards the skyscraper, showing the group tumble down its side. The shot zooms after them, before cutting to a lateral shot from the other side of the skyscraper following the group down. While in this shot, the camera still follows the movement of the group, more movement is introduced by means of a lens flare, which shoots a beam of light across the group. Then there is a higher framed, low angle shot to show Sam and Carly falling, which cuts to a shot from above. The soldiers shoot the glass in several sliding shots, before they all fall through it. The cut is once again to a camera moving in the opposite direction of the bodies' fall, but cuts then to a tracking shot that follows the group sliding across the floor, crashing into chairs, with lots of flying paper and sparks. Before we get our bearings, a desk careens through the window, and an intrepid soldier falls outside again in a slow-motion, computer-generated, animated tracking shot down towards Shockwave. (*See Figure 6.1 in the insert.*) The continuous shot speed ramps down to super-slow, while also shifting from an overhead shot to a lateral shot, only to cut to a wide shot of the group hanging on to the walls of the skyscraper.

This sequence constantly cuts between wide shots and medium close shots, replaying the same events from different angles and allowing shot trajectories not only to clash with the trajectories of bodies going in the opposite direction but also with each other, joining a camera movement of down with a camera movement of up and thus producing a crash cut smashing the different camera movements together. Furthermore, the tumble into the building is edited so quickly as to make any kind of spatial orientation not only impossible but also irrelevant: the shots are not made for spatial consistency but for the flurry of images and objects within the frame. We are not meant to know exactly where we are, only that we are in danger. Bay's concussive editing adds to the intensifying affects of shots already rife with the modes of construction I've described in previous chapters. Practically every single shot obeys the vectoral power of images to project feelings into us, pushing our senses into hyper-perception due to the immense deployment of kinetics within the frame of each shot. The speed of editing alongside the speed within each image makes it difficult for us to keep pace with all the movements going every which way.

Even the wide shot meant to anchor us after the fall and provide a brief respite is in fact a zoom with debris floating in the air in front of us. There is no respite from movement and agitation in the destructive audio-vision of Bay. Immediately, we are cast into the next droning sequence, which features the most massively computer-generated animation in the film franchise so far: the Driller. A kind of giant robotic earthworm with fangs, the Driller is announced not with shrill stingers, the way monsters have often been sonically introduced, but with a drone-like roar. The Driller is seen in an extreme wide shot high above the city, coming up a street. As such, the soundtrack mixes together a range of diegetic sounds, the ambient sound of the battle in general low in the mix. Since the Driller is burrowing through the asphalt, debris and stonework fall all over, providing direct sound of explosions and crashes. Yet to invoke the Driller itself, a strange metallic clanking sound like a winch is used combined with an electronic whine-scream.

However, as we cut to a reaction shot from one of the soldiers, all the ambient battle noise, the direct sound of wreckage and the winch-clanking sound, dissipates to make audible the soldier's panicked breathing. A Doppler shift is maintained, though; a thin echoing sound, which must come from the Driller but otherwise does not seem to have a direct source, is heard moving in the distance. This peculiar Doppler shift is what Chion calls acoustic or offscreen sound.[11] Nominally the purpose of acoustic sound is to provide spatial orientation for offscreen space: where is the character or creature that emits that sound. But since the sound employed is a Doppler shift, meaning that the sound source moves, space is actually not oriented. In fact, we cut back to the Driller to see its ferocious nature, and then back to the soldier screaming in panic. The Doppler sound goes away when we cut to the Driller, as it should, since we now are closer to the creature emitting the sound. Yet when we cut back to the soldier, the sound audio-pans from screen right, which is the direction of the Driller going by the soldier's eyeline, to screen left, which indicates imminent arrival. But the Driller does not come. Instead, it writhes its way to Megatron before burrowing into, constricting and crushing the skyscraper. (*See Figure 6.2 in the insert.*)

In other words, sound is used to dislocate us, rather than provide a sense of where characters are located in relation to each other and us. The sound of the Driller is not simply passive offscreen sound, but instead active, energetic sound that serves its own purpose of unsettling us. Mark Kerins dubs such unsettling sound effects the ultrafield, in reference to Chion's superfield, which "creates the impression not of viewing the action from a distance, but rather of being in the middle of the action and looking around quickly."[12] The Driller is thus sonically threatening before it becomes visually threatening. Here, I agree with Stork's argument that the unsettling sound effects makes the ultrafield's "ability to overwhelm even more powerful. The ultrafield amplifies the viewers' sense of physical risk in the precarious chaos space." But I disagree with his assessment that the "aural specificity of the soundtrack provides stability".[13] I believe, conversely, that the turbulence of the sound design precludes the possibility of stability. The Driller's Doppler shift reveals this, since there is no direct aural specificity to be gained from the sound effect, only the opposite.

Similarly, in an earlier scene in the film, Decepticons are racing to kidnap Simmons (John Turturro), while also chasing Sam. Such scenes of Transformers driving and transforming at high speeds on the freeway are mandatory for the franchise, providing a perfect environment for speed, movement and crashes. Generally, these scenes are kept dynamic by having shots move back and forth alongside the other cars, while also swerving laterally across the lanes. Simmons sits in the back of his car with the roof down as a big, black government car drives up behind him and transforms into a Deception as the camera pulls away, showcasing the transformation. Two more Decepticons show up, transforming into four-legged beasts that chase after Sam, sitting in Bumblebee and accompanied by Dino. As is usual for these freeway chase scenes, there is plenty of speed ramping, shifting to slow-motion whenever a robot transforms or crashes.

Once again, the cuts match against action, disrupting object and camera trajectories by smashing them together. The panning and tracking movement of the camera often loops back around in long takes and shifting perspectives, first looking ahead, then looking back, shifting angles and framings on the vehicles, constantly keeping the shots moving. One of the Decepticons also starts flipping cars, causing more objects within the frame to fly around at canted trajectories. The camera is also within a part of the action, as is the crash-cam in the Bourne Movies. All in all, the effect is quite overwhelming visually, and this sensation is only compacted by the sound design.

The soundtrack is dominated by the direct sound of cars crashing, robots tearing up the asphalt and guns firing. The score is dramatic; a combination of string bass and cellos set an overarching mood, while violins set a steady beat. The violins slowly increase their pitch as the tension grows, while the bass and cellos keep their pitch. The score here adds tension, while also driving the pace forward. The slow-motion sequences are interesting, however, in that they block direct sound in favor of the roaring, stretched sound effects that both emulate the slowing down of time and intensify the slow-motion sequences. For instance, when one of the Decepticons leap over Bumblebee, speed ramps down and sound drops off. All the offscreen trash-sound effects employed to increase the sense of action disappear, as does the score, which literally cuts off. What we do hear is the direct sound of Bumblebee's tires screeching, the deep crash of the Decepticons' clawed feet stomping on the freeway and the dull roar of the primary Decepticon as it flies over Bumblebee. *(See Figure 6.3 in the insert.)*

We get what Chion calls a "null extension," in which sonic space shrinks to only those three sounds.[14] However, Chion's argument pertains to subjective point of audition, i.e. what an individual character can hear. What occurs in the slow-motion leap is that sonic space contracts into the singular occurrence of the slow-motion leap, thus highlighting the impressive visual nature of the leap. Here, sound is used to bolster the image by contracting attention around the spectacular display in a process Chion calls synchresis: "the spontaneous and irresistible weld produced between a particularly auditory phenomenon and visual phenomenon when they occur at the same time."[15] And yet, the Decepticon does not make the sound, since it is a sound from nowhere. Instead, the two impacts – affectiles, if you will – of sound and vision conjoin in our experience and intensify it.

A minute later, Bumblebee has to partially transform to leap over a crashing truck loaded with gas canisters. This ejects Sam from his seat, and again the shot ramps to slow-motion. A low-angle tracking shot moving back shows Sam flailing wildly through mid-air with Bumblebee in humanoid shape above him. Gas canisters, wheels and random debris fly chaotically around, as once again all sound drops off. A drone tone begins pealing in the soundtrack, slowly increasing in pitch as objects almost seem to converge on Sam. There are a few direct sounds in real-time as Bumblebee swats away wheels to protect Sam, and a thud when Bumblebee grabs Sam, and Sam's corresponding groan. In a flurry of images, Sam is placed back inside Bumblebee during its transformation back to car. That transformation is expressed sonically by a series of loud, metallic clangs indicating Bumblebee is skidding across the asphalt. Speed ramps back up during the transformation, and we end with a stable shot of Sam sitting inside Bumblebee, screaming in panic.

Again the null extension effect is used, this time to indicate Sam's subjective point of audition. However, the drone tone increasing in pitch not only suggests imminent impact, it also diffuses where this impact might originate. Since noise reverberation by definition does not indicate a source, every point of offscreen space is a threat to Sam. Similarly, the churn of images of Bumblebee's transformation is too fast to provide spatial orientation, and the clanging peals of metal striking asphalt can also not provide any clear sense of direction.

At stake in both sequences is the turbulent experience of the sound design. Although space is compressed during the slow-motion sequences, this only serves to amplify our sense of anxiety and tension. The concussive editing, alongside the crash-cam, produces a huge number of vector trajectories flying all through the frame, suggesting that any point in the cinematic space might be at risk of crashing objects. The turbulent sound design amplifies this sense by producing more kinetic movement without a clear point of origin. Space implodes into impact, overpowering any sense of time and space we may have. Sound is not used to anchor the actions or movements on screen but to provide its own form of action and movement *on us*. This is why the slow-motion sequences use null extensions, anchoring us directly to *this* sequence, *this* moment, with no regard for greater spatial or narrative continuity. There is not even a sonic continuity, since both offscreen sound and the score cut off without motivation. Chion and Kerins both make much of the fact that sound is exactly the great continuity maker, tying together separate, distinct and at times even fragmented shots and images. For Bay, however, sound is simply another vehicle for sensory overload.

With the velocity exhibited in Bay's sound-images, it is evident to me that watching his films is a form of audio-vision machine, whereby perception becomes automated through sheer intensity of speed. Paradoxically, this excessive sense of audiovisual pyrotechnics becomes in itself a kind of blindness, "the industrialisation of the non-gaze."[16] We sense, but we see nothing: audiovisual technologies "confuse, destroy, and challenge our assumptions about movement".[17] While we watch *Transformers*, the sound-images before us move with such celerity that we perceptually cannot keep up. The transformation of Bumblebee mentioned above is one extreme case of a blur of colors and shapes. However, all the action set pieces move at a pace that is exhausting. While there are of course quiet periods in the films, giving us a chance to catch up with what has happened, when we are in the thick of action, the entire purpose is to move at such a pace as to make perception impossible.

There is, then, a sense of continuity in Bay's films, but it is a visceral continuity rather than a visual one. To put this another way, we do have a continuity of experience while watching Bay's films, but it is not an experience of a hierarchical continuum, expressible through a clear progression through spacetime and narrative. Instead, the experience is of a rhythmic continuity of a surfeit of sensations one moment and a lull or waning of sensations the next. *Transformers'* visceral continuity is affective not cognitive; it reproduces a certain kind of affective entrainment of shifting between two extreme states: dreary stasis or euphoric, delirious movement. Either extreme, of course, serves as kind of monotonous drone; they are two ends of the same spectrum.

Considering the excessive and destructive nature of *Transformers*, Bay's films are extremely anemic. Despite the grandiosity of the imposing wreckage, hardly anyone ever gets hurt. We mostly see grime and dirt cover the human characters, possibly beside a stylishly bleeding cut. Much like contemporary extreme horror is called torture porn, we could call *Transformers havoc porn*, interested in extreme spectacles of utter destruction, without humans getting hurt. Whereas torture porn fetishistically displays the complete ruination of human bodies, *Transformers* displaces its appetite for destruction onto buildings, vehicles and robots. This reveals another paradox for the films. Their intention is to provide the most intense and excessive experience of pure mayhem, yet they must obtain a PG-13 rating in order to demolish the box office. It is therefore desirable to wreck as many buildings as possible, crash as many vehicles as possible, smash as many robots as possible, but never actually show any blood. The desire for violence and injury is thus displaced onto the robots, since robots bleed liquid electricity, which the MPAA has no compunction about. What we are left with, then, are some of the most destruction-filled films in all of film history, yet no one gets hurt. In fact, considering the amount of slapstick comedy interspersed into the films, there is a sense in which these films truly are like amusement park rides: all the adrenaline and excitement, but still good, clean, family entertainment you can trust. We are, in other words, affectively entrained to the fact that devastation is fun and safe.

And yet, if we begin to perceive devastation as fun and safe, as impressively imposing but mostly bloodless, surely this might also inure us to other, real spectacles of destruction. If *Transformers* whets our appetite for destruction, might some form of this appetite not carry over into everyday images of death, war and havoc. Such a scenario is Virilio's fear, because our perception is trained not to recognize the atrocities of war in so far as they resemble the pleasures of cinematic spectacle. Obviously we are aware of when we are watching a *Transformers* film and when we are watching a newscast, but if the one induces a drone state, can we be sure that the other does not? To reiterate, not all viewers will respond to the drone vibrations by carrying them out of the movie theater, but the rhythms of destruction and war increasingly blur between cinema and reality. The issue is not that we cannot distinguish between film and reality, but that our perception is conditioned to not discern between them, to see shock-and-awe strategies on a continuum with shock-and-awe aesthetics.

Sonic Dominance: *Battle: Los Angeles*

While *Transformers* might be the most famous and well-known example of films that attune us to the excitement of destruction, it is far from the only one. Military action films have particularly emphasized extreme versions of audiovisual spectacles as a means of replicating the intensity of combat. The best example of this new war intensity is Steven Spielberg's *Saving Private Ryan*, where the opening scene of Allied troops storming the Normandy beaches became justly famous for its hectic camerawork and frantic editing providing a deeply unsettling experience of being right there on the beaches. From today's perspective, however, *Saving Private Ryan* (1998) might in fact come off as a little vanilla, which only underlines the way it set a new standard – such as its lack of establishing wide shots, instead keeping us tightly in the action, and its shutter angle shots turning live motion into seeming stop motion. Similar camera techniques were used in Ridley Scott's *Gladiator* (2000) during that film's opening battle sequence. The result is hectic and disorienting, seemingly a perfect presentation of war.

However, one aspect easily overlooked is the sound design of these films. As Kerins argues at length, the development of Dolby Digital Sound (DDS), as an improvement on Dolby Surround Sound (DSS), produces an active soundscape rather than a passive one only capable of

155

providing ambient sound. With DDS, sound can move around the cinematic space, thus producing a form of secondary space that can either enhance or run counter to the visual space. Sound, then, becomes a central tool for the technique of droning: the soundtrack can become so intense as to overwhelm us in its own right. Once again, as Kerins points out, *Saving Private Ryan* set a standard by choosing to cut audio *at the same time* as the image. Such an editing strategy draws attention to the cut itself, rather than providing a smooth transition.[18] Yet the advent of an active soundscape allows for greater flexibility in creating immense sonic impact.

Here, Scott's *Black Hawk Down* (2001) is instructive. In keeping with the film's general interest in presenting the scenario as intimately and closely as possible, the soundscape works to produce sensations of proximity to the action. From a sonic perspective, this is done early on in the film, where the sound design produces a deep rumble that unsettles us. If we pick apart the different aspects of the soundscape, we find a deep, resonant bass line from drawn out cellos that functions as the sonic ground when the film opens. Overlaid are a variety of string instruments that suggest Middle-Eastern music, along with a melancholic song in Arabic. The deep cellos linger right on the boundary between score and sound design. Coupled with images of famine and devastation and text describing the horrible state of affairs in Somalia and Mogadishu, a desolate mood is set. The deep bass tones produce an unsettling feeling contra the lament of the rest of the score. Ambient sounds of sea waves produce a sense of space of location, along with the whistling wind. Slowly the wind starts to modulate and pulse, morphing into the rotor sounds of helicopters. At the same time, the beat of the score picks up, becoming more energetic. Arabic speech is heard as the helicopter sounds increase, and the sound becomes distinctly more militaristic. We hear English spoken over radios, and an electric guitar joins the score. We find a tension between the opening dirge, the tension of the bass, the atmospheric sounds that become helicopter sounds and the arrival of US troops. We are slowly introduced to the place of the narrative, pulled in primarily by the sound, with the images working primarily to accentuate the unsettling feelings produced by the sound design.

The film's constant sense of proximity is highly significant. Decontextualizing the conflict, the film focuses solely on one day's events, and the pathos of the troops' actions. We are placed in close proximity to the troops through an emphasis in the sound design on voices, ambience and gunfire. First, the voices of the troops are modified in post-production and enhanced with reverberation, suffusing all the voices with a sense of enormous space, as if they were all speaking within a huge room. The effect makes all the voices appear right next to us, their resonance enveloping us. In a sense, we are brought right into the space of the troops and their dialog, which makes everything feel more intimate. Second, once the assault begins there is no scene which does not feature gunfire in the sonic background. Even in quiet scenes of introspection and self-doubt, where the characters talk about their bad choices and poor decisions, we do not find a lull in the conflict. Permeating the sonic field, the constant presence of gunfire induces a stressful experience of constant and imminent threat. Third, in the combat scenes, when the gunfire is in the forefront of the sound mix, the individual shots are deep, with a limited overhead of higher-pitched tones, and plenty of reverb making the shots sound even deeper. Furthermore, to intensify the sonic mood, constant rumbling bass notes that do not have a direct sound source are added to the mix. This produces a depth of sonic space, but also makes the gunfights more overpowering, sonically. Add to this that the ultra-field is employed to make individual shots come from all around the characters, and we have a full-on auditory overload, which does not reproduce a realistic three-dimensional space, but instead constructs an immersive, energetic soundscape. That we cannot orient ourselves clearly in the cinematic space based on sound direction makes the experience more chaotic. There are sounds that suggest direction, but the majority of undertones and bass drones from nowhere make for a fraught, energetic space rather than a clear, stable one.

This production of an immersive sound emphasizes visceral impact over spatial clarity and falls in line with what we saw at work in *Transformers*, but it has been developed even further in recent films. Sound takes on such expressive potential because it creates a contrast to that of moving images in isolation. Rather than only support, extend and augment the moving images, sound can in fact run counter to or completely color the entire experiential field of watching a film. Furthermore, sound envelops us in a different way than images suffuse us. We can turn away from the moving images, or even close our eyes if the intensity becomes too much. However, it is far more difficult to turn away from sound. With the current emphasis on bass in action films, even covering our ears make little difference, since the bass tones will still vibrate our entire body, acting directly on our nervous system.

One of the best examples of how sound-design bass tones can permeate a film's atmosphere, and even dominate our entire impression of it, is found in *Battle: Los Angeles*. While the film's narrative is quite conventional, its audiovisual design sets it apart from earlier alien invasion films. The plot is straightforward: aliens invade Earth along a number of coastal cities. In Los Angeles, a platoon of Marines is assigned to rescue civilians out of Santa Monica before an air raid levels it. The platoon encounters a group of soldiers trying to escape Santa Monica along the way. Learning that the aliens seek out and kill humans by the use of drones, the platoon tries to leave in a bus, leading to a massive shoot out on the I-10 freeway. They reach the evacuation point, but learn that the military is retreating from Los Angeles and also that there is an alien vessel that commands all the drones. The platoon heroically recons the area and paints the vessel with an electronic target so that air support can blow it up. Returning to base, the heroic Marines relay how to defeat the aliens to the other coastal cities, thus saving Earth.

Ideologically, it is easy enough to see the film as a recuperative trauma narrative dealing with 9/11 and the subsequent wars in Afghanistan and Iraq. Consider the setup of unknown enemies striking suddenly and unexpectedly, without any immediate motivation or reason. Furthermore, it is impossible to communicate with this unknown enemy, who does not even seem to have a language. Our main protagonist Michael Nantz (Aaron Eckhart) has not only served in Iraq and Afghanistan, but is in fact 2/5, or 2nd Battalion 5th Marines, the most highly decorated battalion of the Marine Corps. The alien invasion offers an easy way to engage with a situation similar to 9/11, but one in which the US military can be victorious. The Marines are cast as heroes who race to protect civilians in Santa Monica, only to discover, almost accidentally, how to vanquish the enemy. As such, the film offers the opportunity to "get it right" this time and to show "what the troops are really doing" during war time. Gone are all the complicated issues of invasion, weapons of mass destruction and anything else that might stand in the way of battle heroics. Precisely for this reason, the film's audiovisual shock-and-awe technique of completely overloading our senses becomes a way to wash away any objections or hesitations one might have about war. In other words, the film drones away resistance by overpowering our senses and leaving us dumbfounded through its immense sound design.

Taking place in a spectacular vista of destruction in the middle of Santa Monica, the location looks like a war-torn Middle-Eastern city, thus activating memories of newscasts from Iraq and producing resonances with the war on terror. The audiovisual style throughout the film is a handheld mockumentary style. However, this is interspersed with a number of more conventional shots that provide a sense of clarity and stability. The technique is clear: provide a few stable medium to medium wide shots that allow us to orient ourselves in space and give us a sense of the destruction and mayhem taking place. Similarly, many of these shots, and even the tighter shots, use depth of field to provide glimpses of a broader canvas of devastation. There are several instances when we glimpse collapsed buildings, alien drones, smoke and other signs of mayhem over the shoulders of the characters. Or a shot cranes up from a medium shot to give us a wide shot of a wasted urban landscape. The film thus manages to provide a general mood of wreckage, while mostly staying close to the troops.

The handheld camera style employed in most of the action sequences thrusts us into the action and often makes it feel claustrophobic and tight. We often feel that aliens may be lurking right around the corner and only get brief glimpses of the surrounding area. Several camerawork techniques are employed to make the scenes feel frantic. Tight framing with a shaky, handheld style makes everything shift and tilt, providing a sense of movement but no sense of what is actually in frame. Similarly, the camera often settles on a framing, only to swerve and then reframe or, alternatively, zoom in on the subject. All these techniques indicate movement and tension, and while we get a general notion of what the characters are doing and where they are, the blurry images of the constantly shifting camera make it impossible to get a clear orientation. This has the added value of making it hard to distinguish the set design, the acting and the blocking. The camera essentially obfuscates more than it reveals, working primarily to create a sense of agitation and urgency, while covering any goofs or continuity errors that might creep in.

Once again, continuity is not the primary concern for this film. The production of energy that comes from a rapidly moving camera and equally rapid editing works to generate an impression of extreme speed and frantic movement. As such, one might be led to believe that the sound design would be essential in terms of creating a coherent whole. And to some extent, that is true, but not in the way of classical continuity. The sound design establishes a general mood and atmosphere, a larger sonic environment that the characters move around in. However, this sonic environment works in a similar fashion to the obscuring camera; we hear indirect sounds constantly, and with the use of the ultrafield, sounds move around. These sonic trajectories clearly establish a full environment, but since most of the sounds are indirect, they actually work to unsettle us: we have no idea whether the sound objects will hit us and the characters, or if they fly past us.

Chion's term acousmatic sound helps us understand what these sounds are, but it only goes so far. Chion explicitly defines acousmatic sound as sound that is not visualized.[19] He goes on to argue that these sounds, even when they are never visualized and remain offscreen, work to establish an ambience, and he calls offscreen sounds territory sounds.[20] However, this distinction depends on the sounds being passive, i.e. that they only work to suggest space and location, such as bird-song in a forest or church bells near a cemetery. The sonic trajectories in *Battle: Los Angeles* are active: they move around the aural environment and work to produce an environment of tension and agitation. These sounds, then, are not territory sounds but *ecological sounds*, part of a holistic whole that cannot be separated into passive and active pieces: all the sounds are active, moving around to suggest a lively, if tension-filled, ecology. In fact, it is this sonic ecology that produces a sense of tension and fear.

Nowhere is this sonic ecology clearer than in the film's climax. The climax presents us with the intrepid Marines attempting to "paint the target," i.e. shining a laser light on the alien craft so that automated missiles can hit it. Hopefully, destroying this craft will cut off the alien drones that seek out any humans and kill them. The scene starts with Nantz getting out of the helicopter to recon the area where the alien craft is believed to be. Although Nantz at first does so alone, his platoon chooses to follow him. As the Marines run below ground, the scene kicks into gear when the immense alien craft is revealed in a wide shot that shows the top just jutting out from the freeway bridge. Sonically, the soundtrack moves from a restrained, tension-filled slow score to a huge booming crescendo as the craft comes into view. This conventional use of music is supported by a rumbling drone tone that wobbles around the audio channels. At first the rumbling drone tone is masked by occupying the same frequency as the score, but as the score recedes, the drone tone becomes more prominent. This functions as a kind of switch-over, where the soundscape moves from score to drone tone almost unnoticeably. To further this sensation, the mix has scooped out the mid-range, which means that, for the introduction shot, there are only deep and high tones. All the mid-range tones have been removed to further the impression of scale and grandeur. What the opening shot of the alien craft does, then, is to sonically produce size and scale. The booming sounds and the wobble of the drone tones create the impression of an immense craft, which is difficult to do otherwise, since most of it is underground and there is nothing on the horizon to provide a visual sense of scale.

Nantz and his Marines crawl up a ladder to the road with aliens in hot pursuit. To gain a little time, Nantz hurls a grenade down the ladder tunnel, and the explosion comes right as the score reaches a high crescendo, with strings and bright brass horns. The booming of the explosion roars up, immediately followed by a decrease in amplitude of all environmental sounds, as well as the score. This effect depends on the ear's acoustic reflex. Our ears instinctively contract their muscles to protect the cochlea from loud noises. By reducing the sound immediately following the explosion, the sound design reproduces the same result, in effect tricking our ears into thinking that we have just heard a deafening boom. As the Marines all run from the explosion, dust showering over them, low rumbling noises are heard, but the score reduces in amplitude, employing only strings. Again, these low amplitude sounds make the sound sources appear far away, creating a lacunae in the middle of all the chaos. The voices of the Marines all appear closer to us, reproducing the kind of intimacy we found in *Black Hawk Down*. For us to hear what they are saying as they discuss their plan, there needs to be a bit of calm, but low rumbles keep a sense of tension in place. We are brought into close proximity with the Marines, though, which establishes an emotional alignment with them, making the scene more tense.

The hectic pace continues above ground as the Marines disperse to blow up the alien craft. Lieutenant Corporal Kerns (Jim Parrack) moves to a high point to radio in for air support. From this vantage, he shoots an alien, saving the other Marines. However, this has revealed his position to the alien drones, and one of them blasts the tower, killing him. As the alien drone hovers right next to Kerns, there is a high amplitude drone tone that warbles across all audio channels. The overtones are full of static, electrical sounds that diffuse into garbled noise, making the drone sound alien. Glitch noises and electrical sparks fly all over, providing a tense lead-in to the booming blast. Once again, the boom of the explosion that kills Kerns is followed by a dip in amplitude, increasing the impact of the explosion's sound. A continued rumble leads into a mournful horn section before the scene shifts back to gunfire and higher pitched strings punctuated by drums and kettledrums. Alternating between rapid bursts of gunfire and explosions, the soundtrack is chaotic and exceedingly loud. This reaches a preliminary climax when the first rocket blasts the antenna of the alien craft, making the Marines whoop and rejoice, thinking that it is over.

A deep continuous crackling clamor signals that the battle is not over. The alien craft lifts out of the rubble, and the Marines must scramble to make sure the rest of the missiles hit the craft. With the drones protecting the craft, we hear the sonic trajectories of the missiles whip past, booming as they strike the drones. Swirling peals of explosion move all around the ultrafield, providing a sense of pure chaos. As the last missile streaks toward the craft, Nantz grabs the laser target and yells to Technical Sergeant Elena Santos (Michelle Rodriguez) to blast the drone to clear a path. Selflessly standing up in the middle of the combat zone, Nantz succeeds in lighting up the craft and the missile strikes it. The ensuing explosion is the loudest and deepest crashing roar of the entire film, continuing far longer than the other explosions. Beneath this is a deep, ululating drone tone, which indicates the crash of the alien craft, though it is not otherwise visualized or located in an offscreen sound. *(See Figure 6.4 in the insert.)* Rather, this drone tone is the sonificiation of the crash. Significantly, the craft does not explode as a massive fireball, the way one might expect. Instead, the impact of the crash is rendered through sound rather than image. In other words,

Battle: Los Angeles in fact privileges sound over image, even in a sequence where we would conventionally expect stunning visual spectacles.

The overpowering sound is produced by employing ultra low frequency vibrations, which fall within the infrasound range. Infrasound cannot be heard directly, as it exists on the periphery of human hearing, but it can be felt. As Goodman has shown, filmmakers deliberately add these infrasound ranges to intensify the felt experience of the film.[21] While images can often be endured, since we have all learned to interpret and manage extremely disturbing images, sound has not been culturally curtailed in the same way. What ultra low frequency sounds can do is to make your body shake, even to the point of making you feel nauseous and panicky for no clear reason (since the source is not visible). Admittedly, sensing the ultra low frequency sounds requires either watching the film in a cinema or in a home cinema with the proper audio setup. Yet whether or not an individual viewer can feel the infrasound, it is clear that the film is designed to produce uncomfortable vibrations and rhythms in the viewer.

Sound is intensified into an overpowering force, which seeks to modulate us into a specific bodily state that we cannot escape, because its effect is not visible nor exactly audible, although it is felt. In this way, sound becomes a weapon: as conceptualized by Goodman, "a weapon in a war of perception, a war whose battlefield is the body (its sensations, reflexes, and habitual ticks)."[22] Goodman's argument follows the Italian Futurists and Paul Virilio and is in large part inspired by all of them. Where Goodman extends their argument is in the way he connects sound's vibrational force with a larger affective mobilization that expands from individual responses to larger collective networks. Goodman insists that sound can be one of the strategies through which "mediatic moods" can disseminate and disperse through a culture.[23]

What *Battle: Los Angeles* reveals is that sound can work as a force directly on our bodies, unbeknownst to us. Deploying ultra low frequencies, although not particular to this film, produces what we can call *sonic dominance*. Sound becomes so intense that it is no longer heard, only felt. Such sonic dominance colors our entire sensory-perceptual field and in large part determines how we understand the images we see. *Battle: Los Angeles* sticks out in the way it actually abandons the visual in many places in favor of the audio-visceral. Considering the deployment of ultra low

163

frequencies, it is hardly overstating facts to designate its force as visceral rather than visual. Rattling, clanking and uneven, the film's visual aesthetic becomes a kind of blur, in its own way a form of blindness. Often we only get a vague sense of what is happening in the frame, but we never escape the impact of the sound design. Constantly working to produce a greater sense of tension and anxiety, the ultrafield also works to drone out any response other than pure force.

There is a significant overlap between how the ultrafield works to color the scenes of destruction and how at the same time it brings us close to the Marines. Sonically, Goodman would say vibrationally, we are aligned with the Marines, but we are also made to experience the scenes of destruction as simultaneously unsettling and awe-inspiring. The drone tones are always signals of imminent threat, but they are simultaneously signals of exhilarating action. If there is any kind of conditioning in terms of how these vibrations make us feel, then it is a complex tangle of excitement and tension, both gratifying and intimidating. Clearly a paradoxical combination, this is precisely the state of apprehension: we wish to grasp the moments in the film, as at the same time we are afraid of losing our sensory grip. This apprehension thus explains how we both desire and fear the tension of the drone tones; they provide us with both exhilarating and intimidating sensations. Sonic dominance exerts influence: it is a force to make us feel, despite those feelings not being pleasant.

There is a strong connection, although unstated, between Goodman's affective mobilizations and structures of feeling. The sonic dominance of cinema's sound design can be regarded as one of the ways in which we are positioned within a larger environment of affects that connect us to a collective. As a collective experience, the apprehension enacted by a film's sound design does not designate what we might call emotional determination: the idea that everyone will feel the same thing. Films are designed to make us feel in very specific ways. In *Battle: Los Angeles*, there is a distinctive sense of exhilaration and intimidation mingled in the drone tones of the aliens. Yet we can find similar instances of immense sound design producing variations on these affective moods, such as the near state of frenzy we are placed in during the frantic, never-ending assault of *The Raid* (Gareth Evans 2011). Here, the relentless barrage of bullets induces constant bursts of adrenaline, interspersed only by brief moments of martial arts combat. For *The Raid*, it is the gunfire speed that becomes an adrenaline drone, but the effect is much the same: constant agitation that is both thrilling and menacing.

The sensations produced by the sound design of these films color our perception and tie into a larger, shared environment. While we may not all articulate the sensations in the same way, everyone will recognize the structures of feeling that these films engage with and hook into. The sonic dominance becomes a sub-perceptual mode of inducing specific rhythms in the viewer, rhythms that ripple outward and are not individual but collective. As Goodman argues, this becomes a war of perception, because it connects to a larger feeling or cultural mood. While the drone tones of ultra low frequency are below our threshold of conscious perception, they are not beyond sensory impact. Precisely because they are not consciously perceived, we do not notice that they change and alter our bodily rhythms. We cannot help but feel out of breath and agitated during these films, simply because of the bodily impact the sound has. This state of agitation simultaneously produces and participates in a larger culture of fear.

Goodman uses the term "ecology of fear," taken from Mike Davis' work on Los Angeles, although I have preferred the term culture of fear so far.[24] A culture of fear is one that produces a slow, unsettling rhythm of things on the precipice, a sense that something bad is waiting just around the corner, that disaster can strike at any moment. Goodman broadens Davis' notion in order to suggest that contemporary culture vibrates with this sense of fear and apprehension, the war on terror being the emblematic example. Terrorism is something that can strike at any moment, without warning and for no apparent reason. While the apprehension induced by *Battle: Los Angeles* is a mix of thrill and fear, it is perhaps best to consider the film a compensatory affective resolution of a constant climate of dread. Dread, which Goodman takes to be an affect best elicited by sound, is a diffuse, nonspecific feeling of anxious anticipation. This is precisely the sensation evoked by *Battle: Los Angeles*, but with a solution: the heroic marines. Although they are afraid, they refuse to give up, continuing to fight. The final moment in the film reinforces this: Nantz and his harried platoon return tired and victorious to the base, but when they learn that more troops are going back, they re-up and go back with them. As tireless as they are courageous, these Marines become a kind of substitute or prosthesis for our affective dread. They are the ones who will make us feel better. The film's rhythm educes a similar rhythm of dread in us, but we are rewarded with a victorious thrill by engaging with the film. In other words, the film connects to and participates in the culture of fear: it both produces fear and provides affective relief from it. That is the other side of sonic dominance: although we are dominated, we are also recompensed by the thrill and exhilaration of the film. We recognize in the film the same dread of unexpected attack and catastrophe that we live through every day, yet we leave it feeling better about that, knowing that the military shields us for what might come.

Intimate Rhythms: *The Hurt Locker*

Not all films that so utilize sound design necessarily share the ideological expression of *Battle: Los Angeles*. Some can be said to produce a kind of counter-rhythm to the culture of fear. While sonic dominance can elicit the mixed sensations of thrill and fear, and so connect to a larger sense of anxious anticipation, the rhythms of sound design may also be used to disrupt and estrange us from the images. Just as Brian De Palma's *Redacted* (2007) employs a mélange of different images to produce an irruption of affects that must necessarily make us ponder the engagement in Iraq, so Kathryn Bigelow's *The Hurt Locker* utilizes a distinctive audiovisual design to similarly shake our preconceptions loose. Once again, while individual response will vary, the affective mood of the film is unmistakeable. The central preoccupation of the film's design is clearly contrary to that of *Battle: Los Angeles'* morale-fortifying expression.

The Hurt Locker manages, instead, to interject into and disrupt our bodily rhythms, as well as the conventional, anticipated rhythms of the war film. This arrhythmia is achieved in a number of ways. The narrative form offers no redemption and no heroics for any of the characters. Instead, we find a minimalist, episodic structure that both presents and undercuts the traditional, pleasurable rhythms of war films, in which spectacle joins moral justification and psychological depth to produce a justifiable war, such as in the recent *Edge of Tomorrow* (Doug Liman 2014). Even classic anti-war films, such as *The Deer Hunter* (Michael Cimino 1978) and *Apocalypse Now* (Francis Ford Coppola 1979), delve into the psychologies of soldiers to survey the damage of war. *The Hurt Locker* produces an intimate connection with the soldiers but never engages in overt self-reflection, justification or criticism. Instead, I believe, the film's rhythm is what determines its stance on war and the effects of war.

The Hurt Locker takes its name from military slang originating during the Vietnam War, indicating everything from undergoing a period of physical or emotional pain to being in a painful condition; but more specifically it means to be inside the killing blast radius of a bomb. As far as the film's story goes, all these meanings apply. Focusing on an Explosive Ordnance Disposal unit (EOD) in Iraq, the film opens on the death of the unit's leader, Matthew Thompson (Guy Pearce), during a bomb dismantling gone wrong. William James (Jeremy Renner) takes over, a far more reckless soldier, who often disobeys protocol. During five loosely connected incidents, we follow the unit going about its harrowing job of dismantling bombs. James establishes a rapport with an Iraqi boy, nicknamed Beckham (Christopher Sayegh). When James finds Beckham in a warehouse, turned into a body bomb, he ends up trying to find those responsible. Unsuccessful, James continues with his work, only to encounter Beckham later. James does not acknowledge that he recognizes Beckham, although the reason is unclear. As the unit's rotation ends, they all return back home, but James chooses to go back in rotation, confessing that there is only one thing he loves: dismantling bombs in Iraq. This return to war fulfills the Chris Hedges quote that opens the film: war is a drug. James is incapable of escaping the intense rhythms of war, and so returns. This seems to me to be the ultimate tragedy of the film, although it is not presented directly as such. But we see how out of sync James feels at home, and why he must leave it behind to experience life fully.

In stark contrast to the other films discussed in this chapter and the conventional aesthetic form of most action-oriented war films, *The Hurt Locker* is surprising in its insistence on quietude and drawn-out waiting. Other Iraq war films, such as *Green Zone* (Paul Greengrass 2010) or *The Kingdom* (Peter Berg 2007), not to mention action films dressed up as war films, like *Battleship* (Peter Berg 2011), follow the hectic speed of *Battle: Los Angeles*. There is constant action and gunfire, and even the calmer moments carry the plot forward. *The Hurt Locker* similarly alternates between calm moments and eruptions of intense chaos; however, the sound and the camerawork differ radically from one to the other. Unlike *Battle: Los Angeles*, which consistently employs the handheld camera-style, *The Hurt Locker* shifts between conventional continuity style scenes, which provide clear situational orientation, and extreme handheld camera-style, in which the camera not only follows the character but runs at such a speed that the image becomes too jumbled to perceive.

The opening scene provides a good example of the chaotic visual style of the film. The film opens without a title on a rickety low moving shot of gravel and empty cans. We hear someone speaking Arabic but have no other way of orienting ourselves. Cut to a tracking shot of a small, belt-driven robot and people running around in kaftans and uniforms, and we begin to get a sense of place. The scene is shot in a handheld style, with unmotivated zooms and reframing, which block any kind of situational orientation other than a general impression of this being a war zone. Even wide shots are handheld and often pan around. Abruptly, we shift to the primary action of bomb disabling; the soldiers calmly talk about directing the robot properly to get it to the bomb. All the direct, turbulent sound disappears, and except for a low dirge in Arabic in the background, we can only hear the metallic clink of the robot, the remote control and the relaxed banter of the soldiers. While the camerawork remains handheld, the jittery motion stops, and the editing pace slows down considerably. Calm descends on the scene, and it feels like another day at the office. When an Iraqi man is suddenly seen with a cell phone, it is announced sonically, with a high-pitched tone. Events turn frantic, and the frenetic camerawork returns as the soldiers start yelling. A slow, deep beat begins picking up and grows increasingly louder and deeper, anticipating a blast we now expect to be coming. Thompson begins to run away from the bomb, but the Iraqi man punches a quick sequence of numbers on his phone and the bomb goes off. In super-slow, we see the cloud of smoke rising, a close-up of gravel and dirt lifting, and finally, Thompson falling over, head smashing into the helmet. The sound of the explosion is slowed down similarly, producing a prolonged, rolling thunder effect that reverberates slowly. This makes us feel as if we are inside the blast helmet with Thompson. We can also hear Thompson's breathing under the booming blast, furthering the intimacy and closeness we feel. Just like that, the character of a major, prominent actor has died unexpectedly.

The combination of super-slow images and sound makes the blast waves perceptible. We see the dirt lift off a car, which visually shows the force of impact, otherwise difficult to convey. Overlapping editing shows the explosion from different perspectives and different proximities, possibly suggesting different character points of view, but more likely simply repeating the explosion to increase the effect and prolong both the visual and sonic aspects of the event. A high-pitched rising tone comes in at the end of the boom, after which it fades, leaving us with a deadening quiet of only pebbles and dust falling on the ground. This quiet allows us to absorb what happened as the screen goes black. Unlike *Battle: Los Angeles* and more conventional action and war films, silence is used a lot throughout *The Hurt Locker*, a feature which is highlighted by the predominant lack of score. While there is a score, it does not intrude on every scene, but is used far more sparingly. This restrained use produces a more minimalist effect, which does not guide our emotional responses to the same degree. Without a score to guide or interpret the scenes for us, the film manages to infuse a sense of trepidation into every single shot. Banal dialog scenes take on a different tone without a musical guide, while tense scenes leave us straining to hear anything, since the score does not stress the tempo of the scene.

A good example of this is the encounter with the private military contractors in the desert. Initially a tense sequence, in which we are led to believe that the EOD unit are insurgents, once the mistake is cleared up, we get a placid scene of soldiers talking amongst each other and the leader (Ralph Fiennes) joking with his men. The camerawork is similarly restrained, providing another relaxed lacunae, and we feel ourselves settle into the easy banter. Suddenly a bullet comes from nowhere and kills one of the contractors, and a gunfight ensues against the snipers. The contractor leader grabs a high-powered rifle, attempting to shoot the snipers hiding in a little house. Due to the long distance, both the sniper and the contractor aim carefully, with an assistant guiding their accuracy. The contractor misses his shot, and with no sound except a dull thud and a groan is himself shot dead. Another high-profile actor dead within minutes of being introduced. James and Sanborn (Anthony Mackie) grab the rifle and kill several insurgents. Since they cannot be sure how many insurgents are in the house, a prolonged sequence follows where James and Sanborn do

169

nothing but look at the house through their scope. A total of four minutes are spent, most of the sequence consisting of close-ups of faces, which get more and more sandy, or extreme close-ups of eyes or lips with flies crawling on them. (*See Figure 6.5 in the insert.*) A clear expression of immobility and fatigue settles over the sequence as Eldridge (Brian Geraghty) has to get a juice pack for them and time keeps passing. As the sun begins to set, James acknowledges that it is over.

This scene is followed by a scene of the unit listening to loud music and beating each other, presumably to release the tension of the gunfight and the ceaseless waiting. For us the wait is insufferable, too, the quiet and stillness of the shots in stark contrast to the otherwise frenzied action. This stillness makes the wait tense and often makes even minimal sounds terrifying. Once again, the lack of score makes it impossible for us to really predict what will happen, or if anything will happen. Similarly, the unpredictability of who will be killed is increased by big name actors dying within minutes of being introduced. The unit is portrayed by relatively unknown actors – Jeremy Renner was a rising star at the time, but both Anthony Mackie and Brian Geraghty have mostly played supporting roles. This choice is not in itself usual or particularly meaningful, but audiences recognize big name actors and expect these actors to play significant parts. In the case of *The Hurt Locker*, this expectation is undercut twice. Because there is no specific reason why Guy Pearce or Ralph Fiennes should portray those two particular characters, my contention is that it is solely to increase the surprise of their deaths, since our immediate assumption is that the character is central because of the star power of the actor. Killing them off almost nonchalantly suggests that anything can happen, anyone can be killed at any moment.[25]

In terms of the unit, it is striking how little we see them interact with other soldiers. For obvious reasons, they are isolated from other troops when performing their jobs, but even when they are back at the base we rarely see them interact with others. The main exception is the friendship that James establishes with Beckham, a seeming parallel to his own much younger son. The larger effect of this is to produce a high degree of closeness with the three main characters, simply because we are not given access to other characters' thoughts or feelings. We are brought close to the unit through the intensity of their experiences, something that is expressed primarily through the audiovisual rhythm of the film. Long, drawn-out sequences where nothing happens, but we fear that something might, contrast with frenzied moments of action or tension-filled bomb searches, creating a rhythm of intimacy, of closeness. And yet running counter to that intimacy is the disconnection of always communicating through radios, static hissing, the bomb-suit cutting James off from his environment, which mirrors the disconnect the unit feels from life at home. James mentions that he is not sure if he is in a relationship, since he married his girlfriend, then divorced her, yet she still lives in his house. Sanborn has a girlfriend but does not want a child, and Eldridge constantly talks to the camp's psychiatrist, worrying that for him "to be all you can be" (an old US Army slogan) is to be killed by a roadside bomb.

One of the most intense and intimate scenes of the film comes when the unit is called out to a car bomb, where James has to go inside the car to locate the wires. The scene opens in much the same way that the other bomb dismantling scenes do: the unit is called in on suspicion of a bomb, and a perimeter is cleared. James goes to investigate the car, while Sanborn and Eldridge keep watch. James tries to force open the trunk with a crowbar, but ends up kicking the trunk open in frustration, the loud bang of the reckless act shocking us. The soundscape is quiet, with only the direct sounds of James working, and the score intones a tension-filled whine. As he stops dead in surprise, we hear the sound of a jet passing overhead, which functions as offscreen sound and yet emotes the surprise and suspense of the massive bomb inside the car. James' reckless side is shown as he carelessly flings off his bomb suit and crawls into the car.

James' parts are filmed inside the car in close-ups and medium close-ups as he attempts to find the wires for the bomb. These are contrasted by exterior shots that are far more jittery, with swoosh pans to look at the onlooking Iraqis. The effect is one of uncomfortable claustrophobia inside the car, where at any moment James could die in an explosion, and vulnerability outside, where we feel too out in the open. Two different kinds of threat are navigated in the scene, alternating to produce maximum stress. James cuts up the car seats, making tearing and cutting noises in an otherwise quiet soundscape. Even outside we only hear the direct sound of characters talking. There is no score, and there are no ambient sounds to produce a broader environment. This lack of ambient sounds collapses everything onto the characters, making us feel cut off from the environment we are in. This isolation is doubled when James throws away his headset to be able to concentrate fully on the task at hand, even though all the civilians have been evacuated and he no longer needs to keep working. James' dedication is both heroic and reckless, suggesting a restless excitement in which we both want him to continue and to stop. This excitement is intensified by the lack of sound, the complete stillness making us fear any sound. *(See Figure 6.6 in the insert.)* We jump as much as James when he slowly and carefully pulls out the car radio looking for the wires and the windshield wipers kick in. The frozen reaction that shifts into a relaxed expression, with a raised eyebrow and him saying "Interesting," simultaneously presents James as cocky, in control and possibly having a death wish. His reaction makes us relax a little more, until the score kicks in with its high-pitched whine and bass drums, setting a stressful pace. Sanborn and Eldridge worry about the increasing number of Iraqis gathering to look on, knowing that any one of them could set off the bomb, as we saw in the film's opening scene. The roar of a jet going over the square comes in again, rising to the point where we worry that a bomb will go off in tune with drawn-out bass strings. James continues his work, locates the activating switch and casually throws the box over his shoulder, resolving the matter. We hear James' ragged breathing as the tension concludes.

We are made afraid of sounds, not simply by sounds. Any sound, especially loud noises, shock us because it could be the bomb. Silence, then, becomes the greatest effect of *The Hurt Locker*, because it makes any subsequent sound more of a threat and shock. The silence inevitably draws us in, and we strain to see and hear what James is doing and how Sanborn and Eldridge cope with the onlooking Iraqis. Trepidation mounts through silence rather than extremity of soundscape. Although Chion generally argues that silence separates us from the action, that does not hold true in this case.[26] Every space has its own silence, as Chion argues, but there are a few ambient tones added to the background of the car scene. This produces a null extension which draws us further into the scene: we want more information, yet are worried that we will hear an explosion.

This spare use of sound creates a sense of intimacy with the unit. We experience their vulnerability by projecting ourselves into the environment, feeling as if we are right there. But entering this environment generally means entering through a space of noises, static and hisses. We perceive the ragged breath of James, the crackling of radios, the scrape of metal as sounds that are close to us; they are intimate sounds, sounds we would often not pay attention to in everyday situations and which are rarely prominent in a film's sound design. Integrating the score and the sound design into each other allows for a collapse of the cinematic space, which further pulls us in. There is no safe zone in which we can position ourselves, particularly because the sound design is set up as a full sound envelope, meaning that the sound comes from all angles on a proper sound system. Combine that with the immense subsonic bass of the explosions, which are amplified because of the predominance of silence in the film, and we get a very different soundscape than what we find in *Transformers* or *Battle: Los Angeles*.

In fact, I believe it is the function of what Goodman calls "bass materialism" that ends up estranging us from the situation that the unit is in. Bass materialism, as Goodman defines it, is the "rearrangement of the senses" in which hearing takes on more prominence in a "flatter, more equal sensory ratio."[27] That is to say, our visual over-dependence is reduced in favor of more full-bodied sensory impressions. All the micro-sounds that we rarely pay attention to are amplified to fill up the soundscape, which is what makes the sonic impressions of *The Hurt Locker* so different from other films. We have no choice but to experience the film more intimately than most war films and action films, which includes even a weird intimacy with the bombs. We are placed so close to the bombs and their wires that we do feel a kind of connection to them, even as the connection is antagonistic. It makes sense, therefore, that James keeps all the switches that could have killed him under his bed. Similarly, this intimacy with the bombs also undercuts the traditional control and mastery we feel through the protagonist. As Lisa Purse points out, James often "asserts his mastery over both the environment and the events unfolding within it despite the risks."[28] This is true, yet the bass materialism of the soundscape undercuts that mastery in the way that threats constantly come via sound rather than vision. Clicks, whirrs and rattles are what make us tense up, and no amount of visual mastery can protect us from that.

Clearly James is skilled and in control, but we also sense the way that his mastery comes not only from skill but also from fascination with and desire for the bombs' simplicity and clarity. When James returns home, he is overwhelmed by choices in the supermarket's aisles as infinite variations of pizzas and cereals stretch as far as the eye can see. Cleaning gutters or mushrooms present none of the intensity of experience that deactivating bombs do, and the final shot of James, back in Iraq, walking alone towards another bomb threat, mixes the mythic image of a cowboy riding into the sunset with an isolation and disconnection we have never experienced in James before. Yet it is also an image of leaving, although not necessarily of death. Whereas Sanborn and Eldridge both leave the war and want to go home, in the end James has no mastery over his situation and must go back. We are left with James out of control, completely in the grip of war as drug. We welcome the affective modulation, because fear is what produces energy and intensity of experience. This echoes Bourke's argument that the pain of fear is what produces its pleasure.

The Hurt Locker deliberately plays with the elicitation of adrenaline and trepidation, the intimate rhythms of draggingly slow non-events interspersed with extremes of tension producing a unique feel to the film. There is a constant vibration of stress throughout every scene, an ominous undercurrent even in the scenes with Beckham or when the unit lets off steam that colors our perception of the film. We build intimacy through bodily proximity to the characters, the way they breathe and mumble to each other, or yell and scream. Close-ups of them sweating and waiting also bring us closer to them, and this closeness is what makes the action sequences so tense. Our immersion into their world functions not only on a visual level but on a visceral level, a level we cannot escape from. What the film masters, though, is how it engages us with the rush of adrenaline in its tension-filled scenes but also critiques this rush of excitement. When Eldridge is airlifted out of the war zone because he has been shot in the leg, he blames James' recklessness and need for adrenaline. Earlier, Sanborn even briefly suggests that James might get killed by a bad fuse or other accident in order that the two of them would no longer be at risk because of James' desire for danger.

This adrenaline rhythm places us in a peculiar position. On the one hand, we clearly recognize James' dangerous behavior and the risk he poses for the unit as a whole. On the other hand, his actions are also what produce the most intense engagements with the film. So, either we enjoy the film and accept, at least to some extent, James' daredevil acts, or we reject James' actions, which cuts us off from enjoying the film. We can call this the fundamental choice of the film's articulation of lines of force. Many soldiers have spoken out against the film's representation of the EOD unit, pointing to all the ways that James would be disciplined for his behavior. For this reason, they cannot enjoy the film. As someone who has fortunately never been in a war zone, I have absolutely no insight into the realism of the film's representation of war and soldiers, and can only take the words of those more experienced than I to be true. Yet this does allow me to fully enjoy the film, to plunge myself into the scenes right alongside James, even as I feel uncomfortable doing so. This, I take it, is far closer to the film's intended trajectory: that we are drawn into the force of the film and find it hard to leave, despite the doubts we surely experience in terms of James' actions and the war as a whole. This emulates the notion that war is a drug and the habit is hard to kick. The film's elicitation of sensations of stress, adrenaline rush and trepidation produces a beguiling rhythm that is difficult to resist. Yet in accepting it, I allow my self to be articulated in a very specific way: accept the conditions of war and you will even find some enjoyment in it.

That articulation is exactly the predicament that Chris Hedges constantly debates in his *War is a Force that Gives Us Meaning* from which the film's opening quote is taken. Although no one likes the idea of war, war has a way of becoming its own justification, because war gives "purpose, meaning, a reason for living."[29] Hedges fully admits to having been caught up in this feeling, but also points out that when we inject the drug of war, "we feel what those we strive to destroy feel."[30] While I am sure that many people engaged in war would disagree with this sentiment, for the purpose of *The Hurt Locker*, the point stands, because it allows us to recognize why we might enjoy the film but still feel uncomfortable with this enjoyment. We recognize the algebra of need that James is under because we feel the same bodily surge. The film allows the complexity of war's sensations to come to the forefront, to give us a sense of what it feels like to be caught up in the tension, trepidation and excitement that a war zone is. Clearly, the film is in no way the same as being in a war, but by rhythmically engaging us, pulling us into the complexity of war, it opens up a much broader understanding of military engagement. That, in itself, is its strategy of estrangement, the way we are presented with sensations of war. We are also exposed to the complex articulations of fear, how fear's intensity can entrain us so much that we miss it.

Certainly this is the film's final accusation, then. We continue war because we miss the intensity when it is gone. And considering the criticism that the US Army leveled against *The Hurt Locker*, they clearly agree. Why else would they worry about a marginal film, even if it did go on to win an Oscar? Because the film reveals the inherent structure of feeling that informs war: more. War produces its own cause through its intensities and becomes its own reason for continuing. More intensity, more bombs, more boots on the ground, more of everything. War is excess, which is why war is a machine: it is designed to produce more of itself through the production of intensity. And that is what *The Hurt Locker* exposes, that the intensities of war will only produce more war. But it also exposes the fact that we are all embroiled in this production, and that there is no outside to intensity.

Anaisthesis

The overwhelming, destructive capacities of contemporary action cinema's sound-images produce a deafening roar that, despite the inventiveness and intensity of these spectacular displays, induces a certain repetitiveness that suggest the verb form of drone: a dull, monotonous hum or buzz with no variation. This audiovisual drone has the capacity to drone out our capacity to respond to them with anything but a liminal state, which I will call *anaisthesis*, a state in which we respond automatically to the films, with little space left for reflection. What happens in an anaisthetic state is that reason becomes background noise. Our cognitive function, which is usually focal in terms of how our experience is interpreted and integrated into our bodies, is droned out in favor of pure, unadulterated agitation. By consistently and constantly undercutting any form of stability or spatiotemporal coherence, the droning sound-images deny and reject any form of cognitive integration through their sheer intensity.

By feeling ourselves to be inside the sound-images, yet incapable of making sense of them or orient ourselves in them, we are stunned. This is a bodily experience, in which our own bodily rhythms are pushed aside in favor of the film's rhythms, as manifested both in its editing rhythms and its sonic rhythms. Deeply disturbing, this kind of arrhythmia suggests a battle to see which rhythm will succeed; our's or the film's. Anaisthesis reduces our cognitive functions in favor of immediate, sensorial affective entrainment: we are awed by the sheer magnitude of audiovisual power exhibited by the films. We are worked over by these films, but the work takes place "under our radar," in the interval before affect and sensation become emotion and perception. We are, in this sense, conditioned by the sound-images.

The best way to think about this, I believe, is to draw on Whitehead's distinction between two modes of perception: those of presentational immediacy and causal efficacy. The more classically understood mode is presentational immediacy, through which the world is consciously perceived as a continuum, i.e. we recognize what we see and can place everything in a relational hierarchy.[31] By contrast, the sensory abstractions of contemporary action cinema's droning sound-images are experienced in the mode of causal efficacy, which Whitehead defines as "constituted by its feeling-tones, and as efficacious by reason of those feeling-tones."[32] As Whitehead would have it, these films are not visual but visceral, since "what we ordinarily term visual perceptions are the result of the later stages in the concrescence of the percipient occasion."[33] We only experience films as visual *after* we have felt the images with our entire bodies. Of course, every single experience is made up of both perception in the mode of causal efficacy and presentational immediacy, but in contemporary action cinema we are rarely allowed the time to let the images integrate. Bay said as much when he bragged about distorting the audience's perception by employing movement in multiple directions simultaneously.

The drone of sound-images works by reducing our affective responses, transmitting only certain vectors through which our perception is modulated. Watching these films is often an exhausting affair, in which external cinematic movements produce interior states of action; we leave the film feeling like we have been in a war. The drone of these sound-images leaves room for little else, allowing only a numb state of stunned shock. New sensations of movement are introduced in these films, but only insofar as they render us passive. There is a peculiar blurring of passivity and activity of affect; in other words, action and inaction blur. We feel as if we move even though we do not. Intensively, we do move, however, in the sense that we are made to feel and are affected by the films. This experience of being affected suggests that anaisthesis is a form of affective entrainment, a way of articulating experience with limited means, yet susceptible to the palpable pressures of structures of feeling.

What is really at stake here is *how* and *to what extent* we allow the feelings vectored in our direction to take hold of our sensate experience and the "I perceive"-subject that emerges from this process. Considering that every person is the product of innumerable articulations, there is no predictable way to suggest how any one viewer might respond to these films. However, as I've shown, it is possible to illustrate how these films produce lines of force, which then converge in the production of vectoral power. This vectoral power is the alluring elsewhere that Wark insists participates in what Virilio refers to as "endo-colonization" in *Pure War*.[34] For Virilio, one of cinema's functions is precisely to condition populations by changing the field of perception. This conditioning has very little to do with any kind of intentional procedure, but is instead simply the way that cinema inflects and trains our perceptions, both though its own audiovisual means and through the inevitable conflation of military and entertainment technologies.

The blurring and conflation of military and entertainment technologies is what produces Virilio's logistics of perception, which we can now see is the far more important term, although it still needs to be pushed further. Patricia Pisters updates Virilio's logistics in her book *The Neuro-Image* and points to the fact that through proliferation of media screens the model of perception is different. For her, there is a double logic to the logistics of perception 2.0, in that images of war desensitize us to the atrocities of war by wrapping them up in engaging affects and sensations that turn war into excitement. At the same time war films can contextualize and engage us with these very affects in order to question war.[35]

However, it seems clear to me that we should in fact be talking about the logistics of sensation, not perception: contemporary action cinema's sound-images have become so intense as to exceed our conscious perception. What we are faced with is no longer an optical unconscious of images but the drone non-conscious of sound-images. It is less a question of whether individual viewers are shaped by the cinematic lines of force than of whether, and how, entire affective moods and structures of feeling are augmented by these films. In that sense, the preponderance of droning sound-images blurs any other responses to war, not only because of the over-saturation of our senses but also of box offices.

While *Transformers* and *Battle: Los Angeles* dominated at the box office, *The Hurt Locker* is the lowest-grossing Oscar winner ever.[36] So although I do agree with Pisters' argument that films can and do expose affective entrainment, it remains significant that the films that do expose affective entrainment are generally smaller, more marginal films. Also, *The Hurt Locker* was tellingly made without support from the US Army and publicly denounced several times by military commanders. As opposed to immense science fiction blockbusters such as *Transformers* or *Battle: Los Angeles* that draw praise from the military for the realistic portrayal of what soldiers would do, *The Hurt Locker* remains too unrealistic for the US Army to condone it. This conception of realism has nothing to do with accurately portraying an anterior reality, but rather attempts to accommodate an ideological realism: a war film is deemed realistic by the US military if it conforms to their world view. In any case, the two first films undeniably remain more recognizable for the vast majority of audiences in terms of aesthetic form. The spare minimalism of *The Hurt Locker* has no doubt confounded many a spectacle-hungry cinema-goer.

Perhaps the best way to understand this tension is to return to Whitehead's ecological theory of perception, noticing his distinction between positive and negative prehension. Prehension is Whitehead's term for the process of experience. It is made up of the subject that prehends, that which is prehended and the subjective form of *how* the prehension occurs.[37] The subjective form is what allows for different prehensions between different subjects, i.e. why you and I may understand the same event differently, in this case a film. What is crucial is that Whitehead divides prehension into two different variations, or "species", as he calls them: positive and negative prehensions.[38] Positive prehensions are what we call feelings, while negative prehensions are excluded from feeling. It would be easy to jump to the conclusion that negative prehension is what happens when we do not like something and so refuse the feelings of the experience. For instance, let us say that I do not enjoy Michael Bay's films, so while I watch them I do not open myself to the feelings elicited by the films. Through that negative prehension, I would not be affected by whatever impact the films may have on others.

However, while this formulation is not necessarily entirely wrong, prehension should not be regarded as a fully conscious choice or decision. Instead, it is better to conceive of prehension as an adaption, a way for us to better fit into our environment. As we saw earlier, subjects and objects are not pre-given but emerge through their processual encounter. Instead, the encounter with a film impacts our perception of ourselves and the world, whether it is through integration, confirmation or transformation, as Ivakhiv designates the processes.[39] Not every film will register as a complete transformation of how we understand the world, but some may broaden and alter our worldly awareness. In fact, since our human environment is a complex field, filled with any number of factors that can impinge on us, I propose that we non-consciously prehend films (and many other things) in whatever way best suits the environment we inhabit. Clearly films can and do provide flashes of insight that are at odds with the structures of feeling that make up our cultural ecologies, yet the more we are able to prehend in ways that are congruent with current moods, the more likely we are to fit successfully within the culture of fear. Having the right feelings is a matter of adaption. At times, this is hard work, and there are feelings that run counter which we cannot always bring ourselves to articulate. Films like *The Hurt Locker* may prompt these alternate feelings, and in this way a critical distance sets in: the exuberant sensations of war become disturbingly pathological. Yet most of the time we will find it easier to accept or simply avoid the modulation and somatic markers of how these films are meant to make us feel. This is what Anderson means when he argues that people may have experiences that run counter to a given collective atmosphere. People may feel out of sync with the culture of fear.

Understanding our bodily responses and sensory impressions as part of a larger culture or structure of feeling clarifies how films may work as affective entrainment for war in a culture of fear. The overwhelming presence of these films, both in terms of their perceptual immediacy and bodily impact and also their pervasiveness, makes it difficult for us to avoid or reject the entire cultural mood that these films participate in. While we are free to dislike the films, to feel that the drone of sound-images is a tiring process, what we cannot escape is the fact that they express and produce a particular structure of feeling. On many levels, the films are fun and engrossing, and so cover up the negative aspects of war, the wearying effects of a culture of constant fear, where tension, apprehension and trepidation are permanent feelings that we have to navigate. These films become a lure for feeling; a feeling that releases us from fear, if only for a few hours. Their exhilarating spectacles draw us in and drone us out.

The culture of fear is thus rendered sensible to us, but an affective solution is also presented. Virilio refers to this situation as a polar inertia, in which stillness and immobility overtake us. His argument is that we will become like "*a machine that needs to be constantly revved up.*"[40.] We become contingent on always getting audiovisual energy that will accelerate our bodies.[41] We can see how contemporary action cinema functions by reconfiguring aisthesis. Our bodies are intersected and traversed by action cinema's intense audiovisual energies. Action cinema's production of *anaisthesis* and the culture of fear internally constitute each other. They do not exist as separate domains but are fully imbricated in each other. As Virilio points out, "with excess transmission speed, *control becomes the environment itself.*"[42] The culture of fear gains strength from the *anaisthesis* of contemporary action cinema because it facilitates a fuller integration of fear into our very sensorium. Yet as I have shown with a number of films, the intense production of audiovisual energy can also generate resources for resisting the culture of fear, despite control being diffused across it.

7

Cinematic War Machines

Contemporary action cinema has reached a level of intensity hitherto unimaginable, integrating all manner of audiovisual technologies in order to intensify our experience. Through the film's audiovisual barrage, our bodies are innervated, i.e. set into motion, opening lines of force that traverse and articulate us in ways that are prior to conscious perception. Action films participate in the production of structures of feeling and affective ecologies that we are part of, irrespective of our agreement with them or our desire to join them. I have sketched a line that moves from pre-conscious intensity, through bodily rhythms, to an anaesthesis of drone non-consciousness. This line of articulation is entirely virtual. That is to say, not a single person will be articulated in exactly this way. Not even me (in many ways least of all me). But that does not mean that this line does not have an impact. Parts of the virtual are always actualized and realized along the way. Every person will find their own lines of flight away from the forces and intensities this book outlines; at the same time some of these forces will be articulated in the ways described here. What this means is simply that every mechanism of escape is also a mechanism of capture. We never know if the line we follow will turn out to be one of flight or articulation. What matters is to question it along the trajectory that we become. I understand action films as cinematic war machines because

the intensities of action cinema work as forces that play across our bodies. As cinematic war machines, these films are not about the violence and
destruction that takes place on screen (although certainly that is part of the
genre's attraction), but instead about the focus of those forces of modulation and affective mobilization on crowds and bodies.[1]

War machine as a term originates with Virilio, who delineates how different societies have different war machines, or ways of structuring society
and delegating power. He presents this thesis most extensively in *Speed
and Politics*, outlining the differences between societies that depend on for-
tresses and those that regulate power through city streets. In both cases, it
is a matter of producing specific rhythms of life, as well as bodily rhythms.
It is for this reason that Virilio can switch to argue that cinema works as a
war machine: its production of energies and rhythms in our bodies become
a form of control. In this way, the idea of action films as war machines
also reveals the deeply political nature of action films. While representational issues and ideological formations play across the surface of these
films, their real political work lies in their training of our senses. As action
films' intensities traverse our bodies, reconfigure our senses and entrain
our affective responses, they in fact co-produce the culture of fear as much
as express it, or render it sensible. This co-production should not be confused with a specific ideological formation, since any ideology is necessarily a superstructure of action cinema's sensory assault.

This war machine is most readily associated with Gilles Deleuze and
Felix Guattari, particularly from their nomadology chapter in *A Thousand
Plateaus*. Here they present different forms of war machines, not unlike
Virilio, but their conception is slightly different. Rather than being part
of every society's structure, Deleuze and Guattari conceive of the war
machine as an outside to society: "As for the war machine in itself, it seems
to be irreducible to the State apparatus, to be outside of its sovereignty
and prior to its law: it comes from elsewhere."[2] Not part of society, not
part of all the institutions that makes society hierarchical, instead "the war
machine is of another species, another nature, another origin than the State
apparatus."[3] The force of the war machine comes from the fact that has no
essence or interiority; war machines are only exteriorities, only the relations between entities. War machines are speed machines; they work by
changing and accelerating relations between entities, yet do not exist as

entities in themselves. That is to say, war machines are not nouns or verbs, but they are adverbs and conjunctions: they describe *how* entities relate, and *in what ways* entities enter into relations. They are, in the way that I described earlier, translators.

Action films are war machines and translators because they participate in and change our social relations through their production of intensity. One action film, of course, makes no war machine, but as one of the most popular genres, action films become war machines through repetition, eliminating chance and deploying forces by multiplying them.[4] A war machine functions as a convergence of a host of different forces that together alter a cultural atmosphere or mood. This perspective is quite similar to Anderson's definition of structures of feeling as "collective affective qualities that dispose bodies."[5] Alternatively, Whitehead would call droning a "lure for feeling"; we are invited to participate in this process "providing immediacy of enjoyment and purpose."[6] Other than this immediacy of enjoyment, we should not discount the pleasure inherent in being part of the collective affective qualities of the ones around us: being-with is much easier (and often more enjoyable) than being-against.

Such priming by the sound-images of contemporary action cinema is thus the compaction of energies that allows us to participate in the current collective affective qualities, producing bodily feelings of superiority and dominance. In sum, we find that action cinema attempts to prime us for certain actions, concurrent with larger structures of feeling. However, action films seem a poor fit for feelings of fear; certainly horror films and disaster films seem more aligned with an atmosphere of fear. And indeed, I believe that much like one part of the drone strikes fear in people while the other part exudes power, contemporary action cinema absolves us from fear. The films induce in us a sense of mastery, power and force, offering us a reprieve from fear. While watching these films we inhabit a space of overwhelming sensations, our senses assaulted with the droning of sound-images, yet they all converge on producing a sense of nonhuman capacities that render us immune to fear for the duration of the film. Action films also participate in the administration of fear in the way they absolve us from that very fear in their production of feelings of empowerment through telesomatics. We can drone out fear through intense feelings of empowerment.

As I have shown, contemporary action films make us see the world in different ways, favoring sensations of speed, activating an assemblage embodiment that no longer privileges human sensations but opens our sensory realm to a larger environment. In this way, action films participate in and produce structures of feeling, which on the one hand augment feelings of fear and at the same time sublimate these fears into an engaging and hyper-accelerated blur of intensity. By stepping into these feelings, we are given a reprieve from structures of fear by augmenting our own sense of embodiment into something later and beyond the normal human sensorium. We learn that we can be safe by stepping into a body assemblage which can act at a distance. This atmosphere, or cultural mood, is a legitimation of the drone enterprise through affective entrainment. We can step into certain clusters of affects and sensations as a means of feeling safe, free from fear. While a range of affects and sensations are elicited throughout these films, there is always a return to safety and stability through physical empowerment. Yet as I have also shown, part of the entrainment comes in the form of letting go of one's agency, ceding autonomy to nonhuman affects and sensations in the films. Much of action cinema's attraction comes from this tension between physical empowerment through amplification and a folding of other bodies into our own for the duration of the film. But this empowerment is tightly correlated with and connected to a nonhuman embodiment, which enhances and amplifies our own bodies. As such, these films work as cultural training grounds for habituating us to ceding autonomy to entities and objects, in return for feelings of safety from fear. Habituation occurs through repetition and what I have referred to as affective entrainment: a continuous reiteration of how to satisfy or achieve experience. The best way to think about this habituation is the notion of modulation. Modulation is both inflection and regulation and suggests a behavioral change or tempering.

This leads us to another way in which contemporary action films function as a drone age cinema. In the same way that drones target civilian populations overseas, so drone age cinema targets audiences at home. Through sheer volume of output, action cinema produces an overpowering and pervasive mood not unlike Virilio's "information bomb." Rather than an explosion of unassimilable information, action cinema is an explosion of affect that overpowers audiences and makes entire populations vibrate at the same frequencies. It is in this way that action cinema functions as modulation.

The modulation at work lies in how the films throw out lures for feeling, pulling viewers into audiovisual intensities that inevitably function as sensory training grounds for projections of power and delight in telesomatics, exchanging inertia for affective energies. In this process, we find a switch from power to modulation. You are free to believe anything you want, you can produce any meaning you want, but you cannot feel anything you want. Even frustration is not a free feeling but a response to changes in the environment. Even an attempt to articulate lines of force differently participates in the modulation by contemporary action cinema. But modulation is precisely not an enclosure or a mold, it is an inflection, a rhythmic intervention in our bodies. This is why contemporary action films are war machines: they change relations between elements, and they do so through repetition and intensification.

Action cinema's aesthetic is one of sensory assault, enacted in the hope that its barrage will drone out all resistance, that all individuation will be ruptured into a sameness, an undifferentiated mass of affect that can then be captured and trained. The production of speed blurs our perception and overwhelms our senses, affording only certain lines of articulation. This is the state of *anaisthesis*. But affect is precisely characterized by its volatile and uncontrollable nature, the way it overflows our senses of being and identity and unity. While contemporary action cinema attempts to lure us in with intense sensations and pleasurable throbs of experience, exchanging energies for inertia and the acceptance of motility through bodies other than our own, this production of energy may just as easily engage other forms of expression, other forms of experience.

This is the danger of the war machine. Because it is of a different species and order than ideology, there is no guarantee that the change of relations will serve ideology at all. The war machine is an independent, uncontrollable entity that exists only to deterritorialize bodies, in order that they may be reterritorialized again. That is the real process we have seen here: the ways in which a culture of fear arises from the host of energies and fields of forces that emerge in these film. This is how films participate in and amplify what is already there. Flows and energies converge and diverge and produce new rhythms, new sensations that all flow both above and below the individual level. Aesthetic force is also cultural force: the modulation and priming of our perceptions determines how we inhabit our culture. We cannot escape this process, however we might feel about action films, since they inevitably inflect and are inflected by the flow of energies of our entire culture. In this way, action films participate in producing affective atmospheres, which reach beyond individual responses and color our perception of events. What matters is this priming effect of action films, and the priming is collective.

Contemporary action cinema, more than any other genre of film, renders the culture of fear sensible in audiovisual form. The vectors, kinetics, volatilities and telesomatics all converge on the production of a state of drone nonconscious, which gives us a reprieve from fear by stepping into a nonhuman embodiment. The intensities modulate us in ways that habituate us to the culture of fear, all of which occurs prior to conscious experience. The micro-perceptual impact of action films' affective forms continually in-form our relation to contemporary media ecologies, but also to cultural, ideological ecologies. There is no dividing line between these ecologies, as they continually fold over and into each other. For this reason, any study of action films must begin with the study of how they elicit sensations and affects, and then move to how they integrate us into a larger cultural whole. Their expressive rendering of structures of feeling make them an invaluable resource for understanding current issues of force, power and violence.

Throughout this study, I have deliberately emphasized the formal properties of action films, because they have generally been overlooked or reduced to issues of excess in previous studies. We need to get a much clearer sense of what excess means in terms of our experience of action films, or any film for that matter. Only close attention to form and formal properties can express how and in what ways we understand and receive representations and ideologies. This is why I have emphasized forms such as lines, vectors, rhythms, vibrations and so forth over structures that forcefully delineate between form and experience. The whole point is that experience emerges as a consequence of formal properties. What I have tried to provide is a turn to the experience of action films rather than simply an analysis of their structures. Furthermore, this turn toward experience necessitates the recognition that experience is not a human category but a complex folding of human and nonhuman elements, which through their integration transforms human experience. In doing this, I have suggested that there is always a tension between the process of experience and the system within which that experience emerges. We can only understand action films if we tend to both their experiential forces and the culture they participate in. Only then can we recognize how the nonhuman participates in the human, and only in this way will we begin to recognize that action films have always been stretching the human sensorium, which is why action films have been and remain so fascinating.

Finally, then, we can only understand action films by understanding what they do. They render changes in our culture, and enact them; they reiterate sensations such as fear, while absolving us from those very sensations. As with any form of art, the nonhuman participates in the human experience and makes that experience broader. Action films reveal the limits of our perceptions, and modulate those perceptions to effectuate changes and transformations in the culture of fear. That is what action films do, and it is why they matter. We cannot write off as banal, puerile or simplistic one of the main vectors of our current climate, despite the fact that it might be all of those things. It is always also in excess of those things. Action films are projections of power that reveal and render the lines of force of the culture of fear we are all living through.

Notes

Chapter 1: War of the Senses

1 So far, only music videos have deployed drones but Hollywood is not far behind. There are three significant drone music videos. The most well-known one is OK Go's "I Won't Let You Down" filmed by a quadcopter. More interesting are "97.92" by Flatbush Zombies featuring Trash Talk and Wild Child's "Rillo Talk". These two videos use multiple Go Pro cameras attached to a single drone, subsequently morphing the multiple cameras into one image. as for Hollywood on 2 June 2014, the FAA (Federal Aviation Administration) released a statement, saying that they are in the process of allowing film and TV companies to employ unmanned aircraft systems – drones – in production (www.faa.gov/news/press_releases/news_story.cfm?newsId=16294). While drones are readily available in most electronics stores and can be operated 'for fun' as the FAA terms it, commercial use, including filmmaking, must obtain a Section 333 exemption. By 10 December, 2,518 petitions have been granted (http://www.faa.gov/uas/legislative_programs/section_333/).
2 Rey Chow, *The Age of the World Target: Self-Referentiality in War, Theory, and Comparative Work* (Durham: Duke University Press, 2006), loc. 587.
3 Daniel Frampton, *Filmosophy* (London: Wallflower Press, 2006), 100.
4 Frampton, *Filmosophy*, 101.
5 Robert Sinnerbrink, *New Philosophies of Film: Thinking Images* (London: Continuum, 2011), 4, 5, 8.
6 Steven Shaviro, *The Universe of Things: On Speculative Realism* (Minneapolis: University of Minnesota Press, 2014), loc. 2546.
7 Vivian Sobchack, *The Address of the Eye: A Phenomenology of Film Experience* (Princeton: Princeton University Press, 1992), 205. Emphasis in original.
8 John Mullarkey, *Refractions of Reality: Philosophy and the Moving Image* (Basingstoke: Palgrave Macmillan, 2009), xv.
9 Alfred North Whitehead, *Adventures of Ideas* (New York: The Free Press, 1967), p. 176.
10 Alfred North Whitehead, *Process and Reality* (New York: The Free Press, 1967), 165.
11 Whitehead, *Process and Reality*, p. 109.

189

12 Hansen, *Cinema and Experience: Siegfried Kracauer, Walter Benjamin, and Theodor W. Adorno* (Berkeley: University of California Press, 2012), loc. 254.

13 Hansen, *Cinema and Experience*, loc. 264.

14 Michel Chion, *Audio-Vision: Sound on Screen*, trans. and ed. Claudia Gorman, foreword *by* Walter Murch (New York: Columbia Press, 1994), 109.

15 Michel Chion, *Film, A Sound Art*, trans. Claudia Gorman (New York: Columbia University Press, 2009), 238.

16 Chion, *Audio-Vision*, 112.

17 Brian Massumi, *Parables for the Virtual: Movement, Affect, Sensation* (Durham: Duke University Press, 2002).

18 Shaviro, "'Straight From the Cerebral Cortex': Vision and Affect in *Strange Days*" in *The Cinema of Kathryn Bigelow: Hollywood Transgressor*, eds David Jermyn and Sean Redmond (London: Wallflower Press, 2003), 165.

19 Gilles Deleuze, *The Logic of Sense*, trans. Mark Lester with Charles Stivale, ed. Constantin V. Boundas (London: The Athlone Press, 1990), 107.

20 Chion, *Audio-Vision*, 112.

21 Massumi, *Parables for the Virtual*, 97.

22 Mark B.N. Hansen, *Feed-Forward: On the Future of Twenty-First Century Media* (Chicago: University of Chicago Press, 2015).

23 Steve Goodman, *Sonic Warfare: Sound, Affect, and the Ecology of Fear* (Cambridge, MA: The MIT Press, 2010), loc 907.

24 Hansen, *Feed-Forward*.

25 Raymond Williams, *Marxism and Literature* (Oxford: Oxford University Press, 1977), 132–133.

26 Paul Virilio, *Pure War*, trans. Mark Polizzotti (Los Angeles: Semiotext(e), 2008), 96. Technically, the formulation is Sylvère Lotringer's, who announces this in the extended interviews that make up *Pure War*, but since Virilio not only expresses the same sentiment immediately before and after Lotringer's interjection, I believe that the phrase adequately expresses Virilio's argument.

27 Friedrich A. Kittler, *Gramophone, Film, Typewriter*, trans. Geoffrey Winthrop-Young *and* Michael Wutz (Stanford: Stanford University Press, 1999), 96–97.

28 Kittler, *Gramophone, Film, Typewriter*, 124.

29 Kittler, *Gramophone, Film, Typewriter*, 124.

30 Friedrich A. Kittler, *Optical Media*, trans. Anthony Enns (Cambridge: Polity Press, 2010), 147.

31 For more on this topic, which I will not delve into too much, see Carl Boogs and Tom Pollard, *The Hollywood War Machine* and David L. Robb, *Operation Hollywood*.

32 Paul Virilio, *War and Cinema: The Logistics of Perception*, trans. Patrick Camiller (London: Verso Books, 1989), 11.

33 Virilio, *War and Cinema*, 8.
34 Jonathan Crary, *Techniques of the Body: On Vision and Modernity in the Nineteenth Century* (Cambridge, MA: The MIT Press, 1992, 5. Emphasis in original.
35 Kittler, *Gramophone, Film, Typewriter*, 95.
36 Kittler, *Gramophone, Film, Typewriter*, 132.
37 Goodman, *Sonic Warfare, loc* 517.
38 Yvonne Tasker, *The Hollywood Action and Adventure Film* (Chichester: Wiley Blackwell, 2015), 24.
39 Sobchack, *The Address of the Eye*, 6.
40 Linda Williams, "Film Bodies: Gender, Genre, and Excess," *Film Quarterly*, 44, no. 4 (1991), 4.
41 A wide range of phenomenological, Deleuzian, and affective approaches have flourished in the past two decades, including Steven Shaviro, *The Cinematic Body*, Jennifer M. Barker, *The Tactile Eye*, Anne Rutherford, *What Makes a Film Tick?*, Patricia Pisters, *The Neuro-Image*, Tarje Laine, *Feeling Cinema* and more. Despite their methodological and philosophical diversity all these writers suggest a sensory relation to films and moving images.
42 Yvonne Tasker, *Spectacular Bodies: Gender, Genre and the Action Cinema* (London Routledge, 1993), 5.
43 Harvey O'Brien, *Action Movies: The Cinema of Striking Back* (London: Wallflower Press, 2012), 2.
44 Lisa Purse, *Contemporary Action Cinema* (Edinburgh: Edinburgh University Press, 2011), 45.
45 "aesthesis | esthesis, n.". OED Online. June 2015. Oxford University Press.
46 "apprehension, n.". OED Online. June 2015. Oxford University Press. http://www.oed.com/view/Entry/9808?redirectedFrom=apprehension& (accessed 19 June 2015). Barker does not pick up on the action of laying hold with the senses, although it would fit well with her general analysis. See Barker, *The Tactile Eye*, 106–119.
47 Jennifer M. Barker, *The Tactile Eye: Touch and the Cinematic Experience* (Berkeley: University of California Press, 2009), 108.
48 Tasker, *The Hollywood Action and Adventure Film*, 5.
49 William Brown, *Supercinema: Film-Philosophy for the Digital Age* (New York: Berghahn Books, 2015), 10.
50 Barker, *The Tactile Eye*, 115.
51 Nndalianis, "The Frenzy of the Visible: Spectacle and Motion in the Era of the Digital," *Senses of Cinema* 3 (2000).
52 Edward Branigan, *Projecting a Camera: Language-Games in Film Theory* (New York: Routledge, 2006), 37.
53 Sobchack, *The Address of the Eye*, 195, 184.

54 Denson, "Crazy Cameras, Discorrelated Images, and the Post-Perceptual Mediation of Post-Cinematic Affect," in *Post-Cinema: Theorizing 21ˢᵗ-Century Film*, eds Shane Denson and Julia Leyda (REFRAME Books, 2016).

55 As Dudley Andrews has pointed out, films have been produced without cameras for many years, pointing to both Emile Reynaud's moving images with glass plates and Stan Brakhage's *Mothlight* composed by gluing moths' wings and other objects to raw film stock. Yet these radical practices are a far cry from the mainstream movies that employ these new image technologies.

56 Steven Shaviro, *Post-Cinematic Affect* (Winchester: 0-Books, 2010), 1.

57 Shaviro, *Post-Cinematic Affect*, 137.

58 Gilles Deleuze, *The Fold: Leibniz and the Baroque*, trans. Tom Conley (London: The Athlone Press, 1993), 86.

59 Vivian Sobchack, *Carnal Thoughts: Embodiment and Moving Image Culture* (Berkeley: University of California Press, 2004), 145–146.

60 Sobchack, *Carnal Thoughts*, 140.

61 Deleuze, *The Fold*, 86.

62 Anna Munster, "Transmateriality: Towards and Energetics of Signal in Contemporary Mediatic Assemblages," *Cultural Studies Review* 20, no. 1 (2014), 154.

63 Adam Rothstein, "How to Write Drone Fiction," *The State*, 20 January 2013. Available at www.thestate.ae/how-to-write-drone-fiction/.

64 Massumi, *Parables for the Virtual*, 91.

65 Harun Farocki, "Phantom Images," *Public* 29 (2004), 17.

66 Nasser Hussain, "The Sound of Terror: Phenomenology of the Drone Strike," *Boston Review*, 16 October 2013.

67 Grégeoire Chamayou, *A Theory of the Drone*, trans. Janet Lloyd (New York: The New Press), 12.

68 Warren Ellis, "Editorial," *Superflux* 1 (2015).

69 Hussain, "The Sound of Terror".

70 Shaviro, *Post-Cinematic Affect*, 3.

71 Paul Virilio, *The Administration of Fear*, trans. Ames Hodges (Los Angeles: Semiotext(e), 2012), 45.

72 Michel Foucault, *The Birth of Biopolitics: Lectures at the Collège de France 1978–1979*, ed. Michael Senellart, trans. Graham Burchell (New York: Palgrave Macmillan, 2008), 271.

73 Gilles Deleuze, *Negotiations, 1972–1990*, trans. Martin Joughin (New York: Columbia University Press, 1995), 178–179.

74 Virilio, *The Administration of Fear*, 35.

75 Virilio, *The Administration of Fear*, 14–15.

76 Ben Anderson, *Encountering Affect: Capacities, Apparatuses, Conditions* (Farnham: Ashgate, 2014), 108ff.

77 Brian Massumi, *Ontopower: War, Powers, and the State of Perception* (Durham: Duke University Press, 2015), loc. 3134.

78 Massumi, *Ontopower*, loc. 3377.

79 Joanna Bourke, *Fear: A Cultural History* (London: Virago, 2005), loc. 71.

80 Bourke, *Fear*, loc. 6111.

81 Bourke, *Fear*, loc. 6686.

82 Massumi, *Ontopower*, loc. 3140.

83 Anderson, *Encountering Affect*, 108.

84 Anderson, *Encountering Affect*, 108. This is an argument that Anderson takes from Sara Ahmed in her work *The Cultural Politics of Emotion*.

85 Williams, *Marxism and Literature*, 132.

86 Adrian J. Ivakhiv, *Ecologies of the Moving Image: Cinema, Affect, Nature* (Waterloo, Canada: Wilfried Laurier University Press, 2013), 35.

87 Gilbert Simondon, quoted in Massumi, *Ontopower*, loc 3408.

88 Blackmore, "The Speed Death of the Eye," *Bulletin of Science, Technology & Society* 27, no. 5 (2007), 370.

89 James Der Derian in Paul Virilio, *Desert Screen*, preface James Der Derian, trans. Michael Degener (London: Continuum, 2002), viii.

90 Virilio, *Pure War*, 96.

91 Paul Virilio, *The Vision Machine*, trans. Julie Rose (London: British Film Institute and Bloomington: Indiana University Press, 1994), 62. Emphasis in original.

92 Paul Virilio, *The Art of the Motor*, trans. Julie Rose (Minneapolis: University of Minnesota Press, 1995), 138.

93 Paul Virilio, *Speed and Politics*, trans. Mark Polizzotti (Los Angeles: Semiotext(e), 2006), 29.

94 Virilio, *Pure War*, 88. Emphasis in original.

95 Paul Virilio, *The Aesthetics of Disappearance*, trans. Philip Beitchman (Los Angeles: Semiotext(e), 1991), 35.

96 John Johnston, "Machinic Vision," *Critical Inquiry* 26 (1999), 27.

97 Johnston, "Machinic Vision", 27.

98 Johnston, "Machinic Vision", 44.

99 Shaviro, " 'Straight From the Cerebral Cortex' ", 164.

100 Hansen, *Cinema and Experience*, 136.

101 Hansen, *Cinema and Experience*, 137.

102 Hansen, *Cinema and Experience*, 101.

103 Virilio, *Pure War*, 89.

104 William E. Connolly, *Neuropolitics: Thinking, Culture, Speed* (Minneapolis: University of Minnesota Press, 2002), loc. 256.

105 Dirk Eitzen, "Effects of Entertaining Violence," in *Cognitive Media Theory*, eds. Ted Nannicelli and Paul Taberham (New York: Routledge, 2014), 162.

106 Massumi, *Ontopower*, loc. 1186. Emphasis in original.

107 Brian Massumi, *The Power at the End of the Economy* (Durham: Duke University Press, 2015), 41.

Chapter 2: Vectors and the Transfer of Affect

1 Virilio, *Negative Horizon: An Essay in Dromoscopy*, trans. Michael Degener (London: Continuum, 2005), 73.

2 Gilles Deleuze, *Cinema 1 The Movement-Image*, trans. Hugh Tomlinson and Barbara Habberjam (London: Continuum, 2005), 222.

3 Sean Cubitt, *The Cinema Effect* (Cambridge, MA: The MIT Press, 2004), 80.

4 Cubitt, *The Cinema Effect*, 85.

5 Cubitt, *The Cinema Effect*, 91.

6 Mackenize Wark, *Telesthesia: Communication, Culture, and Class* (Cambridge: Polity Press), 207–208.

7 Beth Coleman, "Everything is Animated: Pervasive Media and the Networked Subject," *Body and Society* 18, no. 1 (2012), 83.

8 Mihailova, "The Mastery Machine: Digital Animation and Fantasies of Control," *Animation* 8, no. 2 (2013), 132.

9 Lisa Purse, "Gestures and Postures of Mastery," in *Cinephilia in the Age of Digital Reproduction: Film, Pleasure and Digital Culture*, vol. 1, eds. Scott Balcerzak and Jason Sperb (London: Wallflower Press), 222.

10 Barbara Creed, "The Cyberstar: Digital Pleasures and the End of the Unconscious," *Screen* 41, no. 1 (2000), 86.

11 Ian Bogost, *Alien Phenomenology, or What It's Like to Be a Thing* (Minneapolis: University of Minnesota Press, 2012), 124.

12 Although beyond the scope of this work, there are countless Iron Man fan vids in circulation that centers solely on the suit and its various actions. Significantly, while there are equally many vids that focus on a fetishistic desire for Robert Downey, Jr/Tony Stark, the suit vids are divested of any interest in Downey/Stark and does not even feature his face.

13 Scott Bukatman, "Spectacle, Attractions and Visual Pleasure," in *The Cinemas of Attractions Reloaded*, ed. Wanda Strauven (Amsterdam: Amsterdam University Press, 2006), 76.

14 Rachel O. Moore, *Savage Theory: Cinema as Modern Magic* (Durham: Duke University Press, 2000), 73.

15 Vivian Sobchack, "Animation and Automation, or, the Incredible Effortfulness of Being" *Screen* 50, no. 4 (2009), 384.

16 Scott Bukatman, *The Poetics of Slumberland: Animated Spirits and the Animating Spirit* (Berkeley: University of California Press, 2012), loc. 502.

17 Coleman, "Everything is Animated", 94.

18 Patricia MacCormack, *Cinesexuality* (Farnham: Ashgate, 2008), 21.

19 Sarah Wanenchak, "Toward a Drone Sexuality – Part 2: Boundary conditions," *Cybergology*, 19 December 2013.

20 Goodman, *Sonic Warfare*, loc. 1016.

21 Aylish Wood, *Digital Encounters* (London: Routledge, 2007), 48.

22 Alexander R. Galloway, *Gaming: Essays on Algorithmic Culture* (Minneapolis, University of Minnesota Press, 2006), loc. 975.

23 Wood, *Digital Encounters*, p. 45.

24 Brown, *Supercinema,* 21.

25 Wood, Digital Encounters 49.

26 For more on character morphs, see Vivian Sobchack (ed), *Meta-Morphing: Visual Transformation and the Culture of Quick-Change* (Minneapolis: University of Minnesota Press, 2000).

27 Wood, *Digital Encounters*, 50.

28 Wood, *Digital Encounters*, 53.

29 Wood, *Digital Encounters*, 54.

30 Wood, *Digital Encounters*, 66.

31 Wood, *Digital Encounters*, 55.

32 Whitehead, *Process and Reality*, 116.

33 Whitehead, *Process and Reality*, 116.

34 Virilio, *Negative Horizon*, 111.

35 Virilil, *Negative Horizon*, 116.

36 Virilio, *Negative Horizon*, 118.

37 Erin Manning, *Relationscapes: Movement, Art, Philosophy* (Cambridge, MA: The MIT Press, 2009), 6.

38 Manning, *Relationscapes*, 105.

39 Whitehead, *Process and Reality*, p. 21.

40 Wark, *Telesthesia*, 82.

41 Chamayou, *A Theory of the Drone*, 53.

Chapter 3: Kinetics and the Force of Movement

1 Enda Duffy, *The Speed Handbook: Velocity, Pleasure, Modernism (*Durham: Duke University Press, 2009), loc 139.

2 Duffy, *The Speed Handbook*, loc 215.

3 A short list would include Marshall McLuhan in *Understanding Media*, Friedrich Kittler in *Gramophone, Film, Typewriter*, Jonathan Crary in *Techniques of the Observer and Suspensions of Perception*, Vivian Sobchack in *Carnal Thoughts* and more, including of course Virilio. Despite belonging to very different theoretical and philosophical camps, all agree that our senses are historical and inflected by technologies.

4 Virilio, *Speed and Politics*, 29.
5 "kinetics, n.". *OED Online*.
6 Barker, *The Tactile Eye*, 110.
7 Tom Gunning, "An Aesthetics of Astonishment: Early Film and the (In) Credulous Spectator," in *Viewing Positions: Ways of Seeing Films*, ed. Linda Williams (New Brunswick: Rutgers University Press, 1995).
8 Maria Walsh, "The Immersive Spectator," *Angelaki* 9 (2004), 178.
9 Bukatman, *Matters of Gravity: Special Effects and Supermen in the 20th Century* (Durham: Duke University Press, 2003), 89
10 Bukatman, *Matters of Gravity*, 114, 115–116.
11 N. Katherine Hayles, "Hyper and Deep Attention: The Generational Divide in Cognitive Modes," *Profession* (2007), 188.
12 Richard Maltby, *Hollywood Cinema*, 2nd edition (Malden, MA: Blackwell Publishing, 2003), 372.
13 Gunning, "The Cinema of Attractions: Early Cinema, Its Spectator and the Avant-Gade," *Wide Angle* 8, no. 3/4 (1986), 68.
14 David Bordwell, "Camera Movement and Cinematic Space," *Cine-Tracts* 1 (1977), 23.
15 Gunning, "An Aesthetics of Astonishment", 121.
16 Karen Pearlman, *Cutting Rhythms: Shaping the Film Edit* (Burlington: Focal Press, 2009), 52.
17 Bordwell, "Camera Movement and Cinematic Space", 23.
18 Barker, *The Tactile Eye*, 107. Emphasis in original.
19 Sara Ross, "Invitation to Voyage: The Flight Sequence in Contemporary 3D Cinema," *Film History* 24, no. 2 (2012), p. 211.
20 Kristen Whissel, *Spectacular Digital Effects: CGI and Contemporary Cinema* (Durham: Duke University Press, 2014), 22.
21 David Bordwell, *The Way Hollywood Tells It: Story and Style in Modern Movies* (Berkeley: University of California Press, 2006), 144ff and Matthias Stork, "Video Essay: Chaos Cinema: The Decline and Fall of Action Filmmaking," *Press Play*, 22 August, 2011.
22 Shaviro, *Post-Cinematic Affect*, 124.
23 Barker, *The Tactile Eye*, 113.
24 David Bordwell, "Unsteadicam chronicles", 17 August 2007.
25 Geoff King, *Spectacular Narratives: Hollywood in the Age of the Blockbuster* (London: I.B.Tauris, 2000) and Shaviro, *Post-Cinematic Affect*.
26 Shaviro, *Post-Cinematic Affect*, p. 123.
27 King, *Spectacular Narratives*, p. 97.
28 Eisenstein quoted in King, *Spectacular Narratives*, p. 98.
29 David Bordwell, "[Insert your favorite Bourne pun here]", 30 August 2007.
30 Bordwell, "[Insert your favorite Bourne pun here]".

31 Matthias Stork, "Chaos Cinema: Assaultive Action Aesthetics," *Media Fields Journal* 6 (2013), 8–9.
32 Anderson, *Encountering Affect*, 111.
33 MacKenzie Wark, "Fury Road," *Public Seminar*, 22 May 2015.
34 For more on 3D filming and basic vocabulary, see Lenny Lipton, *Foundations of the Stereoscopic Cinema*, especially chapter three "The Stereoscopic Field", pp. 91–118.
35 Yvonne Spielmann, "Elastic Cinema: Technological Imagery", p. 65.
36 The primary example is *Return Of Kings*, a blog that reads like a parody of masculinity but is apparently heart-felt. Aaron Clarey, self-styled asshole consultant, wrote a screed suggesting that *Mad Max: Fury Road* should be boycotted because it was feminist propaganda. Yet even mainstream journalists seemed incapable of understanding the film, such as Peter Howell from *Toronto Star* who asked Tom Hardy during the Cannes press conference if Hardy wondered about the presence of all the women in what was apparently a "man's movie". Hardy said no.
37 Hansen, *Cinema and Experience*, 201.
38 Shaviro, *Post-Cinematic Affect*, 135.
39 Hansen, *Cinema and Experience*, 201.
40 Wood, *Digital Encounters*, 73.
41 Deleuze, *Cinema 1*, 86.
42 Deleuze, *Cinema 1*, 87.
43 Brown, *Supercinema*, 46.
44 Jay David Bolter and Richard Grusin, *Remediation: Understanding New Media* (Cambridge, MA: The MIT Press, 2000), 34.

Chapter 4: Volatility and Flexible Bodies

1 The term "hard bodies" comes from Susan Jeffords' book *Hard Bodies: Hollywood Masculinity in the Reagan Era* (1993), a classic book that exposes the ideology of masculinity in the Reagan era. While not all of the book focuses on action films, it connects action films and nation-building through the lens of masculinity admirably.
2 The term volatility echoes a book by Elizabeth Grosz, *Volatile Bodies*, that deconstructs the supposed natural body devalued by philosophy that Grosz reveals to be a throughly male body. Her use of the term volatile thus indicates all the overlooked aspects of human bodies, such as menstruation, lactation, menopause and more. All these natural phenomena are considered unruly by phallocentric cultures, simply because they are female phenomena. While the unruly bodies that I delve into here are often male, the significance of unruliness is similar because it engages with an idea of the limit between human and nonhuman.

3 Purse, "Gestures and Postures of Mastery", 230.

4 Denson, "Crazy Cameras, Discorrelated Images, and the Post-Perceptual Mediation of Post-Cinematic Affect."

5 Jim Emerson, "Agents of Chaos," *Scanners*, 23 August 2011.

6 Purse, "Gestures and Postures of Mastery", 217.

7 Linda Williams, *Hard Core: Power, Pleasure, and the "Frenzy of the Visible,"* expanded paperback edition (Berkeley: University of California Press, 1999), 36.

8 David Bordwell, *Planet Hong Kong: Popular Cinema and the Art of Entertainment* (Cambridge, MA: Harvard University Press, 2000), 220.

9 Bordwell, *Planet Hong Kong*, 232, 229.

10 Man-Fung Yip, "In the Realm of the Senses: Sensory Realism, Speed and Hong Kong Martial Arts Cinema," *Cinema Journal* 53, no. 4 (2014), 84.

11 Brown, *Supercinema*, 44.

12 Virilio, *The Art of the Motor*, 100.

13 Arthur Kroker, *Body Drift: Butler, Hayles, Haraway* (Minneapolis: University of Minnesota Press, 2012), loc. 63.

14 Paul Virilio, *Open Sky*, trans. Julie Rose (London: Verso Books, 2008), 51.

15 Whitehead, *Process and Reality*, 19.

16 Susan Buck-Morss, "Aesthetics and Anaesthetics: Walter Benjamin's Artwork Essay Reconsidered," *October* 62 (1992), 12.

17 Hansen, *Feed-Forward*, loc. 1028.

18 Hansen, *Feed-Forward*, loc. 1034.

19 Whitehead, *Process and Reality*, 21.

20 Whitehead, *Process and Reality*, 21.

21 Connolly, *Neuropolitics*, loc. 564.

Chapter 5: Corporeal Projections and Drone Bodies

1 Chamayou, *A Theory of the Drone*, 12.

2 Virilio, *Open Sky*, 11.

3 Clark, in Chamayou, *A Theory of the Drone*, 21.

4 Virilio, *Open Sky*, 152.

5 Brett S. Mann and Chrystal Jaye, "'Are We One Body?' Body Boundaries in Telesomatic Experiences," *Anthropology & Medicine* 14, no. 2 (2007), 185.

6 Sobchack, *Carnal Thoughts*, p. 136. Emphasis in original.

7 Tanine Allison, "More than a Man in a Monkey Suit: Andy Serkis, Motion Capture, and Digital Realism," *Quarterly Review of Film and Video* 28 (2011), 329.

8 Drew Ayers, "The Multilocal Self: Performance Capture, Remote Surgery, and Persistent Materiality," *Animation* 9, no. 2 (2014), 216.

9 Massumi, *Parables for the Virtual*, 138.

10 Ayers, "The Multilocal Self", 224.

11 Patricia Clough, *Autoaffection: Unconscious Thought in the Age of Teletechnology* (Minneapolis: University of Minnesota Press, 2000), 57.

12 Surely, this is also why Lev Manovich in his *Language of New Media* (2001) argues that film has now come full circle from animation through live action film and now back to animation.

13 Ayers, "The Multilocal Self", 216.

14 Marshall McLuhan, *Understanding Media: The Extensions of Man*, Critical Edition, ed. W. Terrence Gordon (Berkeley: Gingko Press, 2003), 86.

15 Sobchack, *Carnal Thoughts*, 60.

16 Miriam Ross, "The 3-D Aesthetic: *Avatar* and Hyperhaptic Visuality," *Screen* 53, no. 4 (2012), 385.

17 I am acutely aware that due to technical limitations that depend on very specific eye architectures, many people physiologically cannot watch 3D films. Ironically, the, even the very formal properties of the 3D image reproduces the film's ableist overtones. Insisting to shot the film in 3D actually excludes some people from watching *Avatar* as it was intended. While one might argue that this is no different than color films excluding the colorblind, the audience segment that cannot watch 3D is much larger than the colorblind segment. What truly matters is not so much the percentages, however, as the fact that *Avatar* insists on the full-bodied immersive experience being a transcends experience to be strived for and the only true and proper way to be fully connected with nature.

18 Ross, "The 3-D Aesthetic", 397.

19 Whissel, *Spectacular Digital Effects*, 21ff.

20 Whissel, *Spectacular Digital Effects*, 26.

21 Ross, "Invitation to Voyage", 211.

22 Ross, "Invitation to Voyage", 212.

23 Although these post-*Avatar* depressions now have the feel of hype and apocrypha, there were several reports at the time of the film's release.

24 Virilio, *Polar Inertia*, trans. Patrick Camiller (London: Sage Publications, 2000), 86.

25 Virilio, *War and Cinema*, p. 8.

26 Jane Bennett, *Vibrant Matter: A Political Ecology of Things* (Durham: Duke University Press, 2010), loc. 568.

27 Steven Shaviro, *Without Criteria: Kant, Whitehead, Deleuze* (Cambrdige, MA: The MIT Press, 2009), 38.

28 Virilio, *The Art of the Motor*, 103.

29 Virilio, *The Art of the Motor*, 107.

30 John Armitage, *Virilio and the Media* (Cambridge: Polity Press, 2012), 86.

Chapter 6: Droning and Audiovisual Stun Mode

1 Robin James, "Drones, Sound, and Super-Panoptic Surveillance," *Cybergology*, 26 October 2013.

2 James, "Drones, Sound, and Super-Panoptic Surveillance".

3 James, "Drones, Sound, and Super-Panoptic Surveillance". Emphasis in original.

4 Chion, *Audio-Vision*, 150.

5 Chion, *Audio-Vision*, 150.

6 Chion, *Audio-Vision*, 47, 63.

7 K.J. Donnolly, "*Saw* Heard: Musical Sound Design in Contemporary Cinema," in *Film Theory and Contemporary Hollywood Movies*, ed. Warren Buckland (New York: Routledge, 2009), 112.

8 Miriam Bratu Hansen, "The Mass Production of the Senses: Classical Cinema as Vernacular Modernism," *Modernism/Modernity* 6, no. 2 (1999), 67.

9 David Bordwell has spent much time on his blog, if not his academic output, bemoaning the lax filmmaking, as he sees it, of the contemporary action blockbuster.

10 Adam Cook, "Dialogues: Talking Robots, or Michael Bay's *Transformers: Age of Extinction*," *MUBI Notebook*, 8 July 2014.

11 Chion, *Audio-Vision*, 71.

12 Mark Kerins, *Beyond Dolby (Stereo): Cinema in the Digital Sound Age* (Bloomington: Indiana University Press, 2011), 116.

13 Stork, "Chaos Cinema", 11.

14 Chion, *Audio-Vision*, 87.

15 Chion, *Audio-Vision*, 63.

16 Virilio, *The Vision Machine*, 73.

17 Armitage, *Virilio and the Media*, 93.

18 Kerns, *Beyond Dolby (Stereo)*, 91.

19 Chion, *Audio-Vision*, 72.

20 Chion, *Audio-Vision*, 75.

21 Goodman, *Sonic Warfare*, loc. 841.

22 Goodman, *Sonic Warfare*, loc. 220.

23 Goodman, *Sonic Warfare*, loc. 111.

24 Goodman, *Sonic Warfare*, loc. 292.

25 I recognize that a chance to work with a respected and accomplished director in a film open to criticizing the war in Iraq is also a possible reason high profile actors would participate.

26 Chion, *Audio-Vision*, 57.

27 Goodman, *Sonic Warfare*, loc. 451.

28 Purse, *Contemporary Action Cinema*, 165.

29 Chris Hedges, *War is a Force that Gives Us Meaning* (New York: PublicAffairs, 2014), 3.

30 Hedges, *War is a Force that Gives Us Meaning*, 5.
31 Whitehead, *Process and Reality*, 61.
32 Whitehead, *Process and Reality*, 120.
33 Whitehead, *Process and Reality*, 121.
34 Virilio, *Pure War*, 125.
35 Patricia Pisters, *The Neuro-Image: A Deleuzian Film-Philosophy of Digital Screen Culture* (Stanford: Stanford University Press, 2012), 287.
36 The Transformers series have two entries in the top twenty of films that grossed more than 1 billion dollars, while *Battle: Los Angeles* cleared more than 200 million dollars at the box office on a 70 million budget. By contrast, *The Hurt Locker* had a budget of $15 million and earned almost $50 million. To be sure, not a bad result for an independent film, but nothing compared to the other films.
37 Whitehead, *Process and Reality*, 23.
38 Whitehead, *Process and Reality*, 23.
39 Ivakhiv, *Ecologies of the Moving Image*, 48.
40 Virilio, *The Art of the Motor*, 123. Emphasis in original.
41 Virilio, *The Art of the Motor*, 124. Emphasis in original.
42 Virilio, *The Art of the Motor*, 131. Emphasis in original.

Chapter 7: Cinematic War Machines

1 Here I riff off of Goodman's notion of sonic war machines. Sonic Warfare, loc. 265.
2 Deleuze and Guattari, *A Thousand Plateaus*, 388.
3 Deleuze and Guattari, *A Thousand Plateaus*, 389.
4 Virilio, *Speed and Politics*, 90–91.
5 Anderson, *Encountering Affect*, 119.
6 Whitehead, *Process and Reality*, 184.

Bibliography

"aesthesis | esthesis, n.", *OED Online*. Oxford: Oxford University Press. Available at www.oed.com/view/Entry/3234?redirectedFrom=aisthesis& (accessed 19 June 2015).

Allison, Tanine, "More than a Man in a Monkey Suit: Andy Serkis, Motion Capture, and Digital Realism" *Quarterly Review of Film and Video* 28 (2011), 325–341.

"apprehension, n.", *OED Online*. Oxford: Oxford University Press. Available at www.oed.com/view/Entry/9808?redirectedFrom=apprehension& (accessed 19 June 2015).

Anderson, Ben, *Encountering Affect: Capacities, Apparatuses, Conditions*. Farnham: Ashgate, 2014.

Armitage, John, *Virilio and the Media*. Cambridge: Polity Press, 2012.

Ayers, Drew, "The Multilocal Self: Performance Capture, Remote Surgery, and Persistent Materiality" *Animation* 9, no. 2 (2014), 212–227.

Barker, Jennifer M., *The Tactile Eye: Touch and the Cinematic Experience*. Berkeley: University of California Press, 2009.

Bennett, Jane, *Vibrant Matter: A Political Ecology of Things*. Durham: Duke University Press, 2010.

Blackmore, Tim, "The Speed Death of the Eye", *Bulletin of Science, Technology & Society* 27/5 (2007), 367–372.

Bogost, Ian, *Alien Phenomenology, or What It's Like to Be a Thing*. Minneapolis: University of Minnesota Press, 2012.

Bolter, Jay David and Richard Grusin, *Remediation: Understanding New Media*. Cambridge, MA: The MIT Press, 2000.

Bordwell, David, "Camera Movement and Cinematic Space" *Cine-Tracts* 1 (1977), 19–25.

———, *Planet Hong Kong: Popular Cinema and the Art of Entertainment*. Cambridge, MA: Harvard University Press, 2000.

———, *The Way Hollywood Tells It: Story and Style in Modern Movies*. Berkeley: University of California Press, 2006.

———, "Unsteadicam chronicles", 17 August 2007. Available at http://www.davidbordwell.net/blog/2007/08/17/unsteadicam-chronicles/ (accessed 30 July 2015).

———, "[Insert your favorite Bourne pun here]", 30 August 2007. Available at http://www.davidbordwell.net/blog/2007/08/30/insert-your-favorite-bourne-pun-here/ (accessed 30 July 2015).

Bourke, Joanna, *Fear: A Cultural History*. London: Virago, 2005.

Branigan, Edward. *Projecting a Camera: Language-Games in Film Theory*. New York: Routledge, 2006.

Brown, William, *Supercinema: Film-Philosophy for the Digital Age*. New York: Berghahn Books, 2015.

Buck-Morss, Susan, "Aesthetics and Anaesthetics: Walter Benjamin's Artwork Essay Reconsidered" *October* 62 (1992), 3–41.

Bukatman, Scott, *Matters of Gravity: Special Effects and Supermen in the 20th Century*. Durham: Duke University Press, 2003.

———, "Spectacle, Attractions and Visual Pleasure", in *The Cinema of Attractions Reloaded*. Edited by Wanda Strauven. Amsterdam: Amsterdam University Press, 2006.

———, *The Poetics of Slumberland: Animated Spirits and the Animating Spirit*. Berkeley: University of California Press, 2012.

Chamayou, Grégoire, *A Theory of the Drone*. Translated by Janet Lloyd. New York and London: The New Press, 2015.

Chion, Michel, *Audio-Vision: Sound on Screen*. Translated and edited by Claudia Gorman, foreword by Walter Murch. New York: Columbia University Press, 1994.

———, *Film, A Sound Art*. Translated by Claudia Gorman. New York: Columbia University Press, 2009.

Chow, Rey, *The Age of the World Target: Self-Referentiality in War, Theory, and Comparative Work*. Durham: Duke University Press, 2006.

Clough, Patricia Ticineto, *Autoaffection: Unconscious Thought in the Age of Teletechnology*. Minneapolis: University of Minnesota Press, 2000.

Coleman, Beth, "Everything is Animated: Pervasive Media and the Networked Subject" *Body & Society* 18, no. 1 (2012), 79–98.

Connolly, William E., *Neuropolitics: Thinking, Culture, Speed*. Minneapolis: University of Minnesota Press, 2002.

Cook, Adam, "Dialogues: Talking Robots; or Michael Bay's *Transformers: Age of Extinction*" *MUBI Notebook*, 8 July 2014. Available at mubi.com/note-book/posts/dialogues-talking-robots-or-michael-bays-transformers-age-of-extinction (accessed 16 July 2015).

Crary, Jonathan. *Techniques of the Observer: On Vision and Modernity in the Nineteenth Century*. Cambridge, MA: The MIT Press, 1992.

Creed, Barbara, "The Cyberstar: Digital Pleasures and the End of the Unconscious" *Screen* 41, no.1 (2000), 79–86.

Cubitt, Sean, *The Cinema Effect*. Cambridge, MA: The MIT Press, 2004.

Deleuze, Gilles. *The Logic of Sense*. Translated by Mark Lester with Charles Stivale, edited by Constantin V. Boundas. London: The Athlone Press, 1990.

———, *The Fold: Leibniz and the Baroque*. Translated with foreword by Tom Conley. London: The Athlone Press, 1993.

———, *Negotiations, 1972–1990*. Translated by Martin Joughin. New York: Columbia University Press, 1995.

———, *Cinema 1: The Movement-Image*. Translated by Hugh Tomlinson and Barbara Habberjam. London: Continuum, 2005.

Deleuze, Gilles and Félix Guattari, *A Thousand Plateaus: Capitalism and Schizophrenia*. Translated and with a foreword by Brian Massumi. London: Continuum, 2004.

Denson, Shane, "Crazy Cameras, Discorrelated Images, and the Post-Perceptual Mediation of Post-Cinematic Affect" in *Post-Cinema: Theorizing 21st-Century Film*. Edited by Shane Denson and Julia Leyda. REFRAME Books, 2016.

Donnelly, K.J., "*Saw* Heard: Musical Sound Design in Contemporary Cinema" in *Film Theory and Contemporary Hollywood Movies*. Edited by Warren Buckland. New York: Routledge, 2009.

Duffy, Enda. *The Speed Handbook: Velocity, Pleasure, Modernism*. Durham: Duke University Press, 2009.

Eitzen, Dirk, "Effects of Entertaining Violence: A Critical Overview of the General Aggression Model", in *Cognitive Media Theory*. Edited by Ted Nannicelli and Paul Taberham. New York: Routledge, 2014, 158–176.

Emerson, Jim, "Agents of Chaos" *Scanners* blog, 23 August 2011. Available at www. rogerebert.com/scanners/agents-of-chaos (accessed 3 August 2015).

Ellis, Warren, "Editorial", *Superflux* 1 (2015).

Farocki, Harun, "Phantom Images" *Public* 29 (2004), 12–22.

Foucault, Michel, *The Birth of Biopolitics: Lectures at the Collège de France 1978–1979*. Translated by Graham Burchell, edited by Michel Senellart. New York: Palgrave Macmillan, 2008.

Frampton, Daniel, *Filmosophy*. London: Wallflower Press, 2006.

Galloway, Alexander R., *Gaming: Essays on Algorithmic Culture*. Minneapolis, University of Minnesota Press, 2006.

Goodman, Steve, *Sonic Warfare: Sound, Affect, and the Ecology of Fear*. Cambridge, MA: The MIT Press, 2010.

Grosz, Elizabeth, *Volatile Bodies: Toward a Corporeal Feminism*. Bloomington: Indiana University Press, 1994.

Gunning, Tom, "The Cinema of Attractions: Early Cinema, Its Spectator and the Avant-garde" *Wide Angle* 8, no. 3/4 (1986), 63–70.

———, "An Aesthetics of Astonishment: Early Film and the (In)Credulous Spectator", in *Viewing Positions: Ways of Seeing Films*. Edited by Linda Williams. New Brunswick: Rutgers University Press, 1995.

Hansen, Mark B.N., *Feed-Forward: On the Future of Twenty-First Century Media*. Chicago: University of Chicago Press, 2015.

Hansen, Miriam Bratu, "The Mass Production of the Senses: Classical Cinema as Vernacular Modernism" *Modernism/Modernity* 6, no. 2 (1999), 59–77.

Bibliography

———, *Cinema and Experience: Siegfried Kracauer, Walter Benjamin, and Theodor W. Adorno.* Berkeley: University of California Press, 2012.

Hayles, N. Katherine, "Hyper and Deep Attention: The Generational Divide in Cognitive Modes" *Profession* 2007 (2007), 187–199.

Hedges, Chris, *War is a Force that Gives Us Meaning.* New York: PublicAffairs, 2014.

Hussain, Nasser, "The Sound of Terror: Phenomenology of the Drone Strike", *Boston Review*, 16 October 2013.

Ivakhiv, Adrian J., *Ecologies of the Moving Image: Cinema, Affect, Nature.* Waterloo, Canada: Wilfrid Laurier University Press, 2013.

James, Robin, "Drones, Sound, and Super-Panoptic Surveillance", *Cyborgology*, 26 October 2013. Available at thesocietypages.org/cyborgology/2013/10/26/drones-sound-and-super-panoptic-surveillance (accessed 3 July 2015).

Johnston, John, "Machinic Vision" *Critical Inquiry* 26 (1999), 27–48.

Kerins, Mark, *Beyond Dolby (Stereo): Cinema in the Digital Sound Age.* Bloomington: Indiana University Press, 2011.

"kinetics, n.". *OED Online.* Oxford: Oxford University Press. Available at www.oed.com/view/Entry/103503?redirectedFrom=kinetics& (accessed 29 July 2015).

King, Geoff, *Spectacular Narratives: Hollywood in the Age of the Blockbuster.* London: I.B.Tauris, 2000.

Kittler, Friedrich A., *Gramophone, Film, Typewriter.* Translated with introduction by Geoffrey Winthrop-Young and Michael Wutz. Stanford: Stanford University Press, 1999.

———, *Optical Media.* Translated by Anthony Enns, with introduction by John Durham Peters. Cambridge: Polity Press, 2010.

Kroker, Arthur, *Body Drift: Butler, Hayles, Haraway.* Minneapolis: University of Minnesota Press, 2012.

Lipton, Lenny, *Foundations of the Stereoscopic Cinema: A Study in Depth.* New York: Van Nostrand Reinhold Company, 1982.

MacCormack, Patricia, *Cinesexuality.* Farnham: Ashgate, 2008.

McLuhan, Marshall, *Understanding Media: The Extensions of Man*, Critical Edition. Edited by W. Terrence Gordon. Berkeley: Gingko Press, 2003.

Maltby, Richard, *Hollywood Cinema*, second edition. Malden: Blackwell Publishing, 2003.

Mann, Brett S. and Chrystal Jaye, "'Are We One Body?' Body Boundaries in Telesomatic Experiences," *Anthropology & Medicine* 14, no. 2 (2007), 183–195.

Manning, Erin. *Relationscapes: Movement, Art, Philosophy.* Cambridge, MA: The MIT Press, 2009.

Massumi, Brian, *Parables for the Virtual: Movement, Affect, Sensation.* Durham: Duke University Press, 2002.

———, *The Power at the End of the Economy.* Durham: Duke University Press, 2015.

———, *Ontopower: War, Powers, and the State of Perception.* Durham: Duke University Press, 2015.

Bibliography

Mihailova, Mihaela, "The Mastery Machine: Digital Animation and Fantasies of Control" *Animation* 8, no. 2 (2013), 131–148.

Moore, Rachel O., *Savage Theory: Cinema as Modern Magic*. Durham: Duke University Press, 2000.

Mullarkey, John, *Refractions of Reality: Philosophy and the Moving Image*. Basingstoke: Palgrave Macmillan, 2009.

Munster, Anna, "Transmateriality: Towards and Energetics of Signal in Contemporary Mediatic Assemblages," *Cultural Studies Review* 20, no. 1 (2014), 150–167.

Ndalianis, Angela, "The Frenzy of the Visible: Spectacle and Motion in the Era of the Digital" *Senses of Cinema* 3 (2000).

O'Brien, Harvey, *Action Movies: The Cinema of Striking Back*. London: Wallflower Press, 2012.

Pearlman, Karen, *Cutting Rhythms: Shaping the Film Edit*. Burlington: Focal Press, 2009.

Pisters, Patricia, *The Neuro-Image: A Deleuzian Film-Philosophy of Digital Screen Culture*. Stanford: Stanford University Press, 2012.

Purse, Lisa, "Gestures and Postures of Mastery: CGI and Contemporary Action Cinema's Expressive Tendencies", in *Cinephilia in the Age of Digital Reproduction: Film, Pleasure and Digital Culture*, vol. 1, edited by Scott Balcerzak and Jason Sperb. London: Wallflower Press, 2009.

———, *Contemporary Action Cinema*. Edinburgh: Edinburgh University Press, 2011.

Ross, Miriam, "The 3-D Aesthetic: *Avatar* and Hyperhaptic Visuality" *Screen* 53, no. 4 (2012), 381–397.

Ross, Sara, "Invitation to Voyage: The Flight Sequence in Contemporary 3D Cinema" *Film History* 24, no. 2 (2012), 210–220.

Rothstein, Adam, "How to Write Drone Fiction". *The State*, 20 January 2013. Available at www.thestate.ae/how-to-write-drone-fiction/ (accessed 3 July 2015).

Shaviro, Steven, "'Straight From the Cerebral Cortex': Vision and Affect in *Strange Days*", in *The Cinema of Kathryn Bigelow: Hollywood Transgressor*. Edited by David Jermyn and Sean Redmond. London: Wallflower Press, 2003, 159–177.

———, *Without Criteria: Kant, Whitehead, Deleuze, and Aesthetics*. Cambridge, MA: The MIT Press, 2009.

———, *Post-Cinematic Affect*. Winchester: O-Books, 2010.

———, *The Universe of Things: On Speculative Realism*. Minneapolis: University of Minnesota Press, 2014.

Sinnerbrink, Robert, *New Philosophies of Film: Thinking Images*. London: Continuum, 2011.

Sobchack, Vivian, *The Address of the Eye: A Phenomenology of Film Experience*. Princeton: Princeton University Press, 1992.

———, *Carnal Thoughts: Embodiment and Moving Image Culture*. Berkeley: University of California Press, 2004.

———, "Animation and Automation, or, the Incredible Effortfulness of Being" *Screen* 50, no. 4 (2009), 375–391.

Spielmann, Yvonne, "Elastic Cinema: Technological Imagery in Contemporary Science Fiction Films" *Convergence* 9, no. 3 (2003), 56–73.

Stork, Matthias, "Video Essay: Chaos Cinema: The Decline and Fall of Action Filmmaking" *Press Play*, 22 August, 2011. Available at blogs.indiewire.com/pressplay/video_essay_matthias_stork_calls_out_the_chaos_cinema (accessed 29 July, 2015).

———, "Chaos Cinema: Assaultive Action Aesthetics" *Media Fields Journal* 6 (2013), 2–16.

Tasker, Yvonne, *Spectacular Bodies: Gender, Genre and the Action Cinema*. London Routledge, 1993.

———, *The Hollywood Action and Adventure Film*. Chichester: Wiley Blackwell, 2015.

Virilio, Paul, *War and Cinema: The Logistics of Perception*. Translated by Patrick Camiller. London: Verso Books, 1989.

———, *The Aesthetics of Disappearance*. Translated by Philip Beitchman. Los Angeles: Semiotext(e), 1991.

———, *The Vision Machine*. Translated by Julie Rose. London: British Film Institute and Bloomington: Indiana University Press, 1994.

———, *The Art of the Motor*. Translated by Julie Rose. Minneapolis: University of Minnesota Press, 1995.

———, *Polar Inertia*. Translated by Patrick Camiller. London: Sage Publications, 2000.

———, *Desert Screen*. Translated by Michael Degener, preface by James Der Derian. London: Continuum, 2002.

———, *Negative Horizon: An Essay in Dromoscopy*. Translated by Michael Degener. London: Continuum, 2005.

———, *Speed and Politics*. Translated by Mark Polizzotti. Los Angeles: Semiotext(e), 2006.

———, *Open Sky*. Translated by Julie Rose. London: Verso Books, 2008.

———, *Pure War*. Translated by Mark Polizzotti. Los Angeles: Semiotext(e), 2008.

———, *The Administration of Fear*. Translated by Ames Hodges. Los Angeles: Semiotext(e), 2012.

Walsh, Maria, "The Immersive Spectator" *Angelaki* 9 (2004), 169–185.

Wanenchak, Sarah, "Toward a Drone Sexuality – Part 2: Boundary conditions", *Cyborgology*, 19 December 2013. Available at thesocietypages.org/cyborgology/2013/12/19/toward- a-drone-sexuality-part-2-boundary-conditions/ (accessed 8 July 2015).

Wark, MacKenzie, *Telesthesia: Communication, Culture, and Class*. Cambridge: Polity Press, 2012.

———, "Fury Road" *Public Seminar*, 22 May 2015. Available at http://www.public-seminar.org/2015/05/fury-road/ (accessed 31 July 2015).

Whissel, Kristen, *Spectacular Effects: CGI and Contemporary Cinema*. Durham: Duke University Press, 2014.

Whitehead, Alfred North, *Adventures of Ideas*. New York: The Free Press, 1967.

———, *Process and Reality*. New York: The Free Press, 2010.

Williams, Linda, "Film Bodies: Gender, Genre, and Excess." *Film Quarterly*, 44, no. 4 (1991), 2–13.

———, *Hard Core: Power, Pleasure, and the "Frenzy of the Visible,"* Expanded paperback edition. Berkeley: University of California Press, 1999.

Williams, Raymond. *Marxism and Literature*. Oxford: Oxford University Press, 1977.

Wood, Aylish, *Digital Encounters*. London: Routledge, 2007.

Yip, Man-Fung, "In the Realm of the Senses: Sensory Realism, Speed, and Hong Kong Martial Arts Cinema" *Cinema Journal* 53, no. 4 (2014), 76–97.

Index

Index

sound
  acousmatic, 160
  dislocation, 150
  ecological, 160
  infrasound, 163
  null extension, 152–153, 172
  offscreen, 150
  superfield, 144–145
  synchretic, 145
  turbulent, 145
  ultrafield, 150, 164
  unsettling effect of, 150, 156
space, 30
  agential, 41, 43
  audience, 81
  burlesque, 45
  drone, 55
  excess, 43, 49
  morph, 45
  perspectival, 102, 133
  possibility, 90
  ramping, 84
  screen, 81
  sonic, 145, 152
  stereoscopic, 132–133
  vector, 40, 50, 76

spectacle, 9, 33, 55
  war and 9, 39
stereoscopic cinema, 132–133
structures of feeling, 7, 21,
    182–185
Sucker Punch, 40
superfield, 144–145
synchresis, 145

telesomatics, 121, 138–142
Transformers series, 145
transparency, 135–137

ultrafield, 150, 164

vector, 27–29
  power, 29, 32
  space, 40, 50, 76
visceral continuity, 154
volatility, 95–96, 105, 117–118

war, 8, 175–176
  cinema and, 8–9
  spectacle, 9, 39
war machine, 183–184
wonder, 30, 33–34